WORLD WAR II
B-24
"Snoopers"

Consolidated B-24H "Liberator" USAF Museum Photo Archives

Low Level Anti-Shipping Radar
Night Bombers in the Pacific Theater

63rd Squadron

868th Squadron

~ Stephen M. Perrone ~

The records and exploits of the "Snooper" Squadrons were almost a forgotten adventure of the Pacific War Theater.

Published by NJSG (New Jersey Sportsmen's Guides)
Post Office Box 100
Somerdale, NJ 08083-2642

Library of Congress Cataloging-in-Publication Data

Perrone, Stephen M.

World War II B-24 *Snoopers*

    Low Level Anti-shipping Night Bombers
    in the Pacific Theater

    It was almost a forgotten chapter of the Pacific war.

World War 1941-1945
Campaigns: Asiatic-Pacific, New Guinea, Bismarck Archipelago,
Philippines, West Pacific and China.
63rd Bomb Squadron, 43rd Bomb Group, 5th Air Force,
868th Bomb Squadron, 13th Air Force.
History, Military, 20th Century

ISBN 1-887544-02-X   Library of Congress Control No. 2003090097

Printed in the United States of America

June 2003

First Edition

Dedication

To the men who flew the long night missions and
the ground crews that kept the airplanes flying
over the vast reaches of the pacific
war theater.

And the wives and mothers who waited . . .

To LARRY STEELMAN, YOUR DAD WAS
AN ESSENTIAL CREW MEMBER BECAUSE
RADAR MADE OUR LAB MISSIONS
POSSIBLE.

TABLE OF CONTENTS

TABLE OF CONTENTS (continued)

TABLE OF CONTENTS (continued)

Preface
A WWII
Introspective

Preface/A WWII Introspective

It became apparent in the Spring of 2000 that our long-overdue Group history would not be completed in the year 2000, nor probably the next year. At this time, after an exchange of letters and telephone conversations with members of our crew, I proposed to put together a *Snooper* crew memoir. All crew members responded by letter, telephone or audio tape with their recollections of life in the Southwest Pacific during World War II. During that period I contacted the Air Force Historical Agency at Maxwell Air Force Base in Alabama and with their help located 43rd Bomb Group's 63rd Bomb Squadron archives for that period; and the 13th Air Force's 868th Bomb Squadron archives later that year.

Initially, I purchased several reels of the microfilm copies for review and later bought additional copies, which included the formation of the 63rd Bomb Squadron at Langley Field, Virginia on January 15, 1941. The archives describe the movements of the 43rd Group during 1941 and up to February 18, 1942, when the Group boarded the Queen Mary at Boston, Massachusetts for Sydney, Australia, arriving at Rio Harbor on March 6, 1942.

About four months later, on Tuesday, July 28, at Hamilton Field, California, four new B-17F's (plane numbers 355, 384, 357 and 381) were parked with engines running. The plane commanders Folmer J. Sogaard, James A. Barnett, Edward W. Scott and Kenneth D. McCullar were making last-minute checkups before beginning the long flight to Hickam Field in the Hawaiian Islands. These crews were the advanced echelon of the 63rd Bomb Squadron. The remaining flights of the 63rd would arrive soon after.

More from the archives: Ahead, in a bluish haze lay the Hawaiian Islands. Soon-to-be-famous Waikiki Beach passed beneath the starboard wing. Then the lead plane touched down at Hickam Field, and a few minutes later four tired but happy bomber crews were stretching their cramped bodies. Here at Hickam, the flight experienced a two-day stay while the airplanes were rechecked for any faults and repairs made if necessary. Names were painted on three of the planes; *Dinahmite, Pluto,* and *Momma Maxie* were christened.

A question that might be asked of me is: If you're putting together a history of the B-24 *Snoopers* in the Pacific Theater, why are you discussing the history of the B-17 in this theater? My answer: Because we were connected at the hip like conjoined twins. We followed them into the 63rd Bomb Squadron and we had a common purpose. We were asked to fill the large shoes of   the storied B-17 flight crews and the men who kept them flying, and we did. But we should not forget their accomplishments, because they made it better for those of us who followed.

This item from the archives reaffirms our common purpose.

EXTRACTS FROM FIELD ORDER #1, V BOMBER COMMAND, 8 Sept. 1942 3. e. The 43rd Bomb Group (H) will maintain one squadron (63rd) at Mareeba prepared to attack enemy shipping loaded with bombs and one bomb bay tank. This squadron will go on one-hour readiness at 0230K, 11 Sept. The minimum necessary ground staff and maintenance personnel will be moved to advance base by aircraft of the 43rd Group.

Still reading the archives: In July 1943, many of the crew names and aircraft numbers that had been repeated hundreds of times on combat mission reports (such names as Sogaard 520, McCullar 554, Denault 358, Murphy 384, Dieffenderfer 455, and other names such as Vargas, Butler and Benn, to name a few) were no longer being listed. Many left the combat zone on leave to the states, but many remained in the Pacific Theater as young men forever.

And then in August 1943, after several pages of combat mission reports, the archive pages became unreadable and in some cases, completely blank. According to those final readable pages, Major Folmer J. Sogaard was the last member of the original B-17 crews to fly combat in the 63rd Squadron.

After mid-August 1943, there are no 63rd Bomb Squadron archive records until March 1944, and then only a two-page historical record on the training and flying status of the B-24 aircraft. The March 1944 date is when our crew, one of 12 replacement crews, arrived at Dobodura in New Guinea. But there are no records that document the arrival of the 12 B-24 radar-equipped low-altitude bombing aircraft and crews led by Lt. Col. Edward W. Scott in mid-October 1943. Known as the Scott Project, their first base was at the Jackson Seven Mile Strip out of Port Moresby. It is noteworthy that 15 months earlier, in July 1942, then-Captain Scott flew one of the four new B-17F's to the 63rd Bomb Squadron Base in the Pacific Theater. He flew combat with the squadron and later became Commanding Officer.

Unfortunately, the 63rd Combat Mission Reports received from the Air Force Historical Research Agency for the period August 1943 through much of 1944 are sketchy, difficult to read and lacking in substance. Names are never used and aircraft numbers rarely. I only recognized the names of several members of the Scott Project crews while scanning the archives for the year 1944. And they were listed in the Air Medal and Oak Leaf Cluster Extracts.

In defense of the Intelligence personnel in that period, it was a time of major changes in the theater. A new bomber, the B-24, replaced the B-17 aircraft. Having achieved some air superiority in this area, our air groups were moved to new airstrips on the northern coast of New Guinea to Dobodura, Nadzab and later to Biak, Owi and other locations. Combat mission reports were typed on manual typewriters, stored in file cabinets in tents buffeted by tropical storms, and later moved to another island base. It's a wonder that so many reports survived.

Fortunately, I received a memoir based on the overseas combat diary and log of Arthur H. Millard, pilot of one of the 12 crews brought back to the 63rd Bomb Squadron by Lt. Col. Scott. It is complete. It is personal, thoughtful and from it emerges a brave American airman who was just doing his job, and with distinction. And his diary also recorded the early history of the first 63rd Bomb Squadron *Snoopers*. Captain Millard is the only member of the original Scott Project crews to provide material for this document. I tried to contact others using addresses and telephone numbers from early rosters and other sources but got no other responses. So Arthur Millard's memoir is the only historical narrative of the accomplishments, heroics and combat records of this unique group. And I did not find Arthur Millard, he found me!

Arriving in the Pacific Theater just after Christmas 1943, Roland T. Fisher provided us with another bridge to the original 63rd Bomb Squadron *Snoopers*. His route to the 63rd included RAF pilot training in Spitfires, twin-engine aircraft and, later, training in airborne radar-equipped nightfighters. This radar experience eventually got him to the Seahawks. He flew 17 combat missions with the Steve Ring crew and several other original Scott Project crews out of Dobodura until he assumed command of the Watkin's replacement crew at Nadzab.

Both the 868th Bomb Squadron, 13th Air Force and the 63rd Bomb Squadron, 5th Air Force were descendents of an order given on May 30, 1942, by Army Air Force General "Hap" Arnold. He ordered his Director of Technical Services to establish the Sea-Search Development Unit with headquarters at Langley Field, Virginia. The purpose of this unit was to develop tactics and techniques of anti-submarine warfare. The tactical Sea-Search Squadrons that evolved will be discussed later in this volume.

When researching the Pacific Theater mission reports from the 868th Bomb Squadron, I received valuable material from Col. Crowell "Butch" Werner, Navigator, and a member of one of the original 10 *Snooper* crews trained and escorted to the 13th Air Force Base at Guadalcanal by Col. Stuart P. Wright. An engineer, Col. Wright, and the Radiation Laboratory of the National Defense Research Council were instrumental in the development of the SCR-717B long-range radar search radar and the SCR-729 low altitude (LAB) radar bombsight. Col. Wright and the 10 crews with radar-equipped B-24 airplanes (known as the Wright Project) arrived at Guadalcanal in late August 1943 and began flying combat on August 27. Crowell "Butch"

Werner is the only original Wright Project crew member that I have been able to contact.

In February 2002, in a telephone conversation with Crowell "Butch" Werner, he informed me that there was a third *Snooper* Squadron in the 14th Air Force in China. This B-24 LAB Squadron was led by Lt. Col. William D. Hopson. No other information.

Based on a comment by Radar Technician Floyd Hune, in one of Vince Splane's *Snooper News*, about observing Hal Shirey working alongside Col. Wright in one of the Quonset hut radar equipment bench setups in Guadalcanal, I tried to make contact with Shirey in the early Spring of 2002 for information on Col. Stuart Wright and a photograph of him.

I had just received the official biography of Col. Wright from the US Air Force archives at Maxwell AFB and there was no mention of his leadership role and service with the 868th Bomb Squadron, 13th AAF in the Pacific Theater. Strange, but Low Altitude Bombing Radar applications were classified in the 1940s.

In mid-May I received a telephone call from Hal Shirey's daughter, Becky Wilson, a teacher in Charleston, WV. She explained that her dad died in early April after a debilitating illness. And she promised to send me some overseas documents and other materials in mid-June after the school term ended. She did and I'm grateful.

In a memo dated April 23, 1997 for granddaughter Kelly Wilson's class project, Hal Shirey discusses his World War II overseas experiences. Right after the Wright Project Group became the 868th Bombardment Squadron, the two civilian radar technicians from Bell LABS/Western Electric were returned to the states. At the time Col. Stuart Wright said, "Hal Shirey is the first authority on the low altitude Bombardment radar soon to be of greatly expanded capabilities in the Pacific."

To perform these duties, Staff Sgt. Hal Shirey was put in communication via special courier with Bell LABS/Western Electric and during this period he proposed 14 electronic modifications to the various radar equipments. During his tenure with the 868th he "enjoyed the satisfaction of seeing these improvements arrive on the subsequent replacement aircraft."

The *Snooper News*, written, edited and produced by Dr. Vince Splane, an 868th Squadron pilot and president of the 868th Bomb Squadron Association, Volume 1, 1972 through Volume 22, February 1988, were excellent historical documents for my research efforts. His wife Joanie was the typist and production assistant on all 22 volumes. Vince Splane died in October 1989. And credit is also due to Allan G. Blue, WWII Navy Veteran and an active B-24 writer who wrote a column for the Liberator Club Newsletter

Briefing for 26 years. Al Blue provided Vince Splane with all the 868th Bomb Squadron mission reports and overseas photographs.

I should mention the *Snooper News,* Volume 23, 1991 through Volume 33, June 1996 by former 868th Bomb Squadron Association President, Fred Stanley Howell, are included in my readings and I appreciate his contributions. The present Editor of the *Snooper News* and President of the 868th Bomb Squadron Association, Richard Phelps, has also been helpful.

The basis for the 868th Bomb Squadron memoirs are the mission reports and overseas photographs from the early *Snooper News* volumes, and the archives and the memoirs provided by the 868th Squadron members. The basis for the 63rd Bomb Squadron memoirs are the archives and the memoirs received from the 63rd Bomb Squadron members

Stephen M. Perrone

To close out the Preface, a Commendation:

20 August 1945

To: All Fifth Air Force Unit Commanders

The following message has been received from the Commanding General, Far East Air Forces:

THE FOLLOWING MESSAGE FROM CONGENAIR TO BE PASSED TO ALL UNITS UNDER YOUR COMMAND: "THE BRILLIANT OFFENSIVE OF THE FAR EAST AIR FORCES UNDER YOUR INSPIRING LEADERSHIP WAS AN OUTSTANDING FACTOR IN JAPAN'S DEFEAT. LOOKING BACK TO THE HEROIC OPERATIONS OF THE EARLY WAR IN WHICH, GRAVELY OUTNUMBERED AND UNDERSUPPLIED, YOU AROSE FROM THE DUST OF THE PORT MORESBY STRIPS TO STOP THE AUSTRALIA-BOUND JAPS IN THEIR TRACKS, IT MAY BE TRUTHFULLY SAID THAT NO AIR COMMANDER EVER DID SO MUCH WITH SO LITTLE. ALL THAT YOU HAVE DONE SINCE HAS MADE AIR HISTORY. THE ARMY AIR FORCES HONOR YOUR FIGHTING SPIRIT, TO WHICH WE SO LARGELY OWE TODAY'S SPLENDID TRIUMPH.

SIGNED ARNOLD."

In The Beginning

How It Came About

Author's Notes: Lt. Vince Splane was appointed first pilot of one of the 10 original crews that arrived at Guadalcanal in August 1943 under the command of Col. Stuart "Stud" Wright. At that time Lt. Splane was a B-17 pilot who was checked out in B-24s and took over as pilot of one of the crews because the pilot stopped flying.

Now fast forward to the year 1972 when the 868th Bomb Squadron Association was formed with Dr. Vince Splane as president and editor/publisher of the *Snooper News*. In the first paragraph, first page of Volume 3 (published in early 1974) Dr. Splane expresses his gratitude to the readers as follows:

"First of all, I want to take this opportunity to thank all of those who have contributed to the success of the *Snooper News*, both financially and by sending me material and other memorabilia.

From the beginning of the search for former *Snoopers* and the subsequent organization, there has been excellent cooperation. To date, over 250 men have been traced, 233 of these are living. A solid 50% have made donations – most excellent!!

Since I put out a call for help in July, 61 men have responded with donations and of those 34 were making their second donations. Many thanks to all. This issue of the *News* is being brought to you by your own cooperation."

Volume 2, printed in June 1973, was the first volume with a four-color cover that featured the shoulder patches of the 13th and 5th Air Forces. These patches were featured on 26 covers of the 33 volumes produced by Vince Splane (Vol. 1 through Vol. 22, and Fred Stanley Howell (Vol. 23 through Vol. 33).

Through the years many members of the 868th Bomb Squadron Association were 63rd Bomb Squadron members. Fred Cheuvront, a bombardier from one of the original Scott Project 63rd Bomb Squadron *Snoopers,* and a long-time member of the 868th Association, was praised by Vince Splane and I quote:

"Fred Cheuvront, bless him, is a good worker for the *Snoopers* and I want to thank him for contributing to an article about the closeness of the 868th Bomb Squadron and the 63rd Bomb Squadron. This is why we now have a joint reunion with both squadrons."

And then on several pages of Volume 10, Vince Splane includes the article that describes the history of the *Snooper* Squadrons and how they came together in the Pacific Theater.

In the Beginning
Dr. Vince Splane

Origin of 868th Bomb Squadron (H) and 63d Bomb Squadron (H) –The *Snoopers* and the Seahawks . . .

This is the story of the formation of the two original groups of *Snoopers*. For the following information, I must acknowledge Jim Pope, Butch Werner, Cecil Cothran, and Bob Tressel of 868th Bomb Squadron and Fred Cheuvront, Joe Schwarber, K.N. Carson, Ben Schneider, and Charlie Quinette of 63rd Bomb Squadron. All of these men submitted records, special orders and other data which made it possible for me to present a somewhat chronological story of how it all came about. I will not profess complete accuracy and detail but the dates that follow are accurate.

On Feb. 16, 1942 4th Air Force Headquarters sent out a TWX ordering 42 men from 13 different Squadrons and assignments from California to Washington to form six crews and proceed to different airfields and pick up B-18As. All of these crews were to be at the San Antonio Air Depot, Duncan Field, Texas on or before Feb. 21, 1942 for modification of these airplanes. From San Antonio, they were all ordered to report to Municipal Airport, Boston, Mass., reporting there to the Liaison Officer, Radiation Laboratory Massachusetts Institute of Technology. While at MIT, the crews had technical training on a crude mockup of the crude radar equipment, and flew out of Logan Airport tracking merchant and naval shipping to acquire technique of scope interpretation etc., frequently making runs on subs provided by the navy and various military vessels to attempt to determine size of vessels by blips presented on the scope. This cadre of men was headed up by Lt. Col. William C. Dolan who came from Hqts. Sqdn. 42 Bomb Group, McChord Field, Washington. On Col. Dolan's crew were 2nd Lt. John Scanlon, 2nd Lt. James Pope, 2nd Lt. Francis Boykin. Enlisted men were T/Sgt. Ray Elliot, S/Sgt. Marshall Smith and Sgt. William Hillis. All were from 76th Bomb Sqdn., McChord Field, Washington. Another crew was 2nd Lts. William Foley, Robert Lehti, and Crowell "Butch" Werner. Enlisted men Bernard Illig, Cpl. L.P. Bishop Jr., Sgt. Cecil Ring, and Pvt. Doyle Bradford. These men were all from 30th Bomb Group March Field, California. Others in the group: Capt. Adam Breckenridge, 1st Lt. Leo J. Foster (868), 1st Lt. Francis B. Carlson (868). Foster came from 16th Recon Sqdn., Paine Field, Washington and Carlson came from 48th Bomb Sqdn., Bakersfield, Calif. The other officers were 2nd Lts. Franklin T.E. Reynolds (868), Leroy Tempest, Donald McKay, Clarence Harmon (868), Junior Barney (868), Thomas Wortham, Anthony Leal, John Zinn, Neb Estes (868), Bernard Frizzie, Harold Thiele and William Walker.

On April 13, 1942, all of these men were assigned to 20th Bomb Sqdn. of 2nd Bomb Group, Langley Field, Virginia and then on June 23, 1942 these men were attached to the 1st Sea Search Attack Group, Langley Field. Va. Some new names were added which included: Robert L. Coleman (63), John Herrick, Caleb Mende, and Fred Hartbrodt.

Upon July 26, 1942 all of these men were relieved from attached status and assigned to 2nd Sea Search Attack Sqdn. of the 1st Sea Search Attack Group. While these men were still on attached status, the squadron was being added to constantly. On June 13, 1942, the following men were graduated from navigation school at Turner Field, Ga. and assigned to Langley Field, Va.: Ken Royer, James Alexander, John Burt, Cecil Cothran, George Desko, John Bull, K.N. Carson, Earl Cox, and Lee Cunningham. By all rights K.N. Carson should have ended up with Wright Project, but he was the only one who eventually ended up with 63rd in New Guinea. Burt, Cothran, Desko, Bull, and Cox were all original *Snoopers* of 868th.

Special orders #215 dated August 15, 1942 whereby some personnel were named to proceed to Opa-Locka Airport, Florida and to such other places as necessary show a few more names added: William Hafner (63), Grover Hallman (63), Fred Martus (868), Alvin McGehee (63), Henry Wise (868), Sam Pona (868) and Rose, Plocek, Prosser and Rubin all 868th. On these assignments, these crews were anti-sub out of Trinidad and other areas in the Caribbean. September 16, 1942 on an assignment to quarters order shows Barney (868), Pope (868), Burghoff (63), Coleman (63), Hafner (63), McIntosh (63), Quinette (63), Tillinghamst (868), and Wise (868) all assigned adjacent quarters at Langley Fld. In December 1942, the 3rd Sea Search Attack Squadron was activated in order to test and modify the newly acquired B-24s. On the tactical side, valuable assistance was obtained from an experienced RAF crew which flew two radar equipped B-24s. All of the men who later made up the Wright Project came from the 3rd Sea Search Attack Squadron. . . .

On March 11, 1943, the following Bombardiers graduated from Big Spring Texas School: Robert Ryan, Irving Schechner, Joe Stevens, Fred Cheuvront, Ed Crawford, Hayward "Pete" Schandorff, Charles Feucht, Joe Schwarber, John Shytle, Ben Schnieder, Douglas Wright and Charles Swindler. These men were assigned to Las Vegas gunnery school as a group, assigned to Boca Raton as a group, and assigned to Langley Field as a group. They all, with exception of Shytle, were bombardiers on crews in Scott Project and went to New Guinea as a group.

The Wright Project was formed June 2, 1943, by General orders #2 from men of the 3rd Sea Search Attack Squadron Movement order #1 dated 3 August 1943 assigned Wright Project for movement overseas. They left

Langley August 5, 1943, and Operations order #13 dated 9 August, 1943 Fairfield-Suisun AAF California, further assigned them to report to commanding General 13th Air Force Service Command Esprito Santo, New Hebrides. The Wright Project arrived on Guadalcanal on 23rd of August 1943 and flew first missions night of 27-28 August 1943.

The Scott Project formation date I do not have but we must assume it formed just shortly after the Wright Project. The Project was formed with men from the 2nd Sea Search Attack Squadron.

On 5 October 1943 they were further assigned to 43rd Bomb Group (H) of 5th Air Force thence to 63rd Bomb Squadron on October 15, 1943.

> *Note: According to a Memorandum from Headquarters, First Sea Search Attack Group (H) to the Commanding Officer, 2nd Search Attack Squadron, dated July 20, 1943, which lists all the officers and men that make up 12 LAB crews to be trained "immediately for this assignment." (This memorandum was provided by Arthur H. Millard, a first pilot in the first Scott Project group.)*

Each of these squadrons distinguished itself in the ensuing months of combat by its use of the ASV radar in LAB attacks on enemy shipping.

When the 868th moved from Munda to Los Negros in the Admiralties in April 1944, the living quarters were not ready so seven 868 crews went to Nadzab, New Guinea and spent four days with the 63rd Squadron. They returned to Los Negros on the 4th of May.

On the night of April 28th the 63rd and 868th teamed up to put 17 planes over Mokmer airstrip on Biak. Again on May 10th 1944, four 63rd and three 868 *Snoopers* went on a negative shipping search and bombed Mokmer on Biak again.

On May 27th, 1944, the 63rd and 868th again teamed up, flying from Los Negros – eight planes of 63rd and four from 868th bombed Bosnek defenses on Biak.

There you have a smattering of how very closely the men of the two original Projects were associated, both before they were formed into Projects and after. They went overseas as 868th *Snoopers* and 63rd Seahawk *Snoopers*.

SCOTT PROJECT – 5TH AIR FORCE

Colonel Edw. W. Scott
Photo provided by Arthur Millard

In July 1942, then Captain Scott and three other plane commanders, delivered four new B-17F's and crews to the 63rd Bomb Squadron in Port Moresby, New Guinea. These crews were the advanced echelon, and the remaining flights of B-17F's would arrive soon after.

On September 1942, 5th Bomber Command ordered the 43rd Bomb Group to "maintain one squadron (63rd) at Mareeba prepared to attack enemy shipping loaded with bombs and one bomb bay tank. This squadron will go on one-hour readiness at 0230K, 11 September." The 63rd combat crews adapted to this order by developing low altitude precision bombing tactics for shipping targets. The tactics included night bombing, "crack of dawn" attacks and skip bombing, directly out of a setting sun, from low clouds or poor weather, and on clear nights with the moon below 40° elevation.

Major Scott flew combat with the 63rd and later became Commanding Officer of the B-17 anti-shipping squadron, serving from 11/14/42 to 5/13/43.

On October 1, 1943 the 12 B-24 crews of the Scott Project left Langley Field on the first leg of their journey to New Guinea. On October 16, Lt. Col. Scott and the 12 B-24 crews flew into Jackson (Seven Mile Strip) out of Port Moresby.

On the night of October 21, takeoff at 1900 hours, the first B-24 *Snooper* mission in the 5th Air Force was made with the Art Millard crew. Col. Scott flew as an observer.

WRIGHT PROJECT – 13TH AIR FORCE

How and why radar bombing got its start in South Pacific

Colonel Stuart P. Wright
Photo provided by Radar magazine.

Since Coral Sea and Midway the enemy has learned better than to send out ships in such concentrations as made those whole-sale wreckings possible. Japanese ships now move among the islands in ones and twos and threes; make more of the cover of darkness, of overcast and of fighters. Consequently balance sheets on strike missions have had to be drawn up very carefully indeed. Risks worth taking to blast a convoy might or might not be worth taking for a couple of fog-covered barges, or a fighter-protected ship cargo. Search missions for targets so isolated or so protected could be prohibitive.

What we needed to meet the problems thus presented was obvious: precision – precision in finding the targets and precision in striking. What provided the answer was a new adaptation of radar – a low altitude, high precision bombing attachment. It is now five months since the night when three B-24's took off from an island in the Solomons to give this equipment (APQ-5) its first combat trial. At this writing bombers equipped for such operations are flying regularly with the 5th and 13th Air Forces, and regularly paying their way.

Development of APQ-5 started back in 1942, when laboratory work got underway to crystallize ideas that Japanese dispersal tactics had set in motion. By June of 1943 pre-production models were being put through their paces in experimental flights. And at Langley Field Col. Stuart P. Wright and a selected group of pilots, navigators, bombardiers and radar technicians were readying themselves and 10 B-24's to take the new equipment into combat.

Low Altitude, High Precision
Radar bombing blends them to strike dispersed Jap shipping

Question: There's been a lot of talk about your low altitude project in the South Pacific, Col. Wright. But no report has been made generally available to date. We'd like to tell the story through radar, so Air Force personnel all over the world can know what went on. To begin with, is the project continuing?

Col. Wright: Stronger than ever. The operational period I had charge of – which is all I can talk about here – started on 27 August last year and wound up on 2 October. But many of the people who worked with me are still in the area, and more besides. And there's more of the bombing equipment there now and more use of it, than ever.

Question: About how many equipped bombers have been sent out?

Col. Wright: All told, about 22 planes equipped for this type of bombing have been sent to the South and Southwest Pacific together. Incidentally, these planes are called *Snooper* planes out there.

Question: What are they proving? That is, what have the results of this bombing been since you first gave it a try?

Col. Wright: The results have been the destruction of dozens of Jap ships that wouldn't have been touched, except for this bombing, or even known to exist as targets. You can say that for five months the *Snoopers* have been extending the range and striking power of the Air Forces operating in those areas – extending them by a lot, too.

Question: Before we go any further, how about a thumbnail sketch of what you mean by "this type of bombing?"

Col. Wright: What I mean is low altitude precision bombing by radar instruments alone. By low altitude I mean 1000-2000 feet. By precision I mean planting a bomb on or close to a ship target every time we let one go. By radar instruments alone I mean the whole job was done automatically and without visual means from beginning to end – from locating the target right through to the bomb release. The equipment that made this possible was a standard radar search system, the SCR-717B, plus the APQ-5 blind bombing attachment, which had never been used in combat before. It's adaptable to any microwave ASV set such as the SCR-717B, and it works with the Norden bombsight. Other equipment was involved in our mission, but this was the guts of it.

Question: Is the bombing attachment good only at low altitudes and for ship targets?

Col. Wright: It was designed for use against ship targets at low altitudes and that's how we used it. It employs a computer up to 2000 feet and within that altitude it's precision equipment. However, by extending the slant range release distance you can use the equipment against shore-based land targets at any altitude. We tried this out over there but not in combat.

Question: Why not?

Col. Wright: Because we were there to get ships and there were plenty to keep us busy.

Radar Magazine interviews – Col. Stuart Wright, April 1944 Issue (continued)

Question: Have results been good enough in the five months since you went over to represent a real threat to Japanese shipping?

Col. Wright: Not in the quantities in which the equipment's been used. On the other hand, proper use of this equipment in sufficient quantities could pretty nearly disrupt Japanese shipping lines. That's my feeling about it and it's based on the record.

Question: What do you mean by "sufficient quantities"?

Col. Wright: I'd say that if each Air Force operating in the Pacific had one Heavy Bombardment Group equipped for this blind bombing, that would be minimum.

Question: Is the equipment as useful for other theatres as for the Pacific?

Col. Wright: Draw your own conclusions. It was designed for ship targets and that spells Pacific to me. Situations certainly arise in other theatres in which this type of bombing can achieve important gains not otherwise possible. But in the Pacific it may some day emerge as a really decisive technical factor working for us against the Japs.

Question: Is much special training necessary for the personnel using the equipment?

Col. Wright: Well, the blind bombing attachment does a job that nothing else before it did. It was brand new when we took it over, with the usual quota of bugs to be ironed out. Everyone concerned with the use and maintenance of APQ-5 had to have special training, including first of all the bombardiers who operate it. The rest of the equipment involved was standard and required standard training.

Question: How did the group you took over get its training?

Col. Wright: It got it by going through a special training period at Langley Field. This lasted roughly two mouths – from early June to the end of July. Each bombardier, for example, worked a total of five hours on a blind bombing trainer during this period and dropped 100 practice bombs blind at various altitudes. We simply figured out all the angles we could think of and trained ourselves as well as we could along those lines.

Question: Had any of the men had any of the necessary training before you all got together?

Col. Wright: The technical men knew their particular phases and the combat crews were already trained in all normal operations. Most of them had some radar experience, although not with APQ-5. Only one bombardier was up on the blind bombing technique; he was bombardier on all test flights I conducted during the initial development of this equipment.

Question: What were your conclusions at the end of the training period as to the effectiveness of the equipment?

Col. Wright: We figured we had something. We figured we could get a hit out of three tries pretty consistently.

Question: And when you got into combat?

Col. Wright: We improved; direct hits during the operational period I'm covering averaged 39%.

Question: How does 39% compare with results from other types of bombing?

Col. Wright: 39% is good in any league. But no other bombing is altogether comparable.

Question: How about other types of blind bombing? How about the blind bombing that the 8th Air Force is doing for example?

Col. Wright: That's done under entirely different conditions and with a different type of equipment.

Question: O.K. One more question. Can you tell me exactly what happened during one typical mission with APQ-5?

Col. Wright: Sure. I'll tell you about the first one we ever flew. It was on the night of 27 August ... *(This mission is described under combat mission reports. August 27-28 and September 28-29, 1943)*

Note: The first issue of RADAR Magazine in April 1944 was introduced by a letter from General H. H. Arnold on the Masthead of this new publication.

RADAR: " . . . make solid use of it"

The personnel of the Army Air Force must know as much as possible about radar, and make the greatest possible use of both their knowledge and their equipment, for the perfectly simple reason that by so doing they will be able to fly better, fight better and deal with the enemy more effectively in general. Anything which contributes to these ends is of the first importance, and the publication RADAR clearly comes under this heading. I wish it well, and I strongly urge Air Force personnel to make steady and solid use of it.

H. H. ARNOLD
COMMANDING GENERAL, ARMY AIR FORCE

Dr. Vince Splane

868th Combat Mission Reports

Note: In the "Correspondence" column of Vol. 2, Vince Splane discusses his drive to make the _Snooper News_ a quality publication, the work involved, and his high hopes which he expresses as follows:

"I have talked with many new men and have received letters from some of them. I hope to hear from all eventually. My objective is to let history know the story of the Snoopers and what a job they did during WWII. I for one, am proud of my service and the Snoopers."

An important historical feature of the _Snooper News_ volumes was the inclusion of Combat Mission Reports in most issues. Many of the mission reports and overseas photos were made available to Dr. Vince Splane by Allan Blue, as discussed earlier in the Preface. These will be introduced in the pages that follow:

COMBAT MISSION REPORTS
August 27-28, 1943
The night the *Snoopers* hit the Tokyo Express and come of Age!

The *Snoopers* arrived in south Pacific area the last days of August 1943. The original 10 SB 24's of the Wright Project set up shop on Guadalcanal and the first mission was flown on the night of August 27-28 from Carney Field. The mission consisted of three SB-24s, Aircraft #639 (The Lady Margaret) Tillinghast, pilot and Lt. Col. Unruh, C.O. of 5th Bomb Group as command pilot, #653 (Gremlin's Haven), Martus, pilot and Col. Stuart Wright (C.O. of Wright Project) as command pilot; also accompanied by Col. Matheny, C.O. of 13th Bomber Command; #822 (Bum's Away) Lehti pilot and Lt. Col. Burnam as command pilot took part on this first Mission.

Editor's note: These were the aircraft and command pilots of the mission and I assumed that the pilots and crews who flew these aircraft from the states were the ones on this mission. This could be an erroneous assumption.

The first mission resulted in one hit on an unidentified ship by one SB-24. One of the others sighted nothing and dropped bombs on Rekata while the remaining SB-24 mistook small islands for ships and dropped on them. Not an auspicious beginning, but not a total failure either. Remember this was an entirely new tactical weapon and it took time for all the bugs to be worked out and for radar operators and bombardiers to learn what they were looking at in the scope. In the beginning, many small islands were mistaken for ships and bombed. These errors were gradually eliminated as the men learned. Unfortunately on the night of 31st of August, the *Snoopers* suffered their first casualties. Lt. Robert Easterling and crew made a bomb run and were never heard from again.

NIGHT OF SEPTEMBER 28-29, 1943

Mission: All available A/P of the 394th Bombardment Squadron of 5th Bomb Group (H) were to search for and strike a Task force reported to contain eight DD's coming down N.E. shore of Bougainville to Kiota area. The *Snoopers* at this time were the 394th Bomb Squadron of 5th Group. They did not become the 868th Bomb Squadron until January 1, 1944.

Eight airplanes were available and began taking off from Carney at 1717 LCT. led by Maj. Leo Foster in A/P #832 and followed at one to two minute intervals by Capt. John Zinn A/P #854, Capt. Robert Lehti A/P #822, Capt. Frank Reynolds A/P #833, Lt. Charles Rockwood A/P #838, Lt. Fred Martus A/P #653, Lt. Ken Brown A/P #651 and Lt. Durward Sumner was last to take off, not getting off until 2144 LCT.

Reynolds, Zinn and Lehti were the first to make radar contact with target picking it up at 1920 LCT, followed by Foster and Rockwood who made contact at 1925 LCT. Lt. Ken Brown, due to his route out N.E. of

Choiseul, did not pick up target until his return from Buka. This was at 2300 LCT and there were seven friendly DD's in vicinity, so no bomb run was made. Lt. Sumner and crew had a completely negative search.

Capt. Reynolds was first *Snooper* to make a bombing run, followed immediately by Lt. Rockwood. This was at 1933 LCT. Capt. Zinn made his run at 2012 LCT, and Maj. Foster got over target at 2034 LCT. Capt. Lehti, began a run but broke off and never made another attempt. The following reports are right from the mission reports.

Capt. Reynolds and crew A/P #833:

Our A/P #833, the first plane to locate and attack the convoy, found the target by radar at 1920 LCT at 6°33'S 156°17'E. This convoy was observed by radar to consist of 11 vessels traveling in train on course of 160° at an unestimated speed. Our A/P made its attack on one of the rear vessels of convoy from beam to beam in course of 260° at altitude of 1300' at 1933 LCT. Our bombs were spaced at 75 foot intervals at airspeed of 135 mph. The first four bombs were short, the fourth bomb being a near miss of from 30 to 40 feet. Bombs 5 & 6 were observed to hit the ship amidship leaving it ablaze. This fire could be seen from a distance of 20 miles at 300 feet. The type of this vessel could not be discerned due to hazy condition of the weather. We drew no automatic weapons fire but immediately after leaving target, fire was observed coming up, probably at another of our squadron ships making its run.

Lt. Rockwood and crew A/P #838:

A target of 11 ships was located by radar at 1920 LCT. A run was made on this shipping at 1933 LCT at an altitude of 1000 feet. Three bombs were dropped. The course of this shipping was 160° true, this was a beam run. Two of the three bombs hit the ship to stern of admidship. It is not known which of the three bombs missed the target. This was a very large vessel with a square stern as seen by the bomb flash. The bombs were seen visually to hit the ship. No fires were seen to ensue. This vessel, from the size of its wake and from its general design described by member of the crew could easily have been a converted A/P carrier. A second run was made on this target which now consisted of 9 ships at 2043 LCT at an altitude of 1500 feet. This was a quartering run from stern to bow. As this run was made, a friendly A/P was leaving the target, its bomb run completed. One of its bombs was seen to hit this ship. All the bombs of A/P #838 were believed to have hit the target. After the bomb release, our plane made a tight turn which permitted the top turret gunner to visually get a view of the target. He and the tail gunner saw this ship roll over and sink. It also disappeared from the radar screen. The general consensus of crew was that this ship was a DD.

Capt. John Zinn and crew A/P #854:

An attack on this force was made at 2012 LCT at 1300 feet. The run was made from stern to bow at an angle of 30°. The Force was traveling in perfect train headed down the slot from Bougainville towards Vella LaVella. All our bombs fell over the target, the closest being 30 feet away.

Major Leo Foster and crew A/P #832:

An unidentified target was picked up by radar at 1925 LCT. This was not originally recognized as the Task Force, but appeared on the screen to be reefs. Our A/P did not realize this was the Task Force until it received a message from a friendly plane telling of its sighting at the same coordinates where the reef was thought to be. Our A/P immediately returned to this scene. In the meantime the force had been split up into single targets. An attack was made on a target at 2034 LCT at an altitude of 1500 feet. This run was made from the stern to bow quartering. All bombs were close, three or four dropping on the target. No evasive action was taken by this vessel. From its outline in the bomb bursts it appeared to be long and lean of contour having two slanting stacks. Very intense automatic weapons fire was encountered from the bomb release line till the bombs struck the vessel. Then it immediately stopped. This was accurate as several rounds pierced our A/P. Immediately after our bomb exploded, the enemy fire took a horizontal trajectory 180° from its original. Immediately preceding our run on this target another friendly A/P made a run on it. His bomb explosions were seen but the results were not observed

Editor's note: This friendly A/P immediately preceding Maj. Foster must have been Lt. Fred Martus and crew as Foster made his run at 2034 LCT and Zinn made his at 2012, a time lapse of 22 minutes. The report says "immediately preceding" so we must assume it was Martus.

Approximately 20 minutes before this attack was made, a fire was observed at the northern tip of Choiseul Island. Immediately after another plane made an attack on this target, three fires instead of original one were observed.

Capt. Lehti and crew A/P #822:

Task force believed to be eight in number picked up by radar at 1920 LCT on a course of 160° at an estimated speed of 20 knots. The location of this Task Force was between Choiseul and Bougainville. At first it was thought to be reefs on radar screens. When one mile away. This shipping could be counted visually in twilight. At 1930 LCT a message was sent to OOVI on sighting this target (this was acknowledged). At 1950 LCT when 38 miles from target, a bomb run was set up. At a distance of eight miles from target at an altitude of 1400 feet and IFF interrogator return was picked up.

This was neither yes nor no but maybe. The target was not bombed. Our A/P searched the N.E. coast of Bougainville to the tip of Buka and again returned to Bougainville Strait. So much radar interception friendly was contacted in this area that pilot decided not to go in and clutter it up further.

Lt. Fred Martus, A/P #653 and crew, returning from this mission, crashed on landing at Carney Field and all were killed.

That's the story – eight *Snoopers* went out, seven came back . . . Four *Snoopers* made bombing runs and at least four ships sunk with a possible five. The *Snoopers* were learning their "Trade." In his book, *Japanese Destroyer Captain* by Captain Tameichi Hara, the author states, "I took part in the continuing operations in Solomons waters from March through November 1943 in command of destroyer Shigure. Losses were higher than in the previous six months owing to enemy's growing air supremacy and **improved radar.** My ship was the only one in the "Tokyo Express" to survive these battles without losing a man. Some 30 other Japanese destroyers were sunk in this period."

COMBAT REPORT – The Longest Mission

The following is taken right from mission reports of the 868th for the night of 7-8 May 1945. This mission was one of the longest if not the longest flown by B-24s during WW II. The average time flown by all aircraft was 17 hours, 5 minutes, with the longest flight lasting over 18 hours . . .

A/C 397 Major Harriss–Pilot
A/C 464 Lt. Olsen–Pilot
A/C 395 Lt. McDaniel–Pilot
A/C 808 Lt. Reidy–Pilot
A/C 131 Lt. Workman–Pilot
A/C 358 Lt. Sheely–Pilot
A/C 357 Lt. Smitherman–Pilot
A/C 899 Lt. Sprawls–Pilot
A/C 129 Lt. Thompson–Pilot
A/C 810 Lt. Bartelmes–Pilot

Target: Shipping at Soerabaja, Java, and vicinity. Shipping anchored in Naval Base attacked by two air craft and two other aircraft attacked shipping in Commercial Basin.

Time, Altitude and Heading of Attack: All times item.

Major Baylis Harriss
Photo from the 868th Combat Reports

Naval and Commercial basins. Attacked by four aircraft at 2208-2217 from 11,850-13,500 feet true on headings of 127°, 140°, 157° and 270°.

Shipping in Madoera Straits attacked at 2214-2233 from 300-1000 feet true on headings of 200° to 270°.

Results:

This mission is rated excellent. The four aircraft attacking from medium altitude started five large and three small fires in the Naval and Commercial basin areas. Two bombs were observed to fall on the submarine sheds along the southern edge of the Naval basin starting two large fires. One string of four bombs fell across the quay just to the east of the shipyards along the east edge of the Commercial basin. A large fire with cherry red flame was started which developed into a smoky glow and appeared it spread over the quay area. The remaining bombs fell in close proximity. The fires were visible for 30 minutes after the *Snoopers* left the target.

Six aircraft made low altitude attacks on the following vessels, using LAB equipment: A/C 899 and A/C 358 attacked two vessels at 2214. A/C 899 made a quartering attack from 800 feet dropping six bombs on a single run. One large flash was observed disclosing a direct hit on the bow of a 250 ft. vessel. Further results were unobserved and the plane made a sharp breakaway to the left to a heading of 90°. A/C 358 made a quartering attack on a 200-300-foot vessel from 300 feet. Six bombs were dropped but results were unobserved and the *Snooper* broke to the right to a heading of 90°. A/C 129 attacked a single 300-foot vessel at 2217. One run was made dropping six bombs from 900 feet. A terrific flash was observed with a sheet of flame radiating 200 feet out from the ship. A/C 810 made a single quartering run on a 275-foot vessel, dropping six bombs from 300 feet. Two flashes and explosions were observed on the breakaway. A/C 131 attacked a single 200-foot vessel. Three runs were made dropping six bombs on the third run, from 1000 feet. Three large flashes and explosions were observed and a glow was seen coming from the ship as the *Snooper* made a breakaway. A/C 357 attacked a 300-foot vessel. Three runs were made on the anchored vessel dropping six bombs on the third run. The attack was made on the beam 500 feet. A single flash blue in color was seen as the *Snooper* broke right over Madoera Island. A direct hit on a vessel is claimed wherever a flash and/or explosion was observed. All bombs were fused 4-5 sec-ond delay and would cause no flash or explosion except in case of a direct hit.

Enemy Losses:

Five vessels ranging from 200-350 feet in length damaged by direct hits.

Friendly Losses:

Three aircraft holed by AA: A/C 395 received a direct hit by a 90 mm. shell which passed through the nose of the aircraft. A/C 808 received two holes in the right wing. A/C 397 was holed in the tail sections. No injuries to personnel.

AA Fire and Searchlights:

Moderate, heavy and medium, accurate to inaccurate AA fire was received by the four *Snoopers* at medium altitude. The flashes from heavy fire on the ground appeared to outnumber the bursts seen in the air. It is believed that the Japanese are using point detonating fuses in this area. The direct hit received by A/C 395 was apparently a defective fuse and failed to explode. Tracers from medium fuses were seen to burn out at approximately 15,000 feet. The AA fire is described as generally inaccurate in view of the intensity and the time spent over the target even though three aircraft were hit. The *Snoopers* at medium altitude were drawing fire and searchlights in order to screen the aircraft attacking at low altitude. A total of 17 searchlights were observed. The lights were generally ineffective and the decoy *Snoopers* had to resort to flashing recognition and landing lights to draw the searchlights.

Photos:

Ninety-four scope photos were taken over entire Soerabaja area.

Remarks:

This mission was planned and executed with the utmost proficiency on the part of all participants. The plan was aimed primarily at destruction of shipping known to be in the vicinity of Soerabaja. Six aircraft went in low under protection of four medium-altitude aircraft. A/C 464 was first to leave the initial point. It was at 13,000 feet at the same initial point as the low-altitude aircraft. A/C 464 went west through Straits jamming the enemy's early warning and gun laying Radars and dropping Rope Window. The low altitude aircraft left the initial point 15 minutes after A/C 464 set course. They followed at 30-second intervals, the first low plane heading directly for Soerabaja with the remaining five setting course 2° south of each preceding plane. This gave a fan-like coverage of the Straits area. The 15-minute interval between A/C 464 and the low planes gave the window an opportunity to settle to the altitude of the low aircraft, thus screening their approach when A/C 464 was ten miles from Soerabaja, the three high planes orbiting Pangrah point north Soerabaja were notified. They set course at 60-second intervals and headed for the shipping targets in the inner harbour. Enroute all three dropped rope window and made all efforts to attract the attention of the defenses away from the low planes. Evidence of this is the fact that not one of the low-altitude planes was fired at or tracked by searchlights. The execution of this carefully coordinated plan is a tribute to the Commanding Officers' ability as a tactician and the attention to detail on the part of all participants.

Lt. McDaniel, flying at medium altitude, received a direct hit from a 90 mm. shell in the nose of his aircraft. In spite of damage sustained, he remained in the target area, continuing to disrupt defenses. He remained in the lights and AA fire for ten minutes until the last low-altitude aircraft had cleared the target.

RCM (Radar Counter Measures) were considered very effective by the RCM observers as well as the crews of the planes. It was in great part through their efforts and employments that the defenses were made ineffectual.

The above Combat Mission Report may seem to be detailed to the nth degree but this is just what I wanted to show – i.e., how Baylis Harriss tactically planned this mission and how well it was carried out. Also, this was not the first mission to Soerabaja. Maj. Harriss, Capt. Rogers, and Lt. Putnam had preceded this mission April 24, 1945. Another Soerabaja mission was also flown on 27 April, 1945, with Maj. Harriss again in lead accompanied by the following crews: Capt. Rogers, Lt. Whitehead, Lt. Bartlemes, Lt. Workman, Lt. Upfield and Lt. Olsen.

Combat Mission Report
Snooper – Encounters With Japanese Fighters

I would venture to state that all *Snoopers* at one time or another encoun-tered Japanese aircraft. They were sighted visually in many instances, but often times only on the radar scope. There is even one report of an early *Snooper* (Rocky Brown) flying out of Munda, making a bombing run on a Japanese flying boat that was below him. The following two instances re-   ported here, occurred during daylight hours and in both cases Japanese fighters pressed home their attacks with vigor and accuracy:

Number One:

Lt. Beaver in A/C 081 and Lt. Cole in A/C 397 took off from Morotai at 1010 hours for an armed shipping search and photo reconnaissance mis- sion of Southern Makassar Straits and Southern Borneo. Between 1518 and 1532, while flying at 6500 feet in the vicinity of Makassar Town, the two *Snoopers* were intercepted by two Tojos and one Zeke. All three enemy air-craft were painted black with light undersides. A yellow strip one foot wide was on the leading edge of both wings on the inboard one-third next to the fuselage. Large meatballs were observed on the top and bottom of both wings on all aircraft.

The *Snoopers* were echeloned to the right with the wing plane five lengths behind and 25 feet above the lead plane. A total of five passes were made from between one o'clock and five o'clock. Two were high, two were level and one was low. The first pass was made from one o'clock high on the wing plane. One phosphorous bomb was dropped bursting 1000 feet below the formation. The Tojo closed within 100 yards, then did a "Split S" diving out through the formation. The next attack was on the lead plane from two o'clock high. The Zeke passed over the tail dropping one phosphorous bomb which burst 700 yards out at seven o'clock and 100 feet above. The third plane, a Tojo, was flying parallel to the right of the wing *Snooper*, Lt. Cole and 100 feet above. The Tojo pulled ahead and turned into the lead plane, Lt. Beaver, attacking from one o'clock high in a dive. The Tojo went below the level of the B-24 and the last phase of the attack was from below. Lt. Beaver nosed down and turned into the Fighter, bringing the attack at 12 o'clock low.

Both the *Snooper* and the fighter were firing. Neither aircraft veered from course and the fighter first hit the B-24 under the nose, chewing along the underside of the *Snooper* and nosing up into the bomb bay. The fighter appeared to disintegrate, and burst into a ball of flame, nosing up and falling off on its left wing. It settled into a tail down flat spin and crashed in the water six miles west of Makassar Town.

Approximately five seconds after the collision, one chute, partially opened and on fire, came from the wreckage. It is the opinion of Lt. Cole's crew that this was the pilot of the fighter. As the B-24 went down one Zeke circled, following it to the water, then broke off and followed Lt. Cole at seven o'clock at a two-mile distance. After the ramming of Lt. Beaver's air-craft, Lt. Cole dived to the deck. On the way down the Tojo returned and made a pass from three o'clock level breaking out over and to the left. This Tojo returned again and flew parallel to the *Snooper* at two o'clock and 1500 feet above one mile to starboard. Lt. Cole made three gentle turns to the left to avoid a possible recurrance of the collision pass made in the lead plane. Both fighters followed the *Snooper* for 25 minutes before breaking away toward Makassar. Lt. Cole landed safely at Morotai at 2400.

Number Two: Lt. Mills A/C #899 and Lt. Ober A/C #808.

Lt. Mills took off from Morotai at 0945 and Lt. Ober followed at 1020. The mission was to Mandai Airdrome and shipping reconnaissance of Java and Flores Seas. At 1455, while on the bomb run, Lt. Mills was attacked by two Oscars. A single attack was made by each fighter. The *Snooper* was flying along at 10,000 feet. When sighted, the fighters were in the distance orbiting. As Lt. Mills started his bomb run, the first Oscar made an 11 o'clock level pass, forcing him to turn away to the right and abandon the bomb run. The fighter closed to within 100 yards firing as he came and breaking away to the right and under the wing in a gentle curve. The *Snooper* was holed in the right wing by machine gun fire. The second Oscar made his attack from one o'clock level closing to within 50 yards, firing and breaking away in a gentle curve to the left and under. Again the *Snooper* was holed, this time in the bomb bay and radar compartment knocking out the radar equipment.

Tracers from *Snooper* were seen to enter the fuselage of the fighter on the last pass but caused no visible damage. The first fighter climbed after the attack and continued to orbit. The second plane let down as though landing at Mandai Airdrome. Both enemy planes were identified as Oscars and were painted brown with two yellow strips six to eight inches around the fuselage aft of the cockpit. Lt. Ober, who had been contacted by Lt. Mills and warned of fighters in vicinity, began his bomb run at 1555, one hour after Lt. Mills. During this time, two Oscars flew parallel, on altitude, just out of range but did not close. However, the bomb failed to release and Lt. Ober began circling back around for a second run on Mandai Airdrome. At this point, one Oscar made the first attack from one o'clock high, but soon broke away doing no damage. The same Oscar then made a second attack from five o'clock high breaking out beneath the *Snooper*.

The bomber was attacked for the third time just as the bombing run was begun, the attack coming from ten o'clock high. The fighter made a breakaway, then continued to close to 150 yards breaking out under the bomber at four o'clock; 20 mm and 12.7 mm hits were scored on the left waist, killing the radar operator, Lt. Russell, instantly and wounding the radio operator, Sgt. Hampshire, in the right shoulder. The tail turret hydraulic lines were severed and approximately 35 holes were drilled in the waist and left rudder from explosive shells. Lt. Ober continued his bomb run, scoring hits on center of the runway and remaining six bombs hit in hangar area with excellent results. The top turret and waist gunners scored several hits at the right wing roots of the fighter, which was last seen going down smoking in a wide spiral. Lt. Ober landed safely at Morotai at 2035.

Combat Mission Reports:
Snoopers Versus Submarines

Mission #1. Capt. Brown, pilot, night of 27-28 September 1943.

Capt. Brown took off from Munda at 1845L on a search strike mission in Buka, New Ireland area. At 2245L in position 4°30′S-154°-00′E picked up on special equipment indication of target. Made attack, dropped three bombs in train with negative results.

At .0015L in position 4°50′S-154°-35′E another target was picked up, believed to have been a sub. Our aircraft maneuvered for attack, made bomb run, dropped three bombs in train at 30-foot intervals, making a direct hit with the first bomb, second bomb falling approximately 30 feet past and the third bomb 60 feet past target. Attack was made from 1100 feet altitude. Approximately two miles beyond point of attack, indication on special equipment showed that target had broken into two parts and disappeared.

Mission #2. Capt. Reynolds pilot, A/C 833 SB-24D Coral Princess.

Took off from Munda at 2005L on night of 14 December 1943 to search southwest coast of Bougainville, St. Georges' Channel and New Ireland area.

At 2255L, a target was picked up from a distance of 30 miles at 5°02°S-152°27E. A bombing run was made at an altitude of 1000 feet and at 2309L, three bombs were dropped at 60-foot spacing on a surfaced submarine on a heading of 180°, speed five knots. The attack was on the port beam of the submarine. The three bombs straddled the sub with two bombs falling to port, the second bomb exploding 10 feet from the craft, number three bomb falling 10 feet from the starboard side amidship. At 2338L, a second attack was made on the crippled surfaced submarine which was on a heading of 60° and making no headway. This attack was from stern to bow, the bombs falling to port approximately 100 feet alongside the sub. Four strafing runs were made on the stricken vessel which tried to submerge but could not get completely under the surface. Because enemy aircraft were circling this A/P, the close vicinity of the damaged sub was left for the purpose of sending a radio message. One enemy aircraft was identified by the pilot as a fighter type, Nate. At 0100L, the damaged sub was again contacted at 5°00 S-152°4.0E on a heading into St. Georges' Channel. A three quarter mile long oil slick was left by the sub. Four more strafing attacks were made from 500 to 50-foot altitudes.

At 0225L, the sub was in practically the same position on a heading of 270°. At 0325L, the damaged submarine was sighted with the conning tower only above water making little or no headway. The sub had made only eight knots in four hours.

For this mission Capt. Reynolds and crew received the following communication from Commander Third Fleet through Comairsols: "A pat on the back for the pilots and crew of plane eleven flight twenty-one who left that Nip sub with his stern sheets hanging out."

Signed: Halsey

COMBAT MISSION REPORTS OF EARLY SNOOPERS
12 September, 1943 Mission 94A.

Mission: One SB-24 of the 394th Bomb Squadron of 5th Grp. (H) will search and strike shipping along northeast coast of Bougainville to Buka area.

Takeoff from Carney Field, Guadalcanal 2137 LCT and landed at 0220 LCT, 13 Sept., Carney Field.

Narrative: At 2340 LCT. while searching the northeast coast of Bougainville, an enemy convoy was sighted about 15 miles off shore in the Kieta area. This shipping was first picked up by radar, but due to the clear visibility, was almost immediately observed visually. Automatic weapon fire of 10W trajectory was seen three or four miles ahead, converging on what was taken to be a friendly plane. (This too was a *Snooper* who broke off attack due to intense "wall of fire", as he later put it.) This enemy shipping consisting of four AK and two DD's, was roughly scattered in the form of a square over a one mile area. The AK were approximately 1500 feet apart. The two DD's appeared to be circling them. One run was started and thought to be short, so an immediate turn was made and a second run started from a slightly greater distance. Automatic weapon fire of great intensity and fine accuracy was encountered throughout this bomb run. The same fire seen converging ahead, was now turned on our A/P. Tracers were observed all around our A/P. This was an excellent run made on one of the destroyers. This enemy vessel took immediate evasive action, making a very tight turn. It seemed to run directly into our bombs. These bombs were spaced at 40-foot intervals. The first two were short, but near hits; the third was a direct hit above the vicinity of the bridge; the last three were long. This run was made at 2350 LCT, at an altitude of 1500 feet on a course of 285 degrees. The concussion of the explosions at this altitude was terrific, lifting the tail of our A/P violently. The automatic weapons fire, and also some heaver AA continued with intensity. No more fire was received from the stricken vessel. Some of the heavier AA appeared to resemble our Pom-Pom. Much automatic fire was coming up from the area surrounding the immediate target area. These added vessels were never identified, but thought to be barges. Our A/P climbed to an altitude at 3000 feet taking a course of 100 degrees. Immediately after leaving fire from target area, we were intercepted by six or seven night fighters, first coming from 5 o'clock then observed in all directions. Repeated bursts from the rear blinded the tail gunner. It was only from this sector that the attacks were pressed home. These appeared to be single engine land-based type aircraft. The attacks continued for 15 minutes before attacking aircraft broke off. (The pilot's name was omitted from this report, but it could have been any of the original nine crews left after Lt. Robert Easterling was lost on the night of August 31, 1943. These include: Foster, Carlson, Zinn, Reynolds, Rockwood, Martus, Brown, Tillinghast and Lehti.)

Mission #5-213 A/P, #832, Lt. Splane, Pilot, 20 December, 1943.

Mission: During night of 19-20 December, 1943, this command will send one SB-24 type aircraft to Munda for Prowl mission. Airplane commander reported upon arrival to Col. Pincher XIII Bomb Com for further instructions.

Narrative: Airplane #832 took off from Munda at 1855 L moving directly to St. Georges Channel via Southern route. Moving North and East of Rabaul, preparatory to returning through St. Georges, airplane #832 suddenly picked up on radar screen, an eight ship convoy at #3'25S-131'5'W heading toward Rabaul. A large target believed to be a transport, was taken under attack at 2226. A run was made from seven miles, three bombs were dropped in trail from an altitude of 1200 feet. The first bomb fell just to port. The second and third bombs hit amidship, following which there was a series of powerful explosions and flashes and debris flew several hundred feet in the air. The ship burned fiercely on the water, the fire clearly visible from a distance of 25 miles. The screen revealed that the accompaning ves- sels closed in close to the burning ship for a period of 45 minutes, after which they returned to their former positions. Lt. Splane at 2343 L took a second target, believed to be another large transport under attack. A run was made from a distance of 11 miles. From 1200 feet, three bombs were dropped in trail at 30 feet intervals, falling directly ahead of the vessel. No AA fire was thrown up at attacking A/P by other ships. Visual sighting of the ship clearly revealed it to be a transport type vessel with a tall stack. The other ship had two stacks and a bridge that appeared to be very high. The crew at interrogation was of the opinion that one of the bombs fell directly down the funnel, after which the target resembled a roman candle.

Airplane #832 stopped at Munda and reported result of its mission before returning to Carney.

It seems highly possible that this convoy taken under attack by the "*Snoopers*" is the same one reported in Kavieng Harbor on 17 December by a Baker 25 plane, which sighted three large and one small A.K.'s, in addition to two smaller craft.

COMBAT MISSION REPORT A/C #899 Lt. Bartlemes, Pilot B-24J
TARGET – Armed shipping search of Makassar Straits from Cape Simutang to Laoet Island and thence north to Manggar.

Secondary target: Runway #1 Manggar Airdrome.

NARRATIVE

The *Snooper* entered the search area at 2115, performed the search at an altitude of 1500 feet, and left the search area at 2400. At 2225, approximately five minutes after radar indications of planes attempting to intercept were received, the *Snooper* first observed a large radar indication of a ship at 00°29´N – 117°48°E. This vessel was steaming on a course of 20°

at an estimated speed of 20 knots. The ship was subsequently identified as a CVE due to the fact that:

1. Six airborne interceptors were encountered in the vicinity.
2. The vessel showed on radar scope as a rectangular shape.
3. The vessel was seen by bomb flashes, momentarily, and no superstructure could be observed.
4. Lt. Bartlemes' crew made a radar pickup of a carrier on 8 February 1945 and recognized the scope picture received this night to be exactly the same.
5. The vessel appeared to be 550-600 feet in length, which, assuming it to be a carrier, would place it in the CVE class.

At 2245, the *Snooper* attacked the CVE. The LAB run was made at an altitude of 1100 feet, on a true bearing of 360°. The attack was practically broadside to the vessel, 9 x 500 lb. G.P. bombs were dropped with an intervalometer setting of 25 feet. During the attack, the carrier appeared to be slackening speed. This was thought to be an evasive tactic, designed to throw off the accuracy of the bombing run. The carrier did not change course during the run but maintained a heading of 90°.

The bomb train crossed the ship approximately one quarter of the way forward from the stern. One bomb fell within 25 feet of the starboard side of the vessel, three bombs were direct hits on the vessel, and one bomb fell within 25 feet of the port side. A large reddish explosion instantly followed by a very brilliant white flash, occurred. The pilot stated that he was able to read all of his instruments in the light generated by this explosion. The *Snooper* closely observed the stricken carrier on the radar scope during the next 20 minutes and in that time it did not change its position, but lay dead in the water.

CLAIMS: One CVE 550-600 feet in length approximately 13,000 tons damaged and possibly sunk.

At least six enemy planes appeared to be trying to intercept the *Snooper*, according to radar indications received. The planes were first observed five minutes before the carrier itself was sighted. The enemy planes appeared to approach the *Snooper* very directly. They circled the *Snooper* and then followed it until it was within six miles of the carrier. The planes approached closely, enough so that the exhaust pattern was picked up, in at least one instance, visually. The closest approach was estimated one mile and this plane was above and to right of the *Snooper*. During the whole time the interceptors were following the *Snooper*, Lt. Bartlemes altered course something like 30 times by as much as 25°. In each instance, the enemy planes would be seen on radar to have the new course. If these planes were vectored to the *Snooper* it was a remarkably efficient job. The crew feels that perhaps the interceptors were equipped with some sort of radar.

A subsequent report in the 13th Air Force Intelligence Summary dated 8 March, states that two 5th Bomb Group Liberators conducted a negative search of Makassar Straits on 7 March but did see a large oil slick, 300 x 600 feet. As a result of this sighting, our claim of one CVE damaged and possibly sunk, should be changed to probably sunk.

COMBAT MISSION REPORT – Lt. Wilmer B. Haynes, June 11, 1944

At 0240K Lt. Haynes made a precomputed bombing run on Dublon Town on a heading of 300 degrees true and dropped bombs from an altitude of 11,000 feet true. All bombs were observed to hit in target area. An estimated 10-15 searchlights caught this *Snooper* in their beams. Intense, very accurate anti-aircraft fire was hurled up at the airplane, which as a result of the fire shook and rocked violently. Lt. Haynes took forceful evasive action, dropping his plane down to 4000 feet. Immediately after the run, both the tail gunner and the assistant engineer visually sighted a two-engine airplane pursuing this *Snooper*. The plane opened fire on the *Snooper* as Lt. Haynes made a steep diving turn to the left, losing 100 feet of altitude and thereby successfully evading the night fighter. During the period that Lt. Haynes was being fired upon by the night fighter, intense anti-aircraft fire was being hurled up from a naval vessel outside the Truk Atoll.

Four direct hits were scored in the bomb bay and two hits in the Number 3 engine. As a result of the anti-aircraft fire, the control cables were shot out and the wing gas tank was hit causing gas to flow freely for some time through the bomb bay. The plane caught fire and burned furiously in the bomb bay and on the flight deck for an estimated five to eight minutes before the fire was extinguished by the crew members. Due to hydraulic system being shot out, it was necessary for Lt. Haynes to make a crash landing at Los Negros.

Lt. Haynes and crew were lost over Truk, June 25, 1944, two weeks later to the day. This loss was especially felt because besides Wilmer Haynes, who was a fine young man and other members of his crew, Lt. Charles Ames, bombardier, Sgt. Terpstra, Sgt. Preye and Lt. Bowden, all original *Snooper* members and were the last to be lost from the original members. Butch Werner and Charles Ames lived in the same tent and were very close friends. Butch took it very hard.

COMBAT MISSION REPORT: ENEMY SHIPPING, BRUNEI BAY

Following is an excerpt from mission reports for a mission flown by Capt. Earle M. Smith and crew on 29 January 1945 against shipping in Brunei Bay, Borneo:

Capt. Smith and his crew in A/C #396 took off from our staging area at Morotsi, at 0100, flew a direct route to Miri to conduct a search mission for enemy shipping in Brunei Bay. The *Snooper* entered the search area at 0700 and sighted its first target at 0740, a Sugar Charlie approximately 140 feet long. Two bombing runs were made on this target from an altitude of 100 feet. Three bombs were dropped, the first falling 50 feet over the target. On the second run, the first bomb fell 30 feet short and the third bomb scored a direct hit on the after part of the vessel just forward of the stack. The vessel was then strafed and observed to sink in shallow water.

At 0815 just north of Labuan Island about 300 feet offshore, a Sugar Dog was sighted and taken under attack. Two bombing runs were made. On the first run all bombs fell over the target. On the second run, the first bomb scored a direct hit squarely amidships. The vessel blew up and disintegrated.

Not content with having already sunk two shipping targets, Capt. Smith, with two bombs left, turned the *Snooper* toward Labuan Airstrip for a final attack. The *Snooper* reached Labuan airstrip and took under attack a large building on the western end of the strip. During this run the *Snooper* received intense and very accurate anti-aircraft fire and was severely damaged. Two 40mm hits were received in the nose turret. The #3 engine was hit in three places, knocking out the hydraulic system, the accumulator, all radio equipment and instruments were shot out, the LAB equipment was shot out, and the pump (fuel) damaged so that fuel transfer could not be normally made. The engines were getting gas by tank engine cross-feed.

The gas was low and difficulty was experienced in keeping #1 engine in operation on trip back. Ten miles from Pitoe strip #2 engine cut out completely. Although #3 engine was hit and hydraulic system shot out, it continued to operate. The engineer attempted to crank down the main gear manually. The left main gear came down but the right wouldn't budge. Capt. Smith set the plane down on the north Pitoe strip landing from west to east. The plane swung around and crashed against embankment between north and south strip. The aircraft was a total loss.

The following men were seriously injured: 1st Lt. Charles J. Nichol, copilot, was wounded by flak in the left shoulder, right leg and in the left eye. He suffered severe shock and was given a 50-50 chance of living. (C. F. Nichol survived and resides today in Emsworth, Pennsylvania); S/Sgt. Paul Ramaglia, armorer, was wounded by flak in the left foot and in the left shoulder. All but the heel of the left foot had to be amputated. S/Sgt. Arthur Russo, radio operator, was wounded by flak which shattered the left hand, pierced his left arm, his right shoulder and tore a large hole in his back. S/Sgt. Sidney Palley, Engineer, was pinned in bomb bay during crash landing while still attempting to lower the right landing gear. He suffered a possible fracture of both legs. Capt. Smith, pilot, received several fragments of flak in the right arm. The rest of the crew received minor injuries during the crash landing.

MISSION REPORTS SUMMARY – OCTOBER 1944

The month of October 1944 will always be remembered as the beginning of the invasion of the Philippines. The part played by the *Snoopers* was of utmost importance in the preliminary preparations to pave the way for the invasion. During the first days of October, the *Snoopers* were assigned to obtain weather information between Noemfoor and the route to Balikpapen, Borneo. These missions had a two-fold purpose; first to obtain weather data was essential to assure the success of groups of heavy bombers waiting to smash Japan's most heavily fortified oil base; secondly to substantiate theories that our heavy bombers were capable of flying long-range missions (over 2200 miles), with maximum fuel and bomb load. We flew 53 sorties with only one turnback, 14.5 tons of bombs were dropped on shipping targets, 13.25 tons on Balikpapen. A total of 9.75 tons of bombs were dropped on the following land targets; Gorontalo, Koendang, Jolo Town, Puerto Princessa, Lahug Airdrome and Menado Town.

Hordes of heavy bombers from FEAF began to hit Balikpapen, and in a very short period of time the Pandansari Oil Refinery at Balikpapen, producing approximately 12% of the entire Japanese Aviation Gasoline Supply, was made inoperative. Even after Pandansari was reduced, the *Snoopers* continued to heckle Balikpapen with nightly raids. These raids continued until the Philippine invasion on 20 October 1944. To prevent the Japanese from moving any stocks of oil and gasoline from Balikpapen, it was necessary to set up a blockade from their shipping centers. Again the *Snoopers* were called upon to strike enemy shipping. Daily shipping strikes were made in Makassar Strait and were effective in bottling up any shipping that might try to run the gauntlet between the west coast of the Celebes and the northern tip of Borneo.

When the Philippine invasion began, the 868th Squadron's operations shifted to the inland waters of the Philippines and the Sulu Sea. These long searches taxed the *Snoopers* to the limit of their range. The average time spent on these searches was 16 hours.

On 21 October, Lt. Thompson and his crew sighted a large Japanese Convoy in the Sulu Sea. This was the first indication that the Japanese intended to oppose our landing in the Philippines with their Navy. The sighting prepared our forces that were supporting the landing on Leyte and this preparation made it possible to inflict the tremendous losses that later occurred to the enemy. During the search of the west coast of Palawan Island, Captain Wallace and his crew sighted a newly constructed airfield at Puerto Princessa. This airfield had hitherto been undiscovered and provided a threat to our shipping, our Navy and our planes operating in the Philippine area. During the month, the *Snoopers* sank or destroyed approximately 11,000 tons of enemy shipping and damaged another 5000 tons.

Arthur H. Millard

The Saga of Scott Project Crew #3

Photos provided by Arthur H. Millard

As near as I can remember I believe the Scott Project crew personnel were assigned in July, 1943, at Langley Field, Virginia. Major Edward Scott was a veteran B-17 combat pilot with the 63rd Squadron., 43rd Bomb Group, 5th Air Force, and once was CO of the 63rd. The 5th AAF Commander, Gen. George C. Kenney, had sent Scott back to take charge of this operation, preparing the crews for duty with the 5th AAF Veteran navigators, Lt. Cunningham and Lt. Fred Blair. They had come over with Scott to assist our navigators in training. Ten of the First Pilots were veteran Sea Search Attack Group pilots who had flown B-18s on SUB patrol off the Atlantic Coast and the West Indies. One, Capt. Hamill, a pre-war commercial pilot had gone into the RCAF but was now in our own AAF. The First Pilots were Capt. Coleman, Capt. McIntosh, Capt. Hamill, 1st Lts. Ring, Quinette, Hafner, Harris, Burghoff, McGehee, Biddison, Hallman and finally me, the lone fledgling shavetail, 2nd Lt. Arthur H. Millard. We became Crew #3.

Kneeling, left to right: 2nd Lt. Arthur H. Millard – Pilot, 2nd Lt. Harold C. Way – Co-pilot, 2nd Lt. Mervyn O. Gadwah – Navigator, and 2nd Lt. Charles E. Swindler – Bombardier. *Standing:* T/Sgt. Ralph H. McMillan – Radio Operator, T/Sgt. Rudolph J. Rypyse – Flight Engineer, S/Sgt. Richard Everson – Asst. Flight Engineer, T/Sgt. Leslie G. McCulla – Radar Operator, and S/Sgt. William Desmond – Armorer-Gunner.

Each crew was assigned a ground radar technician, ours being Sgt. Conger. Lt. Brewster was assigned to the project as the radar technical officer. Last, but not least, two very important civilians, Carl H. Jones and G. W. Hutton, Western Electric electronic engineers. Western Electric developed the airborne radar and radar bombsight we would be using.

W. G. Hutton   Carl H. Jones

My first assignment with the project was to check out the other first pilots, as none were qualified on the B-24. It was interesting and I gained good experience doing it. Most of them were serious about it and easy enough to work with. Bill Hamill's broader range of experience was plain to see. McIntosh was probably the least physically coordinated pilot I ever saw, but he more than made up for it with a good head and a lot of perseverance. Then there was McGehee. Purely handling the plane, you'd have to put him in the category of being a natural pilot. But it was apparent from the start that he wasn't about to have a practically new 2nd Lt. tell him of anything.

Too long ago to remember details but I know something about him bothered me, with good reason I believe, as you will learn later on.

Sometime during our training, Scott was promoted to Lt. Col. so I'll refer to him as such from here on out. On August 9th I flew Col. Scott to Wright- Patterson. As I remember, that's where our combat airplanes were being modified and equipped. Enroute, we went on instruments in a fairly heavy rain. Scott became concerned about the engines and I learned that the Wright R1820 engines on the B-17s would sometimes quit in heavy rain. I could only say I'd never heard of it happening with the P&W R1830s we had. Much later I learned that the R1820 ignition harness could short out in rain, a condition subsequently remedied. As he was staying and I was flying back, Scott asked me if I'd been instrument-qualified at Langley Field and is-sued a certificate. I had to say no and didn't know anything about it. He said to go ahead now but arrange to get it right away. While there, by the way, I got a close-up look at the Douglas XB-19, a huge monster at that time.

I flew on a total of 14 days in July and 25 in August, two separate flights on several of those days; mostly giving transition but a few day and night Sub Patrols over the Atlantic.

On September 8th our combat airplane arrived, a B-24D, #42-40896, manufactured at the Consolidated plant in 1942, with modifications. The original D models had a green house nose with a flexible 50 cal. machine gun in the nose, a tail turret and top and belly turrets plus waist window guns. Now the tail turret had been installed in the modified nose section and the radar spinner antenna replaced the belly turret. The radar operator's station was on the right side of the half deck above the trailing edge of the wing center section, the fuel transfer system staying put on the left side. A repeater radar scope was mounted at the navigator's station. And a special radar scope mounted on a standard Norden bombsight stabilizer was in the new nose chin. Additional armor plating had been added, particularly for protection of radar equipment. Normal empty weight was increased appreciably. The radar screens were all full 360 degree PPI scopes, the main ones as I re-member with ranges of 30, 50 and 200 miles and the special bombing scope also had three ranges but from 1 and 3 up to 10 miles. This electronic bomb sighting system was called the Low Altitude Bombsight, LAB for short. The optimum altitude was 1500 feet and that's where we practiced. The final objec-tive was to hunt Jap shipping under the cover of darkness at night, detect and track them with radar until picked up on the 10-mile bomb scope and then the bombardier took over. I forgot to mention two flexible 50 cal. guns were mounted in a small-ported Plexiglas greenhouse in the tail.

Dot Millard pins pilot wings on Art Millard

In the meantime, when first assigned to the 1st Sea Search Attack Group at Langley, my wife Dot and I rented a room in a private home belonging to a couple in Hampton. A nice home and very pleasent middle-aged couple. We sure enjoyed the fresh seafood available in the Chesapeake Bay area, especially soft shell crabs. Had to chuckle though the first time I asked for milk in a restaurant after ordering seafood. The waitress refused to serve it saying the combination would make me sick. Had run across that same theory earlier in Louisiana and had actually alarmed people there by drinking milk and eating fish. One night when thunderstorms had cancelled a sub patrol Dot and I had just turned out the lights and got in bed when there was a violent crack of lightning, a few seconds of an eerie glow in the corners of the ceiling and we were showered with bits of plaster. The bolt had shattered the brick chimney down into the attic and wood framing split and splintered here and there to the four corners of the attic, knocking out chinks of plaster in all the upstairs rooms.

Later, not because of that, we shared a cottage on Buckroe Beach, VA with Chuck and Betty Pomerhn. Chuck was Bill Hamill's co-pilot. The cottage was called the "Forecastle," it had two stories but the living area was open to the ceiling, stairway and balcony leading to the second-floor bedrooms to the rear. Had some good times there with others of our new outfit joining us for parties. One highlight then was going to dinner at the Army's oldest officers club in Fort Monroe.

We haven't come up with a name for the airplane yet so for now it's just 896. Took inventory, stowed tool kits, swung the compass on the ground, and calibrated the drift meter. The plane had just 29 hours when delivered and now we took it up for almost seven more. We swung the compass over the James River bridge, dropped our first 10 practice bombs on a rather indistinct target off Cape Charles. Not too good. Calibrated airspeed between New Point Comfort and York Pit Light. Tried bombing again the next day with Western Electric engineers Jones and Hutton observing, over "Old Joe" this time, a wreck off Virginia Beach. Although high winds set up a lot of sea scatter over the shoals the bombing went quite well and Jones and Hutton were elated with the equipment and results. Other crews out that day but none able to identify the target well enough to complete a single bomb run. Says a lot for McCulla and Swindler. Many practice missions followed, mostly good. One day, to test new resisters in the radar's 200-mile range circuitry, we flew at 8000 feet from over the Atlantic toward New York; picked up a return at 180 miles, a new record.

On Sept 18th we flew a round robin to Mobile and return, a lost test and celestial navigation exercise. Lt. Cunningham on board to check Gadwah. With Gadwah not tracking, Cunningham had me fly 300 miles off intended course and then Gadwah picked it up with no trouble.

The Mobile flight took 10 hours 55 minutes and we burned 1840 gallons of fuel, not bad at all. Flew to Charleston the next day and had my first experience flying in thunderstorms. Penetrated a widespread area of closely packed air mass storms to and from Charleston; mostly on the gauges, dead reckoning and again Gadwah stayed right on the ball. At Charleston, an operations officer almost grounded us because we didn't have a weight and balance form filled out. After that we flew one more practice bomb mission and then a high altitude test flight. Again over the Atlantic flying toward New York but this time at 20,000 feet. A photographer was on board to take pictures of the radar scope. The right nose wheel door kept coming open and it got mighty cold, adding to Co-pilot Way's misery being hungover from the night before. We had been in the soup for some time before letdown and during descent started picking up a pretty good load of ice and no wing de-icer boots. It was assumed they wouldn't be needed where we were going.

Pushed on down to warmer air and then on down to 2000 feet to get under the stuff and headed home.

I remember two previous incidents, one having to be in aircraft 896 because radar was involved. We had picked up an unknown blip on radar while on a sub patrol mission. All friendly shipping off the coast was tracked and this was a stranger and we were instructed by radio to check it out. Being in daylight and drawing closer, we were puzzled that we couldn't see it. Much to our surprise, our unknown ship turned into a large pod of whales. The other incident occurred on a night patrol. I had been fighting sleep and went to the tail to try to sleep leaving Harold Way at the wheel. Wasn't long before I felt it getting too quiet and I sensed the plane approaching a stall, and there was nothing I could do about it! But then everything got back to normal. I returned to the cockpit and got the story. We'd been flying under a scattered to broken cloud base with some faint moonlight and Way was flying visually. Then came a turn in our search pattern and he lost the horizon visually, almost stalling, but then getting back in control and settled on the new course. He hadn't had much stick time yet and limited Instrument training.

By this time we had had the best success in the project with the bombing and Charlie Swindler became Bombardiering Officer. On September 26 we were informed to be prepared to give the Secretary of War a demonstration of LAB bombing, but he didn't show. Then we were to take some generals up the next day and that got called off. Finally on the 29th we did take up two Lt. Colonels who were very impressed with the demonstration. The generals were there but went up with Capt. McIntosh. I have to assume someone decided it wouldn't look good to send them up with a mere 2nd Lt. even though Crew #3 was the showcase of the outfit. The rest of that day and most of the next we were busy loading the planes with spare parts, equipment, etc., for our departure from Langley, our families and our country!

On October 1, 1943, we departed Langley on the first leg of our journey to New Guinea. I made a low pass off the shoreline in front of the Forecastle, a final farewell to Dot and Mother, who had been there the last few days. Made two approaches in heavy rain before landing at Tinker Field, Oklahoma. Took off the following morning for Hamilton Field on San Francisco Bay. Clear weather gave us a good view of a lot of scenic territory from an altitude of 10,000 feet, though we took a southerly route avoiding the High Sierras to the north. Somehow somebody had goofed for after landing at Hamilton we were immediately told to proceed back to Fairfield (Now Travis Air Base).

At this point, the Air Transport Command took over complete control of our next and longest leg to Hickam Field. That evening the crew again tried coming up with a name for the airplane. Among others someone had come up with "Art's   " and now it came up again and everyone jumped on it. Scrounging up some yellow paint and a small brush I painted "Art's Cart" in script on the left side of the nose section.

On October 4th we were briefed for the flight to Hickam. One important item was time enroute. We would not be released unless estimated time fell under 14 hours. Two bomb bay fuel tanks would be used. Only the pilot, co-pilot, engineer, navigator and radio operator were to go on this one. All other crew members, radar officer and technicians, and the civilian engineers were off-loaded to ATC flights. Also off-loaded were spare radar equipment, most of the airplane spare parts, our footlockers, etc. Oh, and even all the airplane's defensive guns. During removal of the guns on our top turret, the Plexiglas was damaged and about then our APU solenoid went out, delaying our departure. One evening I managed to go to San Rafael to visit friends I'd met at Altus, Oklahoma, when in Advanced Training School. On October 6th, four of our planes got off but one returned with a gas leak. The night of the 7th, three more got away, our APU still out.

Finally located an APU solenoid on the 8th, swung the compass again and everything was go. Got off that night, landed at Hickam in the morning after 13 hours 15 minutes. Slept the rest of the day. The area was blacked out and restricted at night but we went into Honolulu the next day. Sent Dot some island perfume and a locally fabricated bracelet. Waikiki Beach was covered with barbed wire and barriers.

New guns were now installed on the airplane. Our crews from here on were mixed up due to the off-loading, our own staggered departures plus the staggered arrival of our people spread out over various ATC flights. Can't remember who but we took the rest of another crew who were there and flew on to Canton Island on the 11th, flight time 11 hours. Canton is just a tiny coral atoll all by its lonesome in the middle of the Pacific Ocean, the largest part of it having just enough room for an airstrip and limited installations.

A bit of humor I've never forgotten was thrown in during the briefing for our next leg to the Fiji Islands. In all seriousness the briefing officer gave us a dissertation on the average Australian's usage of the English language, meant to keep us from offending or being offended when mingling with the Aussies. The Aussies have coined words for things too numerous to remember but he placed emphasis on words and phrases commonly used by both them and us, and even Englishmen, but having entirely different meanings. The briefing officer topped it off by saying don't be surprised if, when asking an Australian girl for a dance, she replies, "No thank ya, I'm all knocked up (tired), go jazz (dance with) my sister awhile."

Off again in the morning, next stop Nandi on Vita Lavu, the big island in the Fijis. Here we saw for the first time Melanesian natives who populated much of the Southwest Pacific including New Guinea and the Solomons. Had my first taste of Australian beer here, very good. Capt. McIntosh already there but held up with a gas leak. On October 14th we flew on to Amberly Field near Brisbane, Australia, 10 hours, 50 minutes. (Canton to Nandi had been short, just 7 hours.) Saw an Australian Troup Show staged there that night. Went into Brisbane the next day and by pure coincidence ran into Bud Morrison from A Battery and he told me old buddies Mike Bakenhauer and Leo Outcelt were at the docks with a detail loading equipment preparatory to moving up into New Guinea again. I lost no time finding Mike and Leo and then lucked into a ride out to their bivouac area some distance out of town. Certainly was good to see the old gang, stayed for mess and part of the evening. Saw Vicksburg's grave with tombstone and all. He had been killed, by a falling tree, during clearing for the camp area. Vicksburg was a starving stray mongrel pup Leo Outcelt picked up on the street in Vicksburg on our way to Louisiana in 1940. Small, sort of dirty brown and scraggly hair. He became our mascot and loved by all. Rode back to Brisbane that night with Major Chisholm driven by his attractive blond Aussie chauffeur.

Welcome to New Guinea

Flew on up to Townsville on the 16th, stopped for lunch and continued to Jackson (Seven Mile Strip) out of Port Moresby, total flying time 8 hrs 15 minutes. The landing was my first on steel matting; felt like driving on a corduroy road and was very noisy. Turned off too short on narrow taxiway and buried the right wheel in deep mud. Embarrassing! Took some doing to get it unstuck. Strip located amid rolling terrain, narrow taxiways winding up and down and around to the scattered revetments. We were driven to our bivouac area and assigned to a pyramidal tent with pole, four corner ropes, four folding canvas cots, blankets and mosquito nets. Setting was in the jungle with minimum clearing, well concealed from the air. After chow and it being well after dark we rolled up the sides of the tent and hit the sack, only to be rudely awakened around midnight by our introduction to an air raid alarm. There was a Jap air raid on Dobodura over the Hump (Owen Stanley Range) but nothing came our way.

In the morning we unloaded equipment and spare parts and then began getting acquainted with our Squadron, 63rd Bomb Squadron, 43rd Bomb Group, 5th Air Force. We were replacing the last B-17s and crews operating in the Pacific area, with the exception of four of those crews who were retained as reserve crews. Their pilots were Harry Park, Herbert Derr, Tex

Moulder and Payne. The B-17s were reassigned to Troop Carrier units and became very useful to them on special missions. The existing administrative and ground support personnel were also retained. I hadn't actually known until later that this was Col. Scott's old squadron. White was assigned as our crew chief, answered to "Whitey" and I don't remember his first name. Next came minor maintenance, cleaning the guns and testing equipment. We were one of the first two planes to arrive and the remainder of our own crew weren't in yet.

On October 20th we flew a practice mission on an old World War I freighter on a reef off Port Moresby. Feucht was bombardier, Benner on radar and Kosch, ass't engineer. That afternoon Scott had us fly to Dobodura to stage a mission from there, and he rode with us. Quinette also went, having Lt. Blair riding with him. (Blair was a veteran 63rd, B-17 navigator.) Let me say here that Col. Scott kept a free rein on our operation for the first few weeks before coming directly under FATF (First Air Task Force), a joint Air Force-Navy operation. I assume then, that Scott went to FATF in some position or other, as he definitely remained in the picture throughout my tour. Anyhow, there were no missions that night because of weather. Saw the movie "Virginia City" instead. By the way, the rest of our crew had arrived before we took off but too late for them to go with us, so, we had the same crew we'd practiced with.

Combat Mission No. 1

On the next night, October 21st, armed with ten 500 lb. H.E. demolition bombs we took off at 1900 hours, starting out on our first combat mission, the first of our crews to do so. Scott was with us as observer. No first pilot went out on his own until he had either ridden with or had a qualified veteran combat officer aboard on his first mission. Early on, we encountered thunderstorms too thickly packed to do anything but bounce and toss along through them. Scott didn't seem perturbed so I just kept on wrestling with the plane. Finally out of the stuff north of New Britain over the Bismarck Sea, it remained very cloudy, but still, one dark black night. We patrolled toward the west end of New Ireland and then back toward Rabaul on the north end of New Britain. Finding nothing, we turned back west again and then picked up a target west of New Ireland. Made two normal LAB runs at 1500 feet in and out of the clouds, dropping sticks of three bombs on each run. Near misses both times, possible damage, but ship, by now identified as a large freighter was still underway. Scott now wanted us to try a skip bombing run. We'd practiced the maneuver a couple of times in daylight but now we'd be solely on instruments until almost the last moment with only the radar operator attempting to guide us. (Wished McCulla had been on the scope.) Replaced the 1/10 second fuzes for 10-second delay fuzes, went to 3000 feet and started a shallow high-speed descent toward the target. Toward the end of the run Benner was repeatedly giving me three degrees right – three degrees right. Now approaching the deck in a right bank I saw the ship broadside to us but we're a bit off his stern, decks lit up by its guns and tracers all around us. I racked the plane hard left and about the same moment Scott hollered "pull out!" Patrolled back abeam Cape Gloucester, east end of New Britain, through the Vitias Straits and back to Dobodura. Made approach over 75 feet high jungle, flared too high, ending with a hard landing, four bombs still in the racks though defuzed. Scott then set up as standard policy that any remaining bombs would be salvoed, before landing and all take-offs be made from the trees and landings toward them. Most of this strip was on what had been a natural kunai grass clearing. It had merely been graded, leaving just the natural bare soil. We had landed at 0300 after 8 hours on the mission.

Later in the day, after getting some sleep, we flew back over to Jackson, only now reunited with the rest of our crew. They were very disappointed to have missed out on the mission but eager to hear all the details. Our sleep was broken up again that night by a big commotion not far outside our tent. Got up to find that two Aussie soldiers tanked up on homemade jungle juice somehow ended up in the tent shared by Lt. Blair and Lt. Skeeter Meade, our intelligence officer. Blair woke up, got popped in the chops and the brawl started. When we got out there Skeeter was sitting on one of them still slapping his head a bit as the guy kept trying to come back up fighting. The average Australian male grew up on athletics of one kind or another, and takes pride in his physical abilities. This Digger was very muscular, but drunk out of his mind. Though now past his prime, Skeeter had been a professional wrestler and the guy didn't have a chance with him. The MPs took over from there.

The next couple of days we had trouble with the LAB calibrator. Ground crew damaged the tailskid turning around in the revetment. Finally installed a new calibrator and had to drop practice bombs to set up a new magic number. At this time, I noticed Bob Mendell's APO number placed him right here at Jackson. Bob was in maintenance with Troop Carrier and when trying to look him up I found his outfit had moved back to Australia.

Combat Mission No. 2

On October 26th we went to Dobodura, loaded four 1000 lb. bombs and took off on our second mission, our own crew now except Harold Way. Burghoff flew co-pilot for his combat indoctrination and Way wasn't permitted to go. Two other crews out on their first missions: Col. Scott rode with

Quinette, with Hallman as co-pilot, Lt. Blair rode with Biddison, Coleman as co-pilot. That way five pilots got their indoctrination on three flights. I can't remember just where but we picked up two targets that night, one large and one small blip. Dropped a flare and identified the larger vessel as a merchant ship but no visual on the other. Made LAB run putting one bomb just off the rail and the other a direct hit. Flew on by to get at least a good ten-mile run at it again. Before completing the second run both targets disappeared from the screen. At debriefing we told the story just the way we saw it and being a bit puzzled ourselves didn't try to make any claims. Quinette and Scott reported setting a merchant vessel on fire and later found a destroyer but missed on that bomb run. Intelligence, trying to unscramble just who was over what ships and when and where was reluctant to confirm any results. Due to weather at Dobodura, we had climbed to 25,000 feet to top weather over the hump, landing back at Jackson. In the morning some of the old hands in the squadron made rather snide remarks to me about claiming a sinking, saying no ship sinks that quickly. I could only say we hadn't made any claim, just reported what we saw.

Two or three days later, however, through intelligence reports, it was learned that a submarine of ours while on the surface was setting up to torpedo a Jap transport and a bomber came in and beat them to it. They reported the ship sank and that they'd submerged to prevent becoming a target themselves. Time, position, everything fit into our involvement and we were credited with a confirmed sinking. Similar to new rookies on a ball club, that went a long way towards acceptance and respect as full members of the team.

We flew back to Dobodura on the 28th but no missions out that night. There was a big daylight raid on Rabaul the next day. Someone and I went down to the strip to watch the 90th Bomb Group B-24s return. Saw a B-25 crackup on take-off and burn. Approaching one of 90ths bombers, we saw someone trying to maneuver a limp figure through the nose wheel well. Seeing us, he hollered, "Hey, give me a hand, he won't bite." Got a hold on a pair of legs and eased the body out on the ground. It was the bombardier with a hole in his temple the size of a half dollar, our first close-up look at death in this war, and luckily for me the last. From the air our job was rather impersonal: seek a target, drop our bombs, and those of us on the flight deck never even saw the bombs strike. We would see the bomb release lights blink on the instrument panel and at 1500 feet we would feel the bomb blast concussions, disconcerting when tracers were flying all around you.

Pilot Grover Hallman was in the hospital with ruptured eardrums suffered when descending from high altitude, as we had the other night coming back from the mission into Jackson. On October 30th Col. Scott flew Hallman's airplane and crew to Dobodura and when taxiing in clipped the right wingtip on a guy wire. Well, even the pros can make a boo-boo. Hamill came over around the same time and got a light pole with his left wingtip. Found out Quinette had sprung bulkheads on a landing at Jackson after a hydraulic failure, temporarily grounding his plane. Not too big a deal, we didn't even go out that night, flying back to Port Moresby in the morning. .

We left Dobo early in the morning and for the first time saw what we were flying over; the only time you could as the clouds usually began building in the forenoon every day. Some of the peaks in the Owen Stanleys were pushing 14,000 feet. Back in Jackson we loaded personal belongings, three tents for crew and ground crew, equipment for 15 men in all, preparing for a permanent move to Dobo. Early on the 1st of November, we took off for Dobodura. Set up our tent, under the trees near the edge of a bank above the bottomlands of a small river. The squadron bivouac was in the U of the river, trees around the perimeter and a natural clearing in the middle, which we put to good use as an athletic field.

By now many of the crew had acquired nicknames. Bombardier Charlie Swindler, tallest of the crew, was "Big Stick," Harold Way, co-pilot and short became "Little Stick," radio operator McMillan was "Grandpa," Bill Desmond, average height, slenderly trim but wiry and tough was "Nails." Rudolph "Rudy" Rypysc was more often called "Rip." Mervyn "MERV" Gadwah, "Ben" Green and Leslie "Mac" McCulla.

I felt extremely lucky to have been blessed with this bunch of guys. They had really proved themselves, working well together with efficiency. In my book the best of the lot. In the very beginning we had had an assistant engineer who didn't fit well. By general agreement among the other crewmen, I requested that he be replaced. Got Ben Greene, a real jewel.

Later on that first evening Little Stick started a fire with dead wood, cooked cans of spaghetti and tomato soup and we topped that off with a can of peaches. When we could get them, canned foods were a treat as most   mess hall food was dehydrated. After debriefing from missions, we could go to the kitchen and get fresh eggs (I usually had six fried eggs); to me one of the best treats over there. Canned C Rations weren't too bad when we could find them and K Rations were provided on missions. From them I rarely ate more than the cheese and kept the cigarettes as they were rationed. Everybody losing weight now, the oppressive heat and humidity a factor as well as diet.

On November 2nd we dug a foxhole beside the tent and put up a pole frame in the tent. Slated for a mission that night but a broken spark plug kept us down. Hafner went out and sunk a transport in the straits near Rabaul. Would have gone out the next night but broken plug was not removed and replaced until too late. Coleman and Biddison out, Biddison sank a Sugar

Charlie. Coleman's bombardier Schechner accidently dropped all their bombs early on a run missing a shot at a destroyer or cruiser. Some of us that evening went over to a B-25 outfit and had cokes with ice at a sixpence Australian for a canteen cupful. Ice very scarce, might have been gotten from a ship at Oro Bay. On the 4th we completed a bamboo wardrobe, stashing everything above ground except our cots. Started out on a mission but suction went out. A bent hose to the flight indicator found and changed and then an APU cannon plug burned out. Hafner went out and reported three direct hits on a cruiser. An hour later they sent a routine position report from near Rabaul, but no further transmissions and they never returned. Hafner and crew were our first casualties.

The next morning I got the "Cart" moved from the end of the runway, where it was subject to a lot of propwash, to a revetment and we gave it a thorough inspection. No footlockers yet so some of us drove to the QM to get some needed clothes. Joe Schwarber, McGehee's bombardier, did the driving and he continually tried to keep to the right when meeting traffic, hairy and upsetting to everyone as traffic there was to the left; that part of New Guinea as well as New Britain and other islands having been Australian territories. Later a rumor went around that an SOS had been heard and everyone hoping it might be from Hafner's crew but nothing came of it. I rigged up a lamp with a tin can of kerosene and a piece of tent rope for a wick. Sometime later we got wired up for lights from a generator. For now the makeshift lamp let us play bridge and write letters after dark. Getting up the next morning, I found hordes of red and black ants in my pants (all of my clothes really) and had one helluva time getting rid of them. Our replacement APU not running right and keeping us grounded. Enjoyed a fine rare treat at evening mess, beefsteaks for everyone, Biddison and McGehee went out. After takeoff McGehee struck a flying fox, knocking out a prop governor. Replaced it with one from the "Cart" and went on their way only to have their bombs hang up on a run at a ship. On November 8th a Sgt. Woods looked at our APU and determined the timing was off. With that remedied and the prop governor replaced we were back in business. Learning the new PX was open, I went there and had just bought cookies, soup, a watch band, Xmas cards when Little Stick showed up to say we were set up for a mission and to get right back for briefing. Supposed to be two Jap convoys west of New Hanover. When ready to go the radar was out. Western Electric engineer and Lt. Brewster got it going. Finally off at 2255 hours. Lt. Epplen, one of the B-17 bombardiers, on board for on-the-job training; intercepted a three-ship convoy between Tingwon Islands and New Hanover, one large, two smaller blips.

Combat Mission No 3:

Weather clear as a bell and a full moon at its zenith, not very comfortable for a 1500 foot bomb run. Figuring at least on the element of surprise, we started our run on the larger target. I checked with Mac and one of the ships was to the left of the target and the other directly beyond it. Much to our surprise, we were fired on well before bombs away. I hung in on the PDI, but when the bomb lights blinked, I racked the "Cart" hard right and pushed her down. All in the same moment it felt like we hit a brick wall. Continued descent, gaining speed and wondering is this it – can she pull out – but then she did respond, leveling out at 500 feet, 260 IAS. But now I found the aileron control pressure light on and had to hold considerable left aileron and some left rudder to stay level and on a track. I checked on the interphone, everyone responding but Charlie. In my mind I thought sure from the feel of it, the hit had to have been right on the nose and I said somebody check on Charlie and then Big Stick came back rather testily, "I said I'm alright." I breathed a big sigh of relief. Now I got reports on the target, identified as a tanker with destroyer escorts. We caught it quartering on the bow, a 500 lb. bomb just off the port bow, direct hit from the 1000-pounder, creating a huge blast of flame obliterating the final 500 lb. bomb blast, most likely another direct hit or at worst barely off the starboard rail.

Those observing said the entire tanker was burning fiercely from stem to stern in short order. Big Stick salvoed the remaining bombs and we started climbing to 10,000 feet. I asked Rip to start checking and he found loose control cables in the bomb bay. Then Mac came on the interphone to say we had a hole in the right wing big enough to drive a truck through. He'd just come up from his scope and glanced out his little window on the half deck. Waist window observers had been concentrating on the target, still burning furiously until out of sight. With things settling down, using the interphone, everyone started singing songs, cracking jokes, anything to relieve the tension, and the boredom; we were on a beeline for and a long way from Dobodura.

As the damage was behind #4 engine (close to the full fowler flap, tucked into the wing where you couldn't see it), I elected to make a no-flap landing for fear of maybe aggravating our situation and it was only 0400 in the morning. Set up a long final approach, maintained 150 IAS for insurance, flared gently, chopped power and touched down at 140. Later we learned Coleman had made two runs over the same convoy a half hour or so before we did and that's how the hornets nest had gotten stirred up just waiting for us. Their bombs had hung up on both runs and they'd gotten return fire on the second run putting a hole several inches in diameter through a wing but fortunately the shell didn't detonate. Their observers identified the escorts as a destroyer and a cruiser. We got credit for destroying the tanker.

After some sleep, I went to check the damage more closely in daylight. It was assumed to have been a 40 millimeter shell striking behind #4 engine, barely in back of the rear spar blowing a hole in the top wing skin about 3 by 3 feet. Most of the skin still there but bent up at a sharp angle to either side, some inboard, some outboard. Rear spar was damaged, aileron control cable severed, right aileron jammed up, top skin of outboard end of right flap punched in. We off loaded a lot of equipment, particularly radar equipment that was highly classified, and taxied it over to the 380th Service Squadron. After studying it, they said they would do temporary patching so it could be ferried to Port Moresby for final repairs and heat treating of the rear spar. In the end, they did the whole job right there but found three fuel cells punctured by shrapnel and none in stock.

A day or two later I tried to burn out a hornets nest in a hole in a fallen tree behind our tent using kerosene. Not having much success with it I got some gasoline in a large tin can. Thinking my initial fire was out I started pouring gasoline and it flared up. Startled, I jerked back, flinging the can but slopping gas down the right side of my fatigues and the flames followed. I hit the deck rolling and luckily smothered the flames quickly. In the meantime, two to four planes were out most nights, weather permitting, with varying results but each important for weather reporting if nothing else. Capt. Coleman is now Squadron Commander, about the time we came under FATF. He advised he might send me to Australia on a "Fat Cat" for parts, supplies, whiskey and whatever. Went over to the 380th on the 13th and found progress on the "Cart" coming along good but no fuel cells yet. Two days in a row my crew officers and I censored mail. Set up corner posts in our tent and now we needed lumber for a floor.

Around 0400 on November 15th, the air raid siren sounded off followed by three loud blasts. I dove out the side of the tent-blanket, mosquito bar and all, hit our foxhole skinning an elbow and shin. In no time other officers came from all sides, as naked as I was, and jam packed our foxhole, light rain falling. No one else had dug a foxhole but they did after that. We could hear the typically unsynchronized engines of Jap planes overhead. A/A bursts glowing profusely in the clouds, some spent shrapnel rained on our tin mess hall roof. Heard bomb bursts that turned out to be at nearby Oro Bay. The initial loud bangs that alarmed me had come from an A/A gun not far past our mess hall that I hadn't known about. No sooner back in the sack when we heard a loner coming from inland so back to the foxhole. Could see him in the searchlights under the overcast with A/A popping all around him but he disappeared in the clouds.

Later that morning I flew No. 666 to Townsville on a "Fat Cat" run. First we found the three fuel bladders needed for the "Cart." At the next warehouse stop the District Supply Officer gave us static, saying we were out of order and that our requisition should have gone through channels. We finally softened him up, left a list of things to be picked up in the morning and went into town for steak and eggs and saw a movie.

In the morning Gadwah and I went to the airport and rounded up the supplies and parts we'd ordered, while Little Stick and Lt. Evans, our supply officer, looked for beer and whiskey and whatever else interesting they could find. All they ended up with was four cases of vegetable soup. We loaded the three fuel bladders, three main landing gear wheels, 1600 lbs. of carbon tetrachloride, 12 sacks of mail, nuts and bolts, starters, meshing solenoids, cannon plugs, pencils, staples, etc. Most of it in the waist section behind the bomb bay and what we could get in the nose to compensate, still had to be tail heavy. This had taken up the whole day so we stayed and saw the movie, "I Married a Witch." Flew back in the morning and Big Stick was in a stew because he couldn't go with us and barely talked to the four of us who had for the next couple days.

The next morning we scrounged a truck and went to Oro Bay looking for dunnage suitable for our tent floor. Found a small freighter with some rough lumber for a subfloor and smooth planks to use as doublers on top of them. It had iced water on the boat. Brought the lumber back, constructed the tent floor and by then all of us were so tired we hit the sack early. After breakfast we built steps, reset the tent and framed the inside. Best tent in the squadron and not quite finished yet. Drove back to Oro Bay that evening to give our donors a bottle of brandy and lined up additional lumber and nails. Nails were very hard to come by and up until then we'd been using old nails, many needing straightening. Before turning in we heated up a can of the soup we'd brought up on the "Fat Cat." In the meantime a number of other officers had really hung one on with booze gotten from somewhere. Spent the next morning washing clothes. Our laundry was a washtub of soapy water heated over an open fire, agitating the clothes with a wooden paddle, rinsing and hanging them out to dry. Our latrines, by the way, were replicas of the old-fashioned outhouse.

An excellent breakfast, on November 21st, steak and eggs. First mail began to come in. Big Stick received 15 letters, none for me yet. Got word the "Cart" was ready so went over to the 380th and taxied it back; everything OK but the batteries were dead. Equipment was reinstalled and the ground crew gave it a thorough inspection and accomplished minor maintenance. Took her up for a test flight on the 23rd. Another of the B-17 bombardiers, Lt. Dillingham, was on board for training. On the first bomb run when accelerating up over 200 IAS, we began to get tail flutter so we went back in. Found control cable tension was too tight.

On the 24th I flew 10 enlisted men in Burghoff's airplane to Port Moresby to appear before an Aviation Cadet Board. Little Stick did the flying, still tending to be left wing low on approach. He, as had all of our co-pilots, came out of single engine school, had a tad of P-40 training and then assigned to our project. The only stick time they got was at the discretion of their respective 1st pilots. While at Port Moresby I tried unsuccessfully to locate Gildermeister, from LaCrosse, and Fred Baker, former Cadet and B-24 transition classmate. Enjoyed a good meal at 43rd Bomb Group's mess. Had a rum and coke, first drink since Brisbane on the way over. Then went to see "Harry Aldrich Swings It."

Thanksgiving Day. Discovered the left main landing gear actuating cylinder leaking on ship No. 050. Finally got off for return to Dobodura with 16 passengers and some liquor for the squadron but by now we were late and missed out on dinner. Everyone remarking how good it had been, turkey with all the trimmings. Well, you win some and lose some. Took the "Cart" out in the morning for another test and practice mission and this time everything went smoothly. While some of us were in Moresby, Charlie had gotten more lumber so we built more shelving for the tent.

Combat Mission No. 4

On November 27th, a 90th Bomb Group, B-24 cracked up on take-off with 13 on board, cutting a long swath through the trees, scattering parts all the way. Miraculously two crewmen got out, one unscathed and the other with a broken arm. We went on a mission that night and made a perfect bomb run on what turned out to be an uncharted reef with a ship a thousand feet away. On the following day, Tex Moulder and his crew, from the B-17s, used the "Cart" for training. I rode along and Tex proved to be a good pilot and his crew did well.

At about this time, it became impractical for crews to always fly their own planes. Rotation of crews and availability of planes became paramount, and of course, the so-called reserve crews now becoming qualified had to fly something. Harris took the "Cart" on a mission that night but the radar went out early on and they aborted. The next morning Bolles, Harris's co-pilot, made it a point to let me know our plane was a real dog, claimed they could only get 148 IAS and had a hard time keeping the right wing up. I felt I knew what had happened but asked permission to make a test flight, just to be sure, and invited Bolles to be co-pilot. Our planes were B-24Ds which had but one aileron trim tab on the right aileron. With its modified Davis wing the 24's had neutral stability, with the inherent tendency to remain in any given attitude it happened to be in at any given moment. Unlike most airplanes, you didn't get immediate reaction when applying aileron trim. When needing trim you had to crank in some and then wait on the airplane as it took its own sweet time adjusting to it. A vivid example of this neutral stability can be demonstrated in a bank. For instance, if one applies the proper initial back pressure rolling into a 45-degree bank he can hold it with his little finger, but if he lets the nose get down it almost takes two men and a boy to haul it back up. I always liked to say when flying a B-24, instead of staying a step ahead of it, stay three steps ahead of this baby and you had a good airplane. Too many pilots had trouble with this characteristic and I believe it was the major reason it had such a bad reputation among Air Force pilots. Now back to the "Cart" for the test I found Harris had cranked in 7 degrees left aileron trim, and 4 degrees left rudder, creating extra drag, another thing the Davis wing was more critical to than conventional airfoils. So I reset the tabs, took off and climbed to 1500 feet. Being light and having early morning smooth air I reduced power at 200 IAS, sat back folding my arms in my lap and looked at Bolles. The "Cart" was boring along pretty as a picture, and he couldn't do much but put on a sheepish grin and take back all he had said about the old crate.

Later in the day we flew ship #050 on an experimental flight with our civilian engineers Jones and Hutton, Radar Technical Officer Lt. Brewster, and Bombardier Freddy Schandorf along. Among other things they had me turn 10 degrees off course when three miles from the target but Big Stick quickly cranked in corrections, I got back on the PDI and we hit the bullseye.

Combat Mission No. 5

During briefing for a mission on December 1st, extremely heavy thunderstorms were in progress, even delaying our ride to the strip. During a lull McIntosh got off from a soggy, rain-puddled strip. We were to follow 50 minutes later and Moulder after us. When I lined up at dusk a wall of rain was marching down the runway toward us. Little Stick and I looked at each other, and I thought "Yours is not to question why, yours is but to do or die," pushed up the throttles. (Big Mistake.) In short order we were on instruments, time seemed to drag so I hauled it off at 120 IAS. Now it was like freezing a simulator, hanging in the air but not one instrument needle moving. Visualizing the trees beyond the clearing I eased pressure, coaxing speed to 130, got a glimpse of the darker outline of the trees and barely eased over them. Guys in the tail said they could have picked leaves off the trees. Now we hit rough air, and averaging out 150 indicated and reaching 800 feet, I called for flaps up. Right then the bottom dropped out and I instinctively grabbed Little Stick's hand on the flap handle. In the blink of an eye we ended up at 200 feet indicating 120 mph (Learned more about that phenomena years later flying airlines). Gingerly got the airspeed back and climbed to 1000 feet and then got the flaps up. Banged and bumped our way, until well out over the Solomon Sea before clearing the rough stuff and heavy rain but still on the gauges. We headed toward New Britain only to have radar pick up more heavy weather and we lost our radios. Attempted to return to Dobodura, but weather straddling the coastline was still so heavy even radar couldn't identify land from sea.

I considered flying east to Milne Bay and following the southern shore into Port Moresby. But Finschhafen had been forecast to remain clear and Gadwah suggested going there to see if we could get right on the coastline and follow it home. Could even go into Finschhafen but it was close to Japanese lines then. We dead reckoned to and sure enough went in the clear at Finsch. Turned back down the coastline back into the weather but were able to keep the coastline on radar and not as rough as earlier. Picked up the Gona Wreck (our practice target) about 17 miles north of the field. Heading for the field we began picking up searchlights one at a time and visibility improved enough to find the strip. Moulder was on final approach as we got to the field. He hadn't been out long, not being able to take off until long after we had because of the weather. Then out over the water he ran into some of the same heavy stuff we had and lost his radios. A junction box or something related was found to have grounded out the radios in that extra heavy precipitation and a fix was done on all the planes. Back at camp we found the rain had washed out a lot of the bank behind the officers' tents felling trees into McGehee's and Coleman's tents.

Coleman, Quinette, McGehee and Burghoff went out on the 3rd of December. Quinette made three skip bomb runs sinking a Sugar Charlie. Burghoff returned early with radar out. McGehee lost generators, returned and on landing snapped off the right landing gear. Number 4 prop came off puncturing the wing and aux fuel cells. Bomb bay doors buckled but all in all didn't look too bad. Coleman reported making a bomb run and missing the target. When returning to base, he got within voice range of the tower on VHP and was talking to the tower. The weather was clear but they couldn't find the strip and asked for searchlights to be turned on. Tower advised searchlights were on and they still didn't see anything. Radio contact was lost before they should have run out of fuel, and the airplane never returned. The best guess was that they may have been in the vicinity of Morobe above Cape Ward Hunt up the coast from Dobodura. On radar the shoreline there could look vaguely similar to the Dobo area. A good navigator with a radar screen in front of him and doing proper flight following shouldn't fall into that trap, but I wondered if with the long night hours we were flying, he had fallen asleep and when waking up misinterpreted what he saw on the screen. Mountains at Morobe were much closer to shore than at Dobodura and they may well have run into one looking for the strip.

Combat Mission No. 6

At 0900 in the morning we took off on a search mission to see if we could find any sign of Coleman and crew. Flew to Finschhafen searching between the shoreline and the foothills. Then all the way back past Dobo to Milne Bay and returned at 1545. Park took off at 1100 and combed the Morobe area in particular, landing just ahead of us. Nothing.

For the most part up until now, our departures had been in the late afternoon, and we returned in the wee hours of the morning before sunrise. As a result of Coleman's disappearance Col. Scott set up a new policy that departures would now be generally made after dark and return to base after sunup. Also, to carry only three bombs and just 2700 gals of fuel, main tank capacity. We'd carried various bomb loads but recently till now had settled on six 1000-pounders. I played dumb on that gas restriction and on the QT kept the extra 400 gals in the outer wing aux tanks. Even so I had the lowest average fuel consumption per hour in the squadron, 180 gals PH. Most crews used up to 200 gallons and more, as I kept track primarily through association with our crew chief, Whitey and others in maintenance as well as my own flight crew enlisted men. Got some sta tic from fellow officers about being too familiar with enlisted men but I never regretted it. Those guys busted their butts for the cause and were never disrespectful. I'd never really had cruise control training but had set up my own simple procedure, and I might add we most always took off on missions well over design gross weight. When starting out heavy on a mission I simply adjusted power needed to maintain 160 indicated. As the load lightened I compromised between increased airspeed and reduced power. On more than one occasion when coming home light after a long mission, we were down to 30" manifold pressure and 1800 RPM and indicating 200.

On December 5th, more than two months since leaving Langley, I received my first mail. A letter from Dot left me a bit puzzled until receiving one she'd written earlier, in which she informed me I was to become a proud Papa.

For a couple of days weather kept everyone on the ground. Lt. Woods shot a flying fox high up in a tree but it stayed up there all night. In the morning Harris shot it again knocking it down. The wingspan measured 5'1". The head looks similar to a fox but they are fruit bats. A group of natives came and took it with them for food. I have no idea why but while at Dobo these huge bats would fly by every evening, and always in the same direction. No system, just scattered all over the sky but all on the same heading. We'd joke about that one buzzing dangerously low, and that one way up there must be on oxygen. A couple of natives came to the river behind our tents and spread a fluid on the water. Soon many small fish bellied up to the surface to be scooped up by hand. The fish stunning liquid was squeezed out of some type of roots.

Combat Mission No. 7

Finally got out on the 9th, our first objective being to hunt for a Jap sub, reported in the vicinity of Sio, up above Finschhafen. When abeam of Sio, without any sightings, we received a message to return to base. Encountered heavy thunderstorms spread down from the mountains blocking our way in. Only 40 miles out and in the clear working back and forth from over the water and back toward the hills and in voice contact with the tower. And ground radar had us. Every time we headed inland the tower urgently advised us to turn back over the water, undoubtedly thinking about Coleman the other night. We couldn't seem to make them understand we were in the clear and just trying to find an opening in the weather. When we were advised the field was improving and we had 1000 feet and 4 miles, we bored into the stuff from over water at 500 feet. Picked up the Gona Wreck on radar heading for the strip. Again began seeing searchlights one at a time and finally the tower beacon. On downwind a cloud bank forced us to 200' and we're back in rain. A bit hairy with that tall jungle so close under us, but managed to bring it on around to a landing. Capt. Herbert Derr, now our CO, and others were there to greet us. They had been concerned and quite relieved we were back safe and sound.

In the meantime, we had been putting the clearing, I mentioned earlier to good use, the various sections of the squadron organizing teams and playing softball, touch football and volleyball. Even had team names coined to befit respective sections and intra-squadron tournaments. A lot of fun, good exercise and certainly was a help toward relieving tension.

Cape Gloucester, across the Vitias Straits from Finschhafen, is being softened up for invasion. On December 14, McGehee went out to shadow the coastline near Gasmata on New Britain, causing more concern when his position reports stopped and they didn't get back. Received a message later on that he had gone to Kiriwina Island on account of weather and hadn't gotten a message through to the squadron. Harris went out that night on the same mission. In their last position report, they advised encountering night fighters. They didn't return. The very next night we were scheduled for the same thing again. That day my nerves were just about shot and for the first time I was actually dreading the thought of making a flight. Then the weather went sour and the mission was scrubbed. I slept better and longer than usual that night. Woke up in the morning feeling fine, and though there was always that niggling bit of apprehension when going on missions I never had another day like that.

Combat Mission No. 8

We flew a mission on the 18th, sent back our usual weather reports, but found nothing moving on the water. Returning to Dobo we ran into a solid wall of nasty weather a little offshore, no holes in sight. Pushed through at 600 feet in heavy rain but not too rough and the field was open. Burghoff and Moulder out the next night, found two convoys, no results on bombing. Park and McGehee went out on the 20th, Park sinking a Sugar Charlie and a Navy Blackcat got another one at the same place. I was Duty Officer that night. Payne, a former B-17 pilot, flew Hallman's crew with Hallman riding co-pilot; McIntosh out also, no action. Biddison and Ring out next, Ring flying the "Cart" for the first time. Weather cut their missions somewhat short and afterward Ring told me he really liked the "Cart."

Combat Mission No. 9

Biddison and crew number 3 out on the 23rd. Decoded a message from a "Black Cat (Catalina) saying they had made a bomb run on ships near Garove Island. Being closer, Biddison got a crack at them; no hits and reported ships. When we got there, we were jumped by night fighters before we could make a run. Two ships close to Garove now, others must have gotten into the harbor. Shook off the fighters but felt that going back for a bomb run could be suicidal. Found three Sugar Charlies later but missed due to LAB malfunction. Slept in the morning then played softball, navigators and bombardiers beating the pilots. Special Services put on a good Christmas Eve show.

Enjoyed a full and busy Xmas day. Two volleyball games, aircrew officers beating aircrew enlisted men. Then a softball game they won. Topped that off with a wild touch football game we lost 6-zip. By then everyone hot, sweaty, grimy and bone tired. Revived with a good Xmas dinner, and the evening was topped off with an excellent variety show staged by a number of our own squadron personnel. A highlight was Sgt. Ridenauer doing a strip act and if you hadn't known him you'd have sworn he was a girl.

In the morning Whitey said he'd found a slug in the bomb bay catwalk. Must have come from the night fighters at Garove shooting without tracers. Through intelligence reports received that day it was learned that a PT Boat had shot down a Jap four-engine flying boat. Everything, time, date, place, fit in too well and we had to feel certain that had been Harris, not a flying boat. Unfortunately, this sort of thing happened occasionally. During the recent landing on Cape Gloucester, some of our B-25s were fired on by friendly gunners on the surface with nervous trigger fingers. Our subs in enemy territory were entirely on their own and unknowingly Quinette bombed one he caught on the surface one night; some damage done but luckily the boat limped to a safe port.

Standing, left to right: Lt. Charlies Swindler, Lt. Art Millard. *Sitting, left to right:* Lt. Joe Schwaarber, Lt. Mauer, Radar Technical Officer.

On December 27th, Gildermeister hitched a ride on a plane from Nadzab to Dobo for a visit. He went with several of us to see a Jap camp area and cemetery nearby. There were foxholes and remnants of huts and shacks. It was in dense jungle and only bare minimum clearing done, bugs and mosquitoes must have been horrible. Found a skeleton, less skull and arm bones, amid a rubble of gas masks, canteens, shoes, saddles, motorcycles, etc. I would imagine souvenirs such as guns, bayonets, swords and the like had been scavenged long since. The next morning we took Gildy on a test flight. Hamill, now Operations Officer, rode as co-pilot and we set up the AFCE to try automated coupled LAB runs. Bombar dier T. B. Allen Jones, made several dry runs that appeared to be good. Though I used the AFCE at times on long missions for cruising, I never coupled it for bomb runs.

It was very complicated and could be quite touchy. It had four adjustments for each flight control, centering knobs, sensitivity, ratio, and turn compensation. To start with there were several steps in setting up and then a 10-minute warm up. Then more steps in engaging each control separately one at a time. Cruising with it, I often engaged only rudder and aileron and would get some hunting on headings a lot. The equipment got its basic information from the bombsight stabilizer. Charlie got sick so we quit early and then I flared too high, landed in nose high attitude and damaged the tailskid. (The skid was really meant to protect the twin rudders if the tail was tipped down on the ground.) Back at camp some young native boys stopped by. They had a limited knowledge of English picked up at a mission in Buna, and were very entertaining and seemed to have sharp minds. Said of our enemy, "Japanese no good" and of us, "'Merican good fella". Played a game of basketball, pilots beating the mess hall. Taxied No. 955 out for a mission but scrubbed on account of weather.

To try a new experiment, on the 29th, Hamill again rode with me in ship No. 904 and bombardier Joe Schwarber dropped practice bombs from 5000 feet using AFCE, results not bad. Pictures were taken of the radar scope while flying over ships off Buna and Oro Bay. McGehee blew a tire on take-off scrubbing a mission. Censored mail the next day. The Electrons, radar technicians, beat the Bombers, ground ordinance personnel, in softball. McGehee set to go again but called off for some reason. More ball games the next day and now it's New Year's Eve. I think everybody in the squadron got into the spirit and the SPIRITS, and I fell off the wagon for that night. Our crew had gin and it got a bit rough when someone got a song session going. Had to put Little Stick to bed early. A few stuck on guard duty including Rip at the "Cart" so two or three of us went to the strip to spend a little time with him. At the stroke of midnight several Colt 45s sounded off in camp. No one hurt but in the morning light holes showed up in a couple of tents.

I was one of the very few up for breakfast New Year's morning. An enlisted man Whitey knew, who had painted many pictures on planes, going way back, on the B-17s. Whitey lined him up and the man consented to do our plane. He came up with a sketch of a girl about to step out of a two-wheeled cart. We liked it and said go ahead. He got started while the tailskid repair was being made. Went over to check on the plane, repair coming along and the base coat of the picture was done, outline looking good. Lost a softball game to the enlisted men, 2-0.

To me a major highlight of our New Guinea Experience came on January 2nd. Spent the day attending a native festival sponsored by the Australians, an annual event started years ago. Natives came from far and wide. The everyday apparel of the natives is next to nothing and of course many came that way. But there were also group representatives of the numerous villages and tribes attired in their best ceremonial finery and each group distinctively different from any other. And there were those there that day I'd never seen before, different than those we were seeing here near the coastline. The majority of the natives lived close to the shorelines and in the major river valleys to the lower foothills, probably as food and water were more plentiful. However, the humid heat, malaria and what have you all took their toll. They did have a partial inherent immunity to malaria but the total environment caused rapid aging and the average life span was said to be in the mid thirties. Adults generally short in stature and to me just didn't really look healthy. Young children appeared healthy but the bloom of youth evaporated quickly. Now the natives who came from high in the mountains were taller, had better skin tone and looked much healthier to me.

There were many games, contests and ceremonies. There was spear throwing, spears simply being long, slender, pointed shafts of wood, but accuracy not too bad. There were obstacle courses, foot races, even boxing, etc. Dressed only with the conventional sort of wrap-around mini-skirts, the girls foot races were nothing short of hilarious. And boxing! No way these guys had ever used this form of self-defense or fighting in their culture. The most comical exhibitions you've ever seen and I'm sure no one got the least bit hurt. Prizes for events were tins of bully beef, a treat for them. We'd been told the New Guinea natives lived in what was probably the unhealthiest climate in the world and as a people were about the most backward. From what I'd seen, I could believe it.

On the 3rd of January, I flew No. 904 over Oro Bay to give gunners on ships some practice, at the same time getting dry run practice on them. Later in the day we had a very comprehensive briefing on the world situation by an Intelligence officer along with what we knew and didn't know about New Guinea. For one thing my old National Guard 32nd Division had landed at Saidor without opposition. The Cape Gloucester invasion on New Britain had been hard fought and bloody, however. The enemy in our theater were half starved and lacked supply vessels and air transport. (We were playing our part in that respect.) The big plan was to jump ahead to strategic positions cutting off supplies to the enemy positions left behind. Too long and too costly to take out the Japanese every step of the way. Rabaul, for example, had been one of the strongest Jap strongholds in the area and now was simply by-passed. New Guinea still largely unexplored. The Papuans under Australia had been tamed the past 50 years and were no longer hostile. Although the Dutch had been there for centuries the western half of New Guinea had only been sparsely settled on the north shore. No white had ever been known to penetrate the interior of Dutch territory and return. Every reason to believe the natives there were still headhunters. At this time the Japanese were occupying the north shore of New Guinea, major concentrations from

Hansa Bay (just above Saider), to Wewak, Aitape, Hollandia, Wadko Island on to Biak Island, near the west end of New Guinea. There again we planned to leapfrog to major positions.

After dark that night we had a joint session with a sub chaser. They could pick us up on their radar at 12,000 yards, see us with binoculars at 5000 (moonlit night) and pick up our sound at 1500 yards. They were surprised when using evasive action how we still got directly over them by LAB alone and the SCs skipper was on board our flight to verify this. When finished with the sub chaser we went on to rendezvous with our modified A-20 nightfighters (called them P-70s). Ground radar would have to initially vector the fighters to within (7) miles of a target before the airborne radar could lock in. With our radar, we picked them up as far as 16 miles. We could easily shake them, before or after they got a radar lock on us. But letting them get a visual lock on us, at about a mile that moonlit night, they stuck like glue. Their firing had to be visual and not then tied in with radar and computers.

The sub chaser skipper had invited us on board and we took him up on it the next day. After a tour of his ship, iced pineapple juice was served, a treat for us. They had been on escort duty, hadn't encountered any subs, but had shot down a dive bomber and a torpedo bomber.

Combat Missions No. 10 & 11

Went out on a mission that night in No. 041 but above Cape Gloucester we lost our liaison transmitter and had two generators on the hook so we packed it in. Went out on the 7th on what we called the North Pole Run, sighted two ships, but being north of our bomb line FATF wouldn't approve bombing. Into a lot of nasty weather on return.

Had an easy day and just relaxed. The squadron was assigned a B-24 from another squadron, the 403rd, to be used as a day recco ship. Some of our crews started making daylight flights, occasionally finding a ship to bomb from altitude with the standard Norden sight. Our crew never did. Though it would have been interesting to see where we were going for a change. Thomas, another B-17 pilot, took Hamill's crew out that night. As I've said Hamill was operations officer and he hadn't been able to hack it as a combat pilot. Went on three missions and that's all she wrote. From the moment he left the shores of the USA his problems started. Though an excellent pilot, he had been too accustomed to being his own pilot, navigator and radio operator. This brand new ballgame, with the necessity for relying on other crewmembers, was too much and his ability to function started on a downhill slide. He flew two or three missions and that slide just got steeper. He was a nice guy, too, but now even his crew had more than they could take and it was all over. It did bother him a lot and he finally came to me asking if I would let him fly my crew with me flying co-pilot. We'd been friends way back in Langley and it was a hard thing to do but I had to refuse him. If Little Stick rode along just in case I wouldn't have minded so much myself but I couldn't see jeopardizing the spirit and morale of the rest of my crew. Everyone knew the situation, no secrets over there, and I just couldn't risk it.

Now Thomas got back in the morning, almost certainly with limited B-24 time. I saw them circling with main gear down and nose wheel up so I went down to the strip. Captain Derr, our CO, was up in the tower and when I tried to go up he refused to let anyone else up; keep in mind he had been a B-17 pilot, not much B-24 time. To make a long story short, Thadys, the engineer, repaired the hydraulic system open center line (had been severed by a bullet) using heater line and then they had used leftover coffee and the crew's urine for fluid and finally got the nose wheel down, landing with fuel all but dry, one engine already starved and feathered. They'd cranked the main gear down with the cables and all they needed to do was manually unlock the nose wheel, push it out and safety the downlock and they could have landed hours earlier. Earlier their bombs had hung up on the run they were on when they got hit. Two correspondents happened to be on the field at the time and the upshot of the story is Thomas and Thadys were awarded the Distinguished Flying Cross, Nuff said about how heroes are made, not all of them of course, but a lot of them. I could tell you more about some of the earlier ones but I won't.

On January 10th, I flew a group from our squadron to New Georgia in the Solomon Islands to compare notes with the 13th Air Forces' 868 Squadron twin to our squadron, the only other one like it. They had gone to the 13th a short time before we went to the 5th, and had trained at Langley. The pilots had all come out of Sea Search as had most of ours, and I had met some of them casually at Langley. One, Easterling, had cracked up at the end of the runway, reason unknown. Another, a former college football player, lost his nerve and was now a tower operator on some isolated island. One of their planes got out of control in a thunderstorm, dove to 500 DAS resulting in permanent damage to structural members, managed to get back but scrapped for salvage. Total results of their operation similar to ours.

We looked over their airplanes, radar shack, discussed tactics and procedures, maintenance, etc. They were using flame dampeners, something we never had. The airstrip sat between the shore and a steeply sloped hill just beyond the other end. Saw a B-24 with its nose on jacks being repaired. This one's hard to believe but true. The pilot had gotten too low on approach striking the water, ripped out the nose gear, skipped up and landed on the runway. It was being repaired to fly again. While at the strip I saw a Douglas SBD land with the left wheel retracted, the pilot keeping it level to the last second and damage next to nil. Real nice job. Returned to Dobo on the 12th.

On the 15th McGehee went out on a daylight recco and Joe Schwarber got a direct hit on a freighter with the Norden bomb sight from 10,000 feet, stopping it in the water.

Combat Mission No. 12

That night we took the milk run covering Duyal Island, New Ireland and New Britain and it was just that, a milk run. The next day the "Cart" was ready and towed back from the 49th but a brake line broken in the process scrubbed a test flight.

Combat Mission No. 13

On the the 15th we taxied the "Cart" out for a mission but the carburetor acted up so we took No. 755 instead. A short way out, we ran into rough weather. With the first bump the gyro compass spun out and the gyro horizon was not operating. A real sweat job, flying needle-ball-airspeed in that stuff. Finally into smooth air but on solid instruments for quite awhile longer, experiencing a weird phenomenon. The airplane lit up with a brilliant display of St. Elmo's Fire, staying there until we got into the clear. Air was smooth as glass and the props looked like big whirling discs of fire. In that first clear area we entered, I got the AFCE set up and got some relief, though we still ended up on instruments a good bit of the night. Radar helped in dodging some heavy weather areas. Landed after 11 hours and 20 minutes and I was as completely beaten as I'd ever been from a flight. The crew knew it and practically hauled me to Doc Mott, our Flight Surgeon.

After missions, crewmen usually went to Doc for an authorized shot of "combat whiskey," which I had never done. One of the guys said, "Hey Doc, Art needs a big one" and without hesitation Doc poured a whole glass full and handed it to me. Feeling this one time that I could use it I drank it neat, nonstop. WOW! Hit my empty stomach like a bomb going off. Was flying high when we got to the kitchen for our breakfast and I had my usual six fried eggs, tasting better than ever. After a good sleep I learned the crew who had flown No. 755 the night before we did had lost the gyro compass and horizon and forgot to write them up. With the carburetor fixed McGehee took the "Cart" out that night and Park the following night, sinking a Sugar Charlie.

Combat Mission No. 14

Back in the "Cart" with three other crews on the 19th. Picked up six night fighters off Wewak and flew 100 feet off the deck before shaking them. This time Clint said he saw some visually and Little Stick saw a burst of tracers overhead. Later we found some Sugar Charlies near Hollandia but reefs close by messed up two bomb runs. Messy weather and rain on return, landing after 11 hours and 40 minutes.

Though I didn't have a combat shot after this one I did sleep fairly well that morning. As a rule I could hardly sleep in the daytime after missions. I would always lie down, maybe catnap a little, but mostly lie there in a bath of sweat due to the tropical heat and humidity. More often than not, I'd give it up in an hour or two. Park took the "Cart" out again that night and sank another ship. On the 21st we flew McGehee's ship No. 041. The note in my diary indicates we "checked" the airplane, for what I don't remember and my Form 5 shows 2:35. With that much time it must have been a practice bomb mission to check the equipment. I also noted it was rather sloppy handling.

Combat Mission No. 15

We took the same ship on a mission that night. Three others out, Biddison, Quinette and Ring. Picked up 10 night fighters near Garove Island. Flew an hour and a half before losing them. Biddison reported bomb runs over a four-ship convoy off New Hanover, missing on both runs. We proceeded to the reported position, spotted the ships and made two runs, both near misses. Our target was slowed way down, maybe stopped. We had returned fire on the first run but on the second we experienced the heaviest fire we'd seen yet. Something like being in the middle of a big fireworks display and how we got through it without being hit at all I'll never know. Had to leave the scene when fighters showed up. I went down on the deck but then tried something different. Started a climbing turn with the extra speed built up, then rolled over and dove, repeating this between the deck at varying altitudes up to as high as 2500 feet, losing them in a fairly short time. Later we flew back to check the convoy and only found three ships so we may have sunk another one but got credit for a probable. Upon getting back we found out Biddison had been jumped by fighters there also and Plexiglas on his nose turret had been hit.

A big backlog of mail came that day. I got 13 letters from Dot, 5 from Mother, one from McDonalds, friends I'd known in Altus, another from Tom Wilson, my primary instructor. Grandma McMillan was in the hospital, exact reason unknown. Dan Clinton, another holdover radio operator, asked if he could finish out his time with us as operator. He had flown with us as an extra gunner and liked the crew

Somewhere along the line we'd lost Ben Greene. Ben tried awfully hard to stick it out but flying was giving his sinuses a fit and finally the pain became so unbearable he had to pack it in and went into ground maintenance. Replaced by Dick Everson, from the B-17s.

Park went out in the "Cart" again that night and got a probable. Seems he gets our plane more than we do lately. Again he was a B-17 holdover and did have pull, became Squadron CO later. Although I never cared much for the man, he was a good pilot. I had to think he liked the "Cart" and may have been using his influence to get it as much as he could.

Went on a practice mission in No. 041 on the 23rd. Little Stick flew two runs for Pete Schandorf, 100 feet low on both but results not bad. I flew the runs for Little Stick and still don't like the plane even after quite a lot of time in it.

Combat Mission No. 16

Went out that night with Clinton at the radio station and it looks like he'll work out OK. Our radar picked up 11 planes off Nubia on the way up the coast. Pattern on the scope indicated one likely had radar on board. Flew between 100 and 200 feet again and they stayed with us to abeam Wewak where more airplanes came out, apparently relieving the first ones. We stayed on the deck patrolling on up past Hollandia and then back. The fighters were relieved again and we never had less than four on our radar screen until passing Hakar Island, five hours after the first ones appeared. We'd been between 100 and 200 feet the whole time. If I hadn't mentioned it before we had 600 feet radio altimeters. As had been my habit whenever returning after sunup I went down to check the radio altimeter, remarking to the crew at 100 feet that this was where we'd been for five hours last night. At 50 feet the waves looked awfully close and I eased slowly lower but at 30 feet it seemed the waves were almost in our lap and I hauled back up. Having been out 11 hours I put it out of my mind, but Little Stick hadn't. On the landing roll he looked at me and said, "Do you know what the radio altimeter read at touch-down" I said no and he came back with "30 feet." Chalk up another "NEVER AGAIN."

McGehee's bombardier, Joe Schwarber, wrangled a ride on a PT boat and went on a raid right into the harbor at Madang at night shooting up everything in sight and scooting out. More guts than I've got.

Combat Mission No. 17

On January 26th, we went on another North Pole run. Biddison and Ring also out. Found a large vessel north of Rabaul in 13th AF area and FATF wouldn't approve bombing. Later to the west and north of New Hanover we found eight ships and again FATF didn't approve bombing. Would like to have gone back to check and see if the ship above Rabaul had gotten below our bomb line but time was running out and we headed back, landing after 13 hours and 35 minutes. Went over to Oro Bay for some reason or other and came across Ray Nelson, an old friend in A Battery from LaCrosse.

Combat Mission No. 18

On the 29th we went out on a mission with 14 aboard, including one of our civilian engineers, Jones, on the QT of course. Found two small vessels in the middle of the Bismarck Sea but the LAB had a short in the bias and dropped the bombs when switching from search to track. Also blew the trace fuzes three times. Out 11 hours 20 minutes and I was fighting sleep a good deal of the time on this one. Although very rare for me, I had a splitting headache on the 31st and had to cancel out on a practice mission.

Combat Mission No. 19

But we still went out on a mission that night. Up above Wewak we found a target, missing on our bomb run. Later we got into some pretty turbulent weather and I tried something I'd heard about doing with a B-24 in turbulence. Being below the freezing level we lowered the gear and put down some flaps. The lower center of gravity seemed to stabilize the airplane better and to me it felt like wallowing through the stuff instead of bumping and banging. Coming in after 11 hours 10 minutes, the Red Cross happened to be at the strip with doughnuts and coffee. Later in the day I bought a camera from Updyke, bombardier from the B-17s. Scheduled out again on the 2nd of February but cancelled for weather.

Combat Mission No. 20

Flew a practice mission on the 3rd, back in the "Cart" again and Charlie was happy with the equipment. Took it on a mission that night going to Manus Island in the Admiralties, then to Wewak and Neptune Point and back to Manus finding nothing. On the 5th I went to the QM again for more clothes, running into Harry Alger, Cadet classmate, flying B-25s out of Jackson.

Combat Mission No. 21

Went out that night along with McGehee and Park, turned out to be an-other quiet night. On the way back we happened to converge on Park in the Vitias Straits. I had the rare opportunity to fly formation on his wing. But Park had over 300 hours, he was grounded by Col. Scott, as 10 replacement crews and planes for our squadron were expected soon. With McCulla, Desmond and Everson I went to visit Grandma in the hospital. He was cheerful enough but still doesn't know what's wrong. Will go to a general hospital in Australia for further testing.

Combat Mission No. 22

I went out again on the 7th as well as McGehee and Burghoff. Our initial route was up the coastline some distance beyond Hollandia. It was a clear, bright moonlit night for a change, could have seen any ship on the water for miles but an empty sea is all we did see, 11 hours 45 minutes worth. The following night I flew a fact-finding experiment in conjunction with the Mugford, a Navy destroyer. Our squadron personnel were given an open invitation to go aboard the Mugford for the exercise and a large number went, including half my crew. A fellow named Hackler, just transferred in from fighters, rode co-pilot. Had 16 on board including four Mugford officers. Weather was scattered to broken cumulus, occasional showers and the moon. On the spur of the moment, after our first normal dry run on the ship, I peeled off steeply to the left and made a skip bomb run, greatly disturbing our ex-fighter pilot. Asking what his problem was, he replied, "I thought these crates were only supposed to fly straight and level." With the ships' radar on us they were able to mess up our LAB runs by evasive action, but at the same time I wished Big Stick had been there instead of the bombardier we had, don't remember who, because I believe he'd have stayed with them as he did before with the sub chaser. With their radar off we had them cold.

The entire operation was conducted by direct communication with the ship and we made numerous dry runs. For a windup I made a pass right on the deck, pulling up over the ship at the last moment. Afterward, our people on board the ship said the radar-controlled guns were dynamite. They could tell the direction we were coming from by watching where the guns pointed and as we went overhead the guns flopped right over and followed us on out. Sure glad the Japanese didn't have that ability. The guys also said our buzz job had people scrambling and jumping from higher vantage points on the ship. The next day, Capt. Hamill, who had been on the ship, said some new radar antennas were now on the "Cart." Asking what they were, I got this reply: "You picked them up from the Mugford last night." All of our people on board the Mugford were served steaks for dinner, ice cream for dessert. Almost wished I'd gone on the ship but it had been an interesting flight.

Combat Mission No. 23

Went on a mission on the 10th of February going to a point one degree 15 minutes north of the Equator due north of Manus Island, Biddison to the same latitude above New Hanover. It put us up toward the Carolines where the Japanese had a stronghold on Truk. There had been a suspicion that something might come down from there and early contact desired, but found nothing. On our way out we lost our liaison transmitter above Harkar Island and turned back. Then got the transmitter back and continued. As it was, we only got one message through to FATF, and back at base they sweated us out until we returned after 12 hours 30 minutes. Now have over 200 hours, 90 to go.

Still participating in sports and we beat the mess hall team in a softball game on the 11th. Several of us have started playing checkers. I'd played a lot in Louisiana when still in A Battery and could hold my own with most here, but Ben Greene was the undisputed champ. Though grounded Ben is doing his share with ground maintenance.

Combat Mission No. 24

Back out on February 14th. Located a Sugar Fox Dog, made a bomb run and missed. Making a second run we had some return fire though not too heavy. Put a 500 lb. bomb right on the bow, a 1000 and another 500 off the rail amidships. Practically blew it out of the water.

Started painting the plane's record on the left side of the nose, Twenty-seven bombs for the number of missions and five ships for confirmed sinkings. Three for us, two for Park. Crew No. 3 had been on 24 missions, not all on the "Cart" of course. Then took a bunch of pictures of the plane and crew who were there at the time, including ground crewmen.

Combat Mission No. 25

Went out on a mission on the 17th, nothing exciting except we were mostly in a lot of stratus clouds and rain. A short mission compared to what we'd been on recently, only 8 hours 10 minutes. Supposed to have gone on leave the day after that mission but the weather prevented it. On February 19th Quinette flew us to Fort Moresby to start our leave. The following day we were flown to Townsville on a Troop Carrier C-47, flown by a Lt. Moran. Had a lot of interesting conversation with him, spending much of the trip in the cockpit. They put on more fuel and on to Brisbane, a long day in the Gooney Bird. Stayed the night at Amberley Field and boarded another C-47 flying to Sydney. At Sydney, we checked into a hotel taken over by the Red Cross for the duration to accommodate personnel on leave. Looked around town, took in a museum, watched bowling on the green. McCulla, the operator (not limited to radar), lined up 1927 champagne and scotch whiskey and learned the whereabouts of Cirro's, a night club run by an American. Went to Cirro's for several nights, letting our hair down and doing a lot of drinking. Then we'd drink milk from all night milk bars on our way back to the hotel. During the day, we could find plenty of good food, steak and egg breakfasts, roasted chicken to take out when you wanted, and restaurants with good dinner fare. To me the food was one of the best things about the leave.

Gadwah, Swindler, Way and I lined up a cab driver, who used his family car, for a trip into the mountains west of Sydney. Started out on February 27th, picking up watermelon, fruit and milk on the way. Well up in the hills we stopped at the Lapstone Hotel for lunch, with very posh, spacious lawns and gardens, swimming pool, tennis courts and golf course. A beautiful view for miles around. Then we went higher into the mountains to Katoomba, picturesque, quaint and very neat. Picnicked at a park overlooking "The Three Sisters," natural rock pinnacles nestled in the mountains. Back to Sydney, after an enjoyable day, a day without alcohol and not even a hangover after a week of drinking. On the next evening, the last day of our leave, I went to a stage play called "Rope." Edwin Styles, said to be Australia's leading actor, was the star. His performance was excellent, the supporting cast mediocre, good plot and overall very entertaining.

We were flown back to Amberley Field on the 29th. Bummed a ride to nearby Archer Field and finally got to see Bob Mendell. On to Port Moresby on March 1st, staying until the 4th. While there Gadwah and I walked five miles each way to see "Du Barry Was a Lady." Quinette picked us up on the 4th and when getting back to camp I found 30 letters from home waiting. While we were gone, McGehee, his co-pilot Kreider, the engineer and radio operator were killed at Cape Gloucester. One of their engines had run out of oil and though shut down he refused to feather it. Eventually they had a runaway prop and now it wouldn't feather, so they headed for Cape Gloucester, the closest strip. That was a short fighter strip with just one string of runway lights. McGehee landed over halfway down the runway on the wrong side of the lights, went over an embankment into a gully wiping out the entire nose section. The rest of the crew were in the waist section and Joe Schwarber suffered broken ribs and had an ear almost ripped off, no one else more than bruised and shaken up. Three new replacement crews had arrived with new B-24Js. Two more ships had been sunk by the squadron. Spent the entire evening reading all those letters.

For the record, let me bring out another advantage of our nocturnal *Snooper* missions. When discovering more than one ship, a single airplane could do just so much but when sending back the particulars and the targets, a flight of B-25s would be sent out to intercept just after dawn. With four, fixed forward firing 50 cal. machine guns mounted on each side of the nose (eight in all) plus bombs they raised a lot of hell with shipping. We had the range and radar to hunt and in numbers they had the combined power when they knew right where to go, do their thing and get home.

On the 5th, the USO brought in a show to 5th BOMCOM HQTRS. John Wayne was emcee and Carol Landis was among the troupe. John Wayne brought the roof down with one skit, explaining he had run out of clean clothes and had borrowed the clothes he was wearing from Col. Scott. Then from various pockets he began pulling out booze bottles, silk stockings, panties, brassieres, etc. On the 7th, I flew an advance party of 14 men and their equipment to Nadzab in the "Dude," a standard B-24 acquired from the 403rd Squadron. We wasted three hours waiting for mess and it turned out to be cold beans and bread. Flew from there over to Lae and finally picked up our footlockers. Little Stick flew back to Dobo and made a nice smooth landing. Back into good old No. 896, on the 8th, for a practice mission. That night Whitey and Nygard broke into the mess hall taking some bread, sausage, ketchup and oxtail soup. They were pretty well boozed up and I found them heating the soup with a blow torch. Tasted real good.

Combat Mission No. 26

Back again to the war on March 9th. Clear weather and a bright moon after a short time in a rough patch of thunderstorms off Cape Ward Hunt. We had gone up past Hollandia and were headed for the Admiralties when Moulder reported bombing and missing a Sugar Charlie between Wewak and Hollandia. Going there we found a target, getting a near miss. Flying back for a look he appeared to be trailing an oil slick, fired at us but tracers all behind us. Started a second run but a mile from the target Charlie discovered the PDI clutch was slipping so we pulled out, again tracers behind us. Made one more run and missed, this time tracers too close for comfort, some zipping by just outside my window. Flew by one more time close enough to check on condition, still floating and firing back, nothing close. Another long night, 12 hours 25 minutes. At noon Whitey came by to say he was going to have to change #1 engine. A slug had hit #12 cylinder rocker arm housing and there were no spare cylinders on hand at this time. Visited Schwarber at the hospital and he was up on his feet and feeling fairly good. I saw a really good colored slide of the picture on the "Cart" and made arrangements to get a copy in the future, couldn't be done there. Never got it however. Whitey and Hygard got bombed again in the evening and Whitey "flew" a mission that was a real scream.

Flew No. 049 to Nadzab on the 13th to stage out of there. No. 2 generator went out and Hamill, already settled in there, radioed for a replacement plane but none available. Returned to Dobo in the morning. Biddison now has his 300 hours as well as Park but can't go home. Due to the big push going on in Europe, the forces in the Pacific are receiving a bare minimum of supplies and almost no replacement personnel or equipment with the exception of our specialized squadron. There is a blanket freeze on all 5th AF personnel and crews, who are normally finished with their tours, now have to keep on flying.

Combat Mission No. 27

Back again to Nadzab in No. 049 on the 14th, also Moulder. Staged a mission from Nadzab and returned, no action, 11 hours. Moulder finished his 300 on this one and will sit down with the others who are done. Flew back to Dobo and started breaking up camp. On the 17th we flew a load of lumber to Nadzab in the "Dude." Way flew back doing another good job of it. On the 18th we took the crew and equipment, got everything transported to the new campsite, cleared out brush and set up our tents. In the morning, we found the construction on the mess hall and operations buildings coming along well. We built a washstand by our tent.

Combat Mission No. 28

Staples took the "Cart" out that afternoon to shadow reported shipping. Then we took off in No. 479, "Miss Liberty," one of the new J models, at 1700, earlier than usual for some reason I've forgotten. We cut off the mission a bit early when the radar malfunctioned but still got 10 hours 35 minutes. No one to meet us after landing in the wee hours of the morning. We had almost gone into Finschhafen because of weather but then gave it a try and got through to Nadzab. For the same reason a little earlier, Staples had gone on to Dobodura. We took two radar maintenance jeeps and drove to the 63rd Service Squadron, talked our way into getting fried eggs, bread, butter and coffee. Burghoff had taken off well after dark as was normal, sinking a ship and damaging another off Hollandia.

Started work on improving our living quarters. Built a clothes rack for starters. Quinette and Ahrens out that night, Ahrens sinking a destroyer. On the 21st I shellacked the painting on the "Cart" and it brought out the colors even better. Added bombs for 38 missions now. The crew has 28 bombs now and approaching the 300-hour mark. Then we got the news the "Cart" was slated to go to Townsville for engine change and overhaul. Could be the last we'll see of her as we should be finished with our combat tour before she gets back.

Combat Mission No. 29

On March 23rd, we flew a mission in No. 041, another of the new J's. Not much to say about the mission other than getting 11 hours and 20 min-utes more time and afterwards slept a little better than usual. My notes and Form 5 show I flew ship No. 035 to Dobodura but I don't remember why. On March 27th our squadron became part of a new strategy. One of our crews flew up to Hollandia at night to act as a pathfinder for normally day-light bombers. The pathfinder would circle a predetermined position, send out MO's with the liaison transmitter for the other bombers to home in on and go to the target area from there. Our plane got there but the others didn't on account of weather. It was tried again the next night and again weather was a factor but four of the bombers got through.

Combat Mission No. 30

On March 29th, for the third night in a row it was our turn. The "Cart" now in Townsville, we flew one of the Js to Saidor for staging from there. By pure coincidence I ran into Major Carl Wang and Lt. Herb Zerneke. Wang, from Chippewa Falls, Wis, had been our battery commander in Louisiana, a real top-drawer man in my book, and Zerneke from B Battery, from LaCrosse. The old outfit was back up in the hills from Saidor. As I recall there were 12 B-24s there, some from our own 43rd Group and others from the 380th Group up from Darwin, Australia, their normal base. Again enroute, weather didn't look good. At the briefing the pilots were very much concerned about the weather, and some asked me if I would advise them if I thought they shouldn't go through. All I could say was that I intended to arrive at the IP and send out our MO's and drop flares for them to home in on and that each of them would have to decide for themselves whether to penetrate or turn back when encountering the weather. I forgot to mention earlier that the bombers were to fly all these missions five minutes in trail of each other. The Saidor field we used to stage from was a 3000-foot fighter strip starting from the water and rising up to 80 some feet to the other end. Fighters were scattered in revetments but the B-24's could only park on either side of the strip. Being the first off we had to run a gauntlet between them with little room to spare between our wingtips and their noses. We were heavy with bombs and fuel as we were to remain after the other bombers were done to harass the enemy by dropping 500 lb. bombs at half-hour intervals. I used most of the runway to get airborne and then just cleared a ship anchored close off shore. As predicted the weather in between was miserable but we'd been through worse. As I recall, I thought all of the planes got to the target that night, but the book *Flying Buccaneers* quotes that seven got there. Due to obscuration in the target area, we couldn't observe results of the bombing from our position. We carried on the harassment and flew back to Nadzab, time 12 hours 40 minutes.

The day before Bob Sheldon, from LaCrosse, and a clerk at 5th BOCOM had dropped by to tell me Charlie Raymond from LaCrosse was in the area. I located Charlie and we filled each other in on the whereabouts of various old friends. Saying I wanted to go to Saidor, if I could, to visit the LaCrosse outfits, he said he would like to go with me if possible.

On the next afternoon, I heard the loudest explosion I'd ever heard in my life. Looked out and saw a huge column of smoke. Rode in a jeep to within a mile of the scene. An ammunition dump had blown up and bombs and tracers were still going off, continuing on into the night. Set off a fire up in the hills. That evening Lt. Horn went to Saidor to be the pathfinder, blew a tire and washed out ship No. 031.

On April 2nd, a 64th Squadron B-24 blew a tire on take-off, wiped out the landing gear pinning a gunner in the bomb bay and caught on fire. Crash trucks put out the fire and left the scene. A crane was lifting the plane when another fire started and eight 1000 lb. bombs blew up. Learned my name was put in for promotion to captain. Scott had gotten my promotion to 1st Lt. right after we got to New Guinea. I had been made a flight leader but with our single airplane type of operation I never really lead anything. Big Stick quit as bombardier officer primarily because he wasn't promoted and certainly should have been.

Another B-24 blew up on takeoff the next day with eight bombs; probably airborne too quickly, settled back with brakes on and struck a B-25 on the ground. Six crewmen got out before it blew, three didn't. Brakes are applied on the B-24 before raising the gear to stop gyro effect on the airplane because the wheels swing outward into wells in the wing. Also this before Category T came into effect in the late '40s.Most pilots flew the airplane by a basic set of airspeed numbers, but I liked to establish an attitude and then let the plane takeoff when it was ready at whatever speed it took.

Combat Mission No. 31

We were set up on the 4th to path find for a strike on Wadke Island but it was cancelled by weather. Same strike set up the next night but McIntosh, now operations officer, wanted us to run a recco instead of being the path-finder in case any ships were in the Wadke area; again weather squelched the whole deal. Finally went out on the 6th on a recco to the Equator north of Hollandia and then to the west end of New Guinea, the first to go that far. Meant to drop our bombs on Wadke as a target of opportunity when returning but weather there prevented that. Got back in with 13 hours and had topped 300 combat hours.

The freeze was still on, those of our crews who were done were still staying on the ground, everyone else in the 5th still having to fly. Giving this some thought I figured if I sat down now, say up to a month as some of crews had, and then had to go back to combat flying, my frame of mind could be in bad shape for it. I was conditioned to it now and might not be later. I got the crew together, told them I intended to go on flying and my reasons why. I didn't in any way ask them to do the same yet to a man they all volunteered to go on flying with me. In the meantime, we still had movies regularly. I did a lot of reading books being available. Sports activity curtailed here as we didn't have an open space like the one at Dobo. All set to go to bomb Wadke and then cancelled at the last moment for some unknown reason, on April 9th.

Combat Mission No. 32

On the 11th we went on a milk run in No. 034, a B-24J, found no action, were out for 11 hours and 15 minutes. That evening I fell off the wagon with some of our crew and ground crew, celebrating being over the 300-hour mark, not meaning anything for the moment but knowing once the freeze was lifted we were gone. The next evening I joined a number of the guys in Whitey's tent after they all were high on the booze again. Had a gully-washer and a river of water came through the tent (no floor). Whitey, who'd been over there a long time, went over the brink, completely out of his mind. Very scary and the others sobered up in a hurry. Finally got him calmed and in bed. In the morning he seemed to be back to his normal somewhat grouchy self.

Combat Mission No. 33

"Black Sunday." That's what April 16th was to the 5th AF. On Saturday night of the 15th, we went on a mission with particular attention to be paid to weather reporting. The Bismarck Sea was covered by a front, thick solid overcast, on instruments most of the night. Checking a number of desired points along the way, we found the coastline open but squeezed between the front over the water and solid thunderstorm activity all along the mountain ranges. On the way up, although at low altitude we bucked up to 50 mph winds. Finding it open we dropped eight 500 lb. bombs on Wadke Island from 6000 feet. Charlie eyeballed the run, toggled the bombs manually, four in the water and four in a dispersal area. Wadke is a tiny island up above Hollandia, 9000 feet long and 3000 feet wide, having a key Japanese airstrip and related installations. The Markham Valley remained open for us to get back to Nadzab in the morning, 11 hours on this one. Found out a full scale strike had headed out to Hollandia despite the weather threat. Quoting from the book, *Flying Buccaneers*, "The previous night a 63rd B-24 (that was us) had been reporting weather in the target area every 15 minutes, and the reports were not good, but with time running out (General) Whitehead decided to get in another Hollandia strike."

Quoting again from the book, "Over the target area the B-24s, B-25s, and A-20s were successful, virtually wiping out the fixed defenses in the Humboldt Bay area. But on the way back the planes met a weather front which had quickly moved in over the Markham Valley, cloaking Nadzab and other fields with clouds and rain." We were listening on a radio monitor on tower frequency and it was pretty disheartening. The nervous excited jabber of pilots trapped in the soup was nonstop.

It was the B-25s, A-20s and P-38 fighter escorts with shorter range who had the major problems. Some pilots managed to find the fighter strip at Saidor but there was a midair collision there. The wreckage was quickly removed to allow others to land, the tower having little control, as frantic pilots running out of fuel were only interested in getting on the ground. There were probably as many stories out of that day as there were pilots in the air, and the *Flying Buccaneers* relates quite a few of them. When it was all over 31 aircraft were lost as well as 32 pilots and airmen. A number of airmen survived crash landings, some walking out of the jungle up to two weeks later. The mission had been a calculated risk and despite the losses, the damage done was determined to have been worth the risk as Hollandia was the next objective for an imminent invasion, a leap-frog jump bypassing everything between Saidor and Hollandia.

Over the next few days I saw Gildermeister again, Wrote a number of letters, went to the movies. Saw a film on the bombing of Salamaua, Lae, Finschhafen, Alexishafen and Wewak, ending with the first big raid on Rabaul. Our bomb line cut down as the Hollandia Invasion about to come off. A P-39 clipped a pole on a buzz job knocking down two tents, luckily unoccupied. On April 23rd, we flew a test flight to work out tables for bombing from 6000 feet with our radar. About the same time a Col. Miller from our 43rd Group flew a B-24 with 12,000 pounds of bombs, 8000 in the bomb bay and two 2000 pounders on wing racks, and 2000 gallons of gas. Never heard that it was carried out on an actual mission. On the 25th we acquired lumber for our tent from a sawmill for a quart of whiskey and three quarts of rum. Balsa wood, believe it or not, but it worked, as we built a tent floor the following day.

Combat Mission No. 34

On April 27th I helped with construction on the Group Officers' Club, named the "Bee Two Dozen." Went out that night on an 18-airplane strike on Wadke Island and, again in single file at five-minute intervals. From there the rest went home and we continued up to Biak Island and near the west end of New Guinea, completing a weather recco for a strike planned there in the morning. Incidentally, we dropped fifteen 260-pound fragmentation bombs in the personnel area on Wadke. Twelve hours, 20 minutes on this one.

On the 29th the officers' club "Bee Two Dozen" opened but being back on the wagon I didn't go. Just about everyone else free at the time did and it ended up in a big brawl. I don't really know what set it off, but it had turned into fisticuffs and several officers displayed the physical evidence of the melee the following morning; many others suffered from head-splitting hangovers. Gadwah and I found a glove, mitt and baseball, tossing it around for some exercise.

Coincidentally on May 2nd we played in a game of baseball, for me the first time in about eight years. I've forgotten just who but one of our higher echelon officers and one from a fighter outfit cooked it up with a bet on the outcome. Years back I'd done a lot of catching but in this game played first base. Had a lot of fun even though we lost. Attending the game was one of their officers still in his twenties and a General no less! The game was played in a clearing in their area that was even larger than the one we'd had at Dobo.

Jensen, one of our new replacement pilots, took Hamill's original plane No. 508 to Saidor for staging on another pathfinder flight. Landed there in a rain squall and washed out the airplane but no one hurt. The next morning I asked to ride on a flight to Saidor, going there to inspect the damage and pick up the crew, as it was a good opportunity to visit my old Field Artillery friends. Capt. Derr, our CO earlier, was flying, don't remember who was in the co-pilot seat but probably an operations officer. As mentioned earlier Derr was a B-17 pilot without much B-24 time. Our Group Executive Officer was on the flight riding in the waist section with me. On final approach into Saidor, the engines started cutting out 1-2-3, and the Exec and I looked at each other for a second or two, but then the engines roared back to life. Derr had pushed the mixture controls to idle cutoff, the right-seat man caught it and pulled them back to rich. For some reason B-24 mixtures were set up in reverse to any other airplane I ever knew; idle cutoff forward and rich back, all other engine controls were normal.

I found a ride out to the Field Artillery bivouac area only to find my old Brigade had moved back to Australia. However, what used to be D, E and F Battery's of the 2nd Brigade were there, now A, B and C Battery's of the 129th Brigade. I had originally enlisted in D Battery in Stevens Point in 1936 and there were a number of the guys from there, still with the outfit. And the Battery Commander was Gus Olsen, formerly an enlisted man in B Battery from LaCrosse. There were other officers I had known before so it was still a worthwhile visit. Torrential rains that evening washed out the roads back to Saidor so I stayed the night. In the morning the Brigade Commander had his Liaison Pilot fly me back to Saidor in their Piper L-4. When getting to the 1000-foot grass strip, I saw some of the planes that landed there on "Black Sunday." Five A-20s and a B-25, all with minor damage but no way to get them out of there. The pilot let me fly the L-4 to Saidor. It was the lightest plane I'd flown to date but I made a three-point landing, dropping it in from two or three feet and he said, "Well it was a positive landing anyway." Caught a flight from there to Finschhafen and another back to Nadzab. A day or two later I got over to Lae to visit Gildy again.

Combat Mission No. 35

On the 8th of May we flew a mission to Biak Island. The radar failed completely on the way up but being a clear, moonlit night we found the island and from 6000 feet Charlie was able to see well enough to eyeball and toggle eight 500 lb. bombs in the dispersal area at Mokmer Airdrome. A long one, 13 hours 30 minutes. Five hours of that was after sunup. Little Stick was in the left seat flying back after daylight. I was slumped down in the right seat trying to sleep with my eyes barely open when something flashed downward right in front of the windshield. I popped up wide awake and there was a large convoy just in front of us. Then a Hellcat tucked in just under our left wingtip. Looking up another Hellcat was hovering a few thousand above us. I waved to the Hellcat pilot indicating a right turn and needless to say we gave the convoy a wide berth. Harold must have been half asleep not to have seen them. If the Hellcats hadn't warned us off we very likely could have been shot down. I believe it must have been a task force involved with the landing on Wadke Island on May 17th.

That turned out to be our last mission. The entire crew was grounded and set up for what was called a 15-day sick leave. Found out later our Group Intelligence officer had gone to our flight surgeon, Doc Mott, and told him to get those guys out of the air, they've done enough.

Hollandia had been invaded on April 22nd and now being secured, three of our pilots went up to visit the area, one being Roland Fisher, another fighter pilot who transferred to the squadron. They went out with an infantry patrol and captured three Japanese. One of them made a move Fisher didn't like and he shot him. Quite a number of Japanese hiding out in the jungle but when captured they seem almost relieved as they were practically starving.

The "Cart" was back from overhaul and I flew it on the 12th to give someone bombing practice. Approval was given to qualify as 1st pilots those co-pilots who had finished their tour. I took Way and Burke up in the "Cart" for transition. Little Stick had no problem as I had given him a lot of stick time, more than any of the others I learned. Burke was the opposite extreme. His pilot, "Iron" George Biddison hadn't let him make the first take-off or landing and it sure showed. George had the habit of pulling the yoke into his lap when starting his roll but obviously relaxing pressure appropriately for lift-off. Being all he had ever seen, Burke did the same thing but held it back to a premature lift-off. I'd let him go to there, took over pushing it back for a normal lift-off. After some verbal coaching and discouraging use of George's technique he did make progress but needed more time. A B-24 took more than usual time to master. Made me think of the Colonel giving us a pep talk when I first went to Tarrant Field for B-24 transition. He said this wasn't going to be easy and would take a lot of work and perseverance to conquer the beast. But if you could learn to fly this airplane well you could fly any plane in the air today. Gave transition to several others for two or three days, most doing fairly well but none up to Way's proficiency, they just hadn't gotten as much stick time.

Orders came on May 15th for our sick leave, transportation to Townsville set for the 17th. Went to Townsville as planned but didn't get out of there to Brisbane until the 22nd. There we sat for about three hours in the American Center Restaurant waiting for ground transportation down the coast to Southport. Here we were in our grubby worn New Guinea khakis, no ties, unshaven and all around us were locally based officers in full uniform, ties and blouses. Finally checked into the San Souci, a hotel on the beach at Southport. As in Sydney the Red Cross operated this hotel for Air Force officers on leave. A short way down the beach was a hotel for Naval officers. Our enlisted crew members went to Coolangatta, a number of miles down the coast, about a 30-mile stretch of very clean beach. Structures were set back leaving the sand dunes to protect the beach, not messed up like so many of ours.

Needless to say we enjoyed that leave. Swimming, horseback riding, beach parties, softball, tennis, ping-pong, and good food, etc. Alcohol was rationed and bottles could be gotten at a designated outlet back near Brisbane.

In bars and lounges, rationing was accomplished by "beer calls" restricting drink sales between 12 noon and 1 pm and again between 5 pm and 6 pm. Usually at noon we'd go to the Naval officers hotel, which had a lounge, for "beer calls," then the horses were brought there for those who wanted to ride. There was plenty of room to ride at will almost anywhere we wanted. On one occasion someone couldn't make "beer call" and told me to drink his share for him. His drink was whiskey and I normally had beer, so this time I ordered shots chased with beer. When the groom brought the horses he said one mare was blind in her left eye and was spooky. Feeling no pain and ready for anything I volunteered to ride her. We started out down the beach, water on the left, and sure enough the surf sound or something spooked her and she reared, at the same time twisting away from the waters. She lost her footing in the loose sand and fell with my right leg pinned under. I got straightened out, mounted and left the beach. Later I stopped to look at some Shetland ponies fenced in at the edge of town. The others went around a corner and when I made the turn Little Stick was halfway down the block sitting on this horse crossways on the dirt street waiting. I nudged the mare to a gallop and unthinkingly tried to pass them to the right. With her blind eye she didn't cotton to that and just before reaching them she put on the brakes with all fours and I went sailing over her head for about 10 yards. The only damage was a grass stain on one knee, but I kept my mind on her blind eye for the rest of that ride.

Those 15 days stretched into six weeks. Personnel, equipment and supplies were now starting to flow into the Pacific Theater to back the advancements now underway. Anything or anyone going on Troop Carrier had to have high priority and we were very low priority under the circumstances. Although the leave had been great, being out of touch as we were, time suddenly began to drag, and I started thinking about how I might get back. Then Jim Bishop, a pilot from another 43rd Squadron, found out his CO was at Amberley Field with a Fat Cat. About the same time, we learned a ship at Brisbane had some room and would be leaving shortly for New Guinea. On June 25th Jim and I went to Amberley and a ride on the Fat Cat was available. However due to the load and weight and balance, they wanted us to ride in the nose on take-off and landing. As much as I wanted to go, I said no way. I can't remember if they backed off or if I lucked into another ride but I got to Townsville the next day. The others were to have boarded the boat that same day. Got back to Nadzab on the 28th.

Had a wire waiting from Dot to say Elsa had been born and all well, and stacks of mail. Fred Baker had tried to see me and was now on Manus Island in the Admiralties. Art Harrod, another Cadet classmate flying B-25s, had been by. I looked him up and could have flown with him but their planes were set up for a single pilot; the right side of the cockpits had been opened up for access to the nose. Bob Sheldon dropped by from BOMCOM to tell me the freeze had been lifted and orders to go home should be cut any day. Caught up on letter writing. My Form 5 record shows I flew a B-24J on June 29th for 1 hour 40 minutes, maybe checking more co-pilots. On July 1st we played in a softball game with the 5th Fighter Command on a bet made by Col. Hawthorne, 43rd Bomb Group CO, during a drinking bout the night before. A very good game but we lost it in the 9th inning, 9-8. On the 2nd, Bob Sheldon came by again to say our orders definitely approved. I went ahead and packed up my footlocker with the butterfly collection, diary and all but an extra change of clothes. On the 3rd Sheldon brought over a copy of the orders on which my name appeared and on the 4th they were received at Squadron Headquarters. By now the rest of the crew were back from Australia.

Those involved began clearing affairs with the squadron. At the same time the squadron was making preparations for its next move to Owi, a small island near Biak. Both Biak and Wadke had been taken while we were on leave, little Wadke having been unexpectedly tough to take, a lot of hand-to-hand combat to rout out very stubborn resistance. Normally, Air Force personnel were flown back to the States by ATC but such a large backlog of people being released all at once made that impossible. Went over to Port Moresby expecting to board the liner Lauroli but it ran aground enroute to Moresby. After a week we were flown to Milne Bay at the east end of New Guinea. While there a couple of us ran into a little Scottish Captain of a Liberty ship. He said he had room for four people and would gladly take us but it would be a six-week cruise in that slow boat to San Francisco. After two weeks in Milne Bay we boarded a converted liner, 500 hospital patients and 500 walking Air Force officers and GIs. Officers shared staterooms and enlisted men slept in tiered canvas bunks set up around the decks. The food was very good, especially the first week before the more perishable foods gave out. For bathing we used a large community saltwater shower room. The trip took 18 days to San Francisco. For about 10 days we were running directly into huge ground swells. Every now and then the bow would come well off a crest and go WHOMP into the trough. Quite a lot of the guys were visiting the rails eliminating some of that good food they'd eaten. Luckily, although I may have gotten occasional nausea, I never had to go to the rail. The last few days we were quartering to the swell on the starboard bow, doing the "Rock-n-Roll." Whether passing anything while sleeping I don't know but I never laid eyes on anything but water and sky until we reached the California coastline. We abandoned ship at Mare Island in San Francisco Bay. Visited Tom and Murldeen again in San Rafael. Nails Desmond wasn't with us. He'd lost time due to illness and had been on a mission with the plane missing when we left the squadron. I had promised him I would go to see his Mother in San Francisco if at all possible. With a sick feeling in my heart I did go to her address, and his Mother and sister were there. To my relief they'd been hearing from Bill and whatever that missing airplane bit was about it couldn't have amounted to much. Unfortunately, I found out he was lost on a later mission.

Four more days on a troop train to Chicago and finally home to family and friends in LaCrosse for a 30-day leave.

Reminiscences: A Very Unusual Occurrence

While in Primary Training at Muskogee, Oklahoma, on a solo flight I made a slow roll in a Fairchild PT-19. Within moments I realized something was wrong. I was holding a tad of left rudder to keep the wings level but, most alarming, I couldn't move the stick! I unbuckled the seatbelt to bailout but then had second thoughts.

At cruise throttle, the elevator was stuck at level flight, ailerons slightly right, and wing down; a bit of left rudder held the wings level. I decided to attempt a wheel landing with the only control features I had – engine power and rudder. I had been at 6000 feet and with somewhat reduced power, I reached a high and wide downwind leg at 3000 feet abeam the landing strip, constantly wiggling that stubborn joystick! Lo and behold, at that point the stick popped free. Advancing the throttle, climbed back to 6000 feet and completed my mission; no more problems.

After landing, I taxied to the maintenance hangar instead of the flight line. My instructor came over and I explained what happened to him and to the Chief of Maintenance. My instructor was scheduled to go on a dual flight with another student in the same airplane. He was told to go ahead and if he had any trouble to write it up in the logbook. By the way, my instructor was the youngest and least experienced on the base; nevertheless a good man.

The following Sunday I was called to the base office and questioned by the Operations Officer. Through the grapevine, word had gotten to the office about my experience. The Operations Officer was very stern, asking many questions to the point where I began to be worried that he thought I had dreamed the whole episode. Then suddenly he asked, "Why didn't you write it up in the log book?"

His demeanor now completely changed and he was concerned whether the experience affected my attitude toward flying "Did I have any fears?" He also explained that an assembly washer had inadvertently been lost in the center section of the wing by some careless mechanic at some earlier date. The washer was the culprit that jammed the controls. I also learned that similar incidents happened twice before (not at Muskogee) during dual sessions and instructor and student bailed out in each instance. Also, orders had already been issued to place boots on the ends of the torque tubes to prevent any more problems.

Kent Zimmerman & Stephen M. Perrone

and the Crew of B-24J Bomber Serial No. 42-100037

DEDICATION

To the Skipper and Crew of B-24J Bomber, Serial No. 42-10037 and the Flight Line Crew Chiefs who kept us flying night after night over thousands of miles of the Pacific over the ships and the many islands occupied by the enemy.

They are listed below:

Lt. Kent Zimmerman	Pilot, Oklahoma
Lt. James Watts	Co-Pilot, West Virginia
Lt. George Burhoe	Navigator, Massachusetts
Lt. Stephen Perrone	Bombardier, Pennsylvania
Sgt. Richard Howard	Flight Engineer, Montana
Sgt. Charles Nunez	Assistant Flight Engineer, New York
Sgt. Kermit Crabtree	Waist Gunner, Kentucky
Sgt. Clifford Grivois	Radio Operator, Maine
Sgt. John Ahern	Radar Operator, New York
Sgt. Harold Donner	Nose Gunner, New York
Sgt. Fred Wharton	Waist Gunner, New York, replaced Kermit Crabtree after he was killed in an aircraft accident on Owi Island.
Sgt. Cleo D. Nelson	Radio Operator, Montana, replaced Clifford Grivois after he was hospitalized and returned to the United States
Sgt. Charles Parker	Crew Chief, North Carolina

A WWII INTROSPECTIVE:
WE WERE JUST DOING OUR JOBS
Photos provided by Crew Members

By Kent Zimmerman and Steve Perrone, with major contributions from the crew of the B-24J Bomber, Serial No. 42-10037, as described in the following pages. **Steve Perrone** will serve as editor and narrator to blend the crew accounts of our experiences into a narrative that represents each of our personal perspectives.

THE BOMBARDIER'S PERSPECTIVE

Steve Perrone: The aircrew joined First Pilot Kent Zimmerman beginning at Clovis, AAF, New Mexico, through to Pueblo, Colorado and Salina, Kansas AAF's where we completed crew training. We were then transferred to Topeka, Kansas AAF for assignment to the European theater of operations. We received our high altitude flight gear, sheepskin-lined leather boots, pants, jacket and helmet, and were among the hundreds of aircrews being processed for shipment overseas.

Topeka AAF was an impressive re-assignment base for thousands of young men eager to go forth and fight the enemy. Of course, in our quiet moments, we reflected on the possibilities that we might not make it back. But it passed over. We were members of a flying crew because we volunteered for flying duty. We chose our jobs back when we joined the Army Air Corps. As I recall it, at one of the large group meetings at Topeka, one of the senior officers challenged all of us to a competition and offered a prize (not disclosed) to the first 26 crews completing the training schedule. The scuttlebutt in the dining halls and the latrines was that the winning 26 crews would get to the 8th Air Force in England first.

Our crew finished in the top 26 crews and our reward was we were transferred to the 2nd Sea Search Attack Squadron, 1st Bomber Command at Langley Field, Virginia. What a change! We went from high altitude formation flights over Europe with hundreds of planes to a "*Snooper*" squadron with black-painted B-24's equipped with a super-secret Low Altitude Radar Bombing system using single planes to search for enemy shipping in the Southwest Pacific theater. First Pilot, Kent Zimmerman, the tallest and oldest member of our crew and a former Oklahoma rancher and farmer, describe training and the first leg of our overseas flight to Hawaii.

At Langley Field, the pilot was given a new radar equipped B-24J and we were ready to deliver it some nine or ten thousand miles across the USA and the Pacific Ocean to New Guinea.

THE PILOT'S PERSPECTIVE

Kent Zimmerman: We trained in Electronic Warfare at Langley in the First Sea Search Attack Group flying Radar search missions out over the

Atlantic looking for enemy submarines and protecting the convoys as they departed the Hampton Roads area for Europe and Asia. This was rigorous flight training for all the crewmembers, especially the pilot, navigator, bombardier, and radarman.

We departed Langley about the 15th of February, 1944 for Mitchell AAF, Long Island, N.Y. to process for our overseas deployment. We had been given a new B-24J aircraft at Langley that had logged only 7 hours. We had test-hopped it at Langley and calibrated it for airspeed and altitude corrections and had rigged the top turret gun with a compass rose aligned with the aircraft so the navigator could obtain azimuth readings when the guns were aimed at the sun or any other celestial body.

We took off on February 18th for Scott Field, East St. Louis, Illinois, but had a runaway prop (a propeller we couldn't control with our switches) and had to go back to Mitchell Field. We took off again and after 6:40 hours, we arrived at Scott AAF. The next day, we took off for Lowry AAF, Denver and stayed the next day. That night, the officers on the crew went into Denver for dinner, then to a dance and some drinks which got to us in a hurry possibly because of the 5300-foot altitude.

The next morning, we all sweated getting off the runway at Denver because of the altitude, the heavy load, and the climb we had to make before we started across the Rockies. I remember Watts was feeling no pain when we took off and we used the entire runway that was available. Then, we climbed for 30 or 40 minutes over Denver, before we headed across the Rockies.

Because of weather at Fairfield-Suisun, I decided to divert the flight and land at Las Vegas. I remember that by this time, we all were short of money, so we pooled our resources and went into town to gamble. I remember Perrone found a pretty woman sitting at the bar and decided to make a play for her! He talked to her, bought her several drinks, and thought he was getting close to her. But she got so drunk she fell off the barstool and a bodyguard that had been hanging around picked her up and took her upstairs to her room. If I remember right, Perrone told me that he had found out she was the girlfriend of the owner of the place and the bodyguard had been watching her all the time! I can't remember but I think Watts and I made a little money that night gambling, but Perrone was not happy.

When we took off at Las Vegas, the gas cap on one of the auxiliary wing tanks popped off and we started siphoning gas. The cap was hanging on by its safety chain and the gas fumes were a real fire hazard, if a spark ever occurred. We circled the base until we had lightened our gas load and then landed.

We stayed over at Las Vegas another night and took off the next day for Fairfield-Suisun AAF. If I remember correctly, we spent three or four days there because of briefings and waiting for the weather to clear enroute to Hickam Field, Hawaii. I do remember, we were confined to the base at Fairfield-Suisun. However, if I remember correctly, one or two of the enlisted members of the crew sneaked out to say goodbye to family or friends. I don't remember for sure, but I think Rich Howard was one of them as Mildred Howard came from Langley Field to Fairfield-Suisun and waited for us to depart for Hawaii.

The night we took off from Fairfield-Suisun for Hawaii was really our first long overseas flight. We had flown out over the Atlantic at Langley AAF, but this flight was a real test of Burhoe's navigating skills and Rich's fuel management ability.

When we were finally cleared to leave Fairfield-Suisun for Hickam, I remember, we took off around midnight with several B-25s flown by the Dutch and three or four B-24s, one of them piloted by Lt. Schlesinger and his crew, who had trained with us at Clovis, and later at Langley. We later heard that one or two of the B-25s and Schlesinger and his crew did not make it to Hickam.

I think everyone remembers that flight from Fairfield-Suisun to Hickam on February 28, 1944. We had a good aerial view of Sacramento, Oakland, San Francisco and the Golden Gate Bridge as we climbed out on our way to Hickam. After we had left the Golden Gate Bridge and had reached our assigned altitude, somewhere around 8,000 to 10,000 feet, we hit a front that was really rough. We got bounced around. I think we picked up clear ice on the wings and control surfaces because the flight controls got really stiff and we started losing altitude. I alerted the crew that we were losing altitude, which shook up the crew, somewhat. In a short time, we either penetrated the front or got below the icing level and things started to get back to normal.

We knew we were going to be close on gas to reach Hickam because we were not making the ground speed we had planned. But none of us, especially me, wanted to go back through that front, so we kept going. We eased back up to our assigned altitude and flew 16 hours and 10 minutes before we landed at Hickam. I know we didn't have much fuel left! I estimated less than an hour!

THE BOMBARDIER'S PERSPECTIVE

Steve Perrone: According to the individual flight records, we arrived at Fairfield-Suisun on February 24, 1944. We were held up there for several days by bad weather and overseas briefings for the pilots and navigator. I was assigned the task of supervising the loading of the aircraft. I was briefed on the procedures and given a slide rule. The idea was to load the aircraft without changing the flight characteristics. The bomb bays of our B-24 were already loaded with thousands of pounds of electronic equipment to be delivered to our squadron overseas. Underneath this stack of electronic equipment, the unmarried officers, the pilot, co-pilot and the bombardier had stashed several cases of whiskey purchased at the Langley Field Officer's Club. I don't recall if navigator George Burhoe was involved. The point is the aircraft was almost too heavy without including the weight of the fuel.

Our Flight Engineer, Rich Howard, was on the flight line when our airplane was being loaded with fuel. This practice extended to all our combat missions where Rich always topped off the tanks with an extra 40 or 50 gallons or more for his wife, Mildred. Pilot Kent Zimmerman recalls that our maximum weight for takeoff was 64,000 pounds and our safe landing weight was 56,000 pounds. However, he said we took off many times, especially in combat, with a gross weight as high as 72,000 pounds. Flight engineer Rich says our takeoff weight for the first leg of our overseas flight was 72,000 pounds.

It was nearly midnight and our overseas takeoff time was drawing near. Earlier in the day, I was assigned a military vehicle with an enlisted driver, a young woman from Ohio, as I recall. We made small talk as she drove me around to pick up various items that had to be loaded on the plane. The last pick-up included several of our enlisted crew and as they clambered off the vehicle and disappeared into the belly of the B-24, I turned to the young woman in the driver's seat beside me as if to say something. I don't recall saying anything but I leaned over and kissed her and she responded. It was quiet and brief. Then I opened the car door and climbed quickly into the aircraft. In retrospect, I suppose I just wanted to say goodbye to someone. Hell, I was only 23.

Another perspective on the dangerous icing on the wings and control surfaces as we left the Golden Gate Bridge and the California Coast discussed earlier by the pilot. I was sitting on the floor of the flight deck between navigator's table and the radio operator's equipment table, thinking about our future combat experiences but also listening to the conversations of the pilot, navigator, and the flight engineer. Suddenly, we lost several thousand feet, something you can feel in the seat of your pants, and the flight engineer who was kneeling between the pilot and co-pilot, stood up and turned facing the rear of the plane; he then reached down behind the Pilot's seat, pulled out his chest pack parachute and snapped it on his harness. I don't recall what I asked him but he said something like "We're icing up and the pilot cannot maintain our altitude."

My parachute chest pack was up front in the bombardier's compartment. Earlier in the flight, the nose gunner, Harold Donner, asked if he could sleep in the bombardier's compartment, which was okay. He had zipped the zipper on the inside of the compartment to eliminate drafts from the retracted nose wheel well. Reacting to the flight engineer's exclamation very quickly, I pulled up the springloaded door at the rear of the flight deck, jumped down onto the catwalk in the bomb bays, got down on my hands and knees and crawled into a tunnel-like crawl space about 15 feet long which was under the flight deck, the pilot's compartment, then around the retracted nose wheel which bounced and whistled in the swirling winds that flooded the compartment because the nose wheel doors did not close completely. The nose compartment curtain was zipped shut. I slapped at it, shouted to wake up Donner, and tried to get underneath the tough tent material. Then suddenly, I was in the compartment. I woke up Donner and snapped on my earphones and got the pilot on the intercom. I asked what was going on. He said something like "Don't listen to Rich, we came through a nasty front but we're now coming out of it."

When we landed at Hickam Field some 15 hours later, several of us inspected the split compartment entrance – it was split several inches from the zipper from top to bottom, but how? Several of us tried to duplicate the split on another section but we could not tear the thick tent material. Back to the flight west.

THE NAVIGATOR'S PERSPECTIVE

Navigator George Burhoe, a married New Englander and the second oldest crew-member, gives his perspective on the first leg of our journey, and then goes on to navigate us all the way to Townsville, Australia:

PREFLIGHT BRIEFING: Exact departure time and final destination were only given to the pilot! The weather forecast highlighted a strong fast-moving cold front, traveling south and east 50 to 100 miles west of San Francisco. The assigned altitude was 8,000 feet. The suggested heading to Hawaii was southwest until clearing the front then set course for Honolulu, Oahu. The alternate destination, Hilo on the big island of Hawaii, is about 200 miles closer to San Francisco. The gas load including bomb bay tanks estimated at 14 hours and the distance 2,100 miles. Those figures would indicate an average ground speed needed of 150 MPH. (The accuracy of these approximations depends on memory after 55 years but they will suffice to illustrate the concerns about making the trip.) The urgent need for equipment and crews in the Pacific precluded postponing the takeoff until the front had cleared. The plane was loaded with a night takeoff scheduled. There were no problems on takeoff although the plane did use a lot more runway than usual. Fortunately, the airport had been designed for such exigencies.

After clearing the Golden Gate Bridge area and starting to climb to altitude it got very rough. There was turbulence and it was much colder than the usual temperature drop due to altitude. Passing through 5,000 feet there was something shining on the wing and engine mounts. A check with the flashlight showed ice forming on the metal surfaces.

Navigator to Pilot, "There is ice forming on the wings!!!"

Pilot to Navigator, "This is too serious a trip for April Fool Jokes. OOPS...

The controls are locking up–we don't have de-icing boots!!!"

A quick appraisal and a quicker descent to 3,000 feet cleared the problem but it would be several hours before making the climb to the assigned altitude.

The intensity of the storm gradually abated and the sky cleared enough to see the stars. Time to check progress. There weren't any global positioning satellites or any other modern navigation aids, so grab the sextant and locate some appropriate stars. Three shots and the lines not too far apart. <u>Ground speed 105 MPH!</u>

Navigator to Pilot, "We may have to swim the last 200 or 300 miles into Hilo!!"

Pilot to Navigator, "Do you think we should go back?"

Navigator to Pilot, "Only if you want to fly back through that front!!"

Another quick conference and a review of the preflight briefing. The information indicated the ground speed should improve as we headed southwest to at least get us to Hilo on our gas load. Another speed check an hour later came in at 112 MPH and the storm was over. We continued on our SW heading and it appeared the weather people were right about a more favorable wind to the southwest. But it was 6 or 7 hours before the speed came up to 150 MPH. The tanks would be nearly empty but Honolulu seemed a reasonable objective. We changed course for Oahu. The autopilot was performing admirably and it seemed at times as if all ten of us were asleep. The flight deck and catwalk were showing signs of serious wear from the flight engineer's trips to check the gas gauges and advise the pilot of fuel level and consumption.

Daylight came bringing a first-time view of the vast Pacific, a light breeze (judging by the almost absence of white caps) and a more relaxed crew. Finally, a distant cloudbank, which soon became the outline of an island, was later identified as Diamond Head. Not much gas left in the tanks but an uneventful landing and the first leg of our trip to New Guinea was completed.

Hawaii: Beautiful Waikiki, Diamond Head, Honolulu, and Pearl Harbor, where the trouble had really started. There were maintenance needs that could not be done in the combat areas, so a two-day layover. Swimming at Waikiki, horseback riding up Diamond Head. Pilot Zimmerman had grown up on a ranch in Oklahoma and riding was no problem for him. Watts and Burhoe had some experience and could control their horses but it was Perrone's first experience and at the first turn his horse headed back to the barn. Fortunately, Zimmerman anticipated such a problem and caught up and headed the horse back in the right direction.

The next leg was to the tiniest dot in the vast Pacific – Canton Island. Weather good and the autopilot, faithful and true, kept us on course throughout the day. On the approach to Canton in the afternoon, more and more clouds covered the sky. If the radio direction equipment didn't function, how to find that little spit of land. But everything worked and landing was no problem. Overnight on the island, then on to Fiji.

We took off early in the morning because clouds tend to build heavy overcast in mid- to late afternoon. The day was March 6, 1944, the navigator's birthday. Crossing the International Date Line at noon, he wondered if he was only 26-1/2 instead of 27. It was March 7th on the western side. No matter, he got the half-day back when he crossed the other way going home. Fuji, another beautiful Pacific Island. The base arranged for trucks to take us to the local fresh water swimming holes. The water was clear enough to call heads or tails on a dime in water ten feet deep. It was much warmer than water back home.

Our next destination, New Caledonia. A routine flight getting us closer to the New Guinea combat zone. More afternoon swimming and tent city quarters. The food situation is very hazy at all the stops but the lush Pacific Islands should have provided some exotic meals. Or did we have c-rations?

Some excitement on departure from New Caledonia. Shortly after takeoff, the flight engineer spotted gas pouring from the left wing tank. The possibility of fire and/or explosion was very real. And the gas load had to be substantially reduced before landing. After flying for a while and also dumping gas into the ocean, the plane landed without incident. The emergency vehicles along the runways were a mixed blessing; fortunately, they were not needed. There were no weather problems, so the tanks were topped again and the caps checked very carefully, and onto Townsville, Australia.

Northern Australia at this time was not very modern. A trip into town for a milkshake was nostalgic for those from small town USA and a nice change from the tiny islands. The stories about the Japanese advance to Port Moresby, not that far north, were a little hair-raising but the enemy positions were all on the north coast of New Guinea by now.

The crew had brought a new airplane and the latest in airborne radar to the 5th Air Force and they were ready to help push the enemy back to Tokyo.

On our way overseas, March 1944, Oahu, Hawaii. From left to right, Kent Zirmmerman, Steve Perrone, Jim Watts, Major North, a pilot we met on his way home, and George Burhoe.

In Nadzab, New Guinea, June 1944. From the left, bare-chested and wearing a pith helmet, Charlie Nunez; seated in the jeep, Kermit Crabtree, and standing with hand on hip, Harold Donner. (On January 9, 1945, Kermit Crabtree was killed in an aircraft accident on Owi Island.)

THE PILOT'S PERSPECTIVE

Kent Zimmerman: When we took off from Hickam for Canton Island before daylight on March 5, 1944, we lost all of our static and ram air flight instrumentation on the aircraft! I didn't have any airspeed or altitude readings but I decided to stay on course for Canton, at least until it got daylight. By the time we had climbed to altitude the problem had cleared up, so we flew onto Canton about eleven and a half hours later. We found Canton by intercepting a Sun Line Burhoe had plotted that led to the island. Another excellent job done by Burhoe! We figured out that it had rained so much in Hawaii that water had got into the Pitot line and knocked out the static and ram air flight instruments.

A recollection from Flight Engineer Richard Howard, a rancher and farmer from Hysham, Montana: Rich recalls that after passing the point of no return on our flight to tiny Canton Island, the number two engine began running rough long enough to cause concern about making landfall. Then suddenly, it began to run smoother and it was fine. Navigator George Burhoe commented that we would name that engine "Skippy."

The next day we took off for Nandi Airport on the island of Viti Levu in Fiji. The runway at Nandi had a slight rise in the middle of it, which made it appear that you were running out of runway after you landed. We were told that one of the aircrews a few days ahead of us had blown his tires trying to stop because he thought he was running out of runway. The thing I remember about Nandi was the native village we visited close to the airfield and the river where we went swimming, that had the clearest water I had ever seen.

On take off from Nandi, I think on March 7th or 8th, the auxiliary gas tank cap popped off again and we had to fly around the field burning up gas before we could land. On the 8th of March, we made it on to Noumea Airfield in New Caledonia. From Noumea, we finally arrived at Townsville, Australia. When I reported into the 5th Air Force Replacement Center at Townsville, they told me to have the airplane unloaded and then check into the Replacement Depot with my crew for assignment to some Bombardment Group. I told them we were on Project 96331-R and we were not giving up the airplane or going to any unit except the 63rd Bombardment Squadron!

After a heated discussion, they finally told me where we would be assigned and that the 43rd Bombardment Group was at Dobodura and to get the hell out of their office. I finally got orders from Headquarters 5th Air Force Service Area Command and the 5th Air Force Reception Center assigning our B-24J Aircraft, #42-100037, and its crew to the 5th Air Force, 5th Bomber Command, 43rd Bombardment Group (Heavy). This order was dated 15 March 1944.

We went to Base Operations, found out where Dobodura was located on the east coast of New Guinea and I think on March 16, 1944 took off. We flew a course to Port Moresby, then climbed over the Owen-Stanley mountain range dodging the clouds. After logging two and a half hours of instrument time we found Dobodura. We could see five or six different airstrips located within an 8- to-10-mile radius.

We had no idea which strip belonged to the 43rd, so we picked out one that had B-24s parked around it in the revetments and landed. Of course, this was the wrong one! Somebody told us which one we should be on and we took off and landed again. I don't know who met us, but I remember we were given tents in the 63rd area, close to a river, not far from the airstrip.

I can't remember if we flew any combat missions out of Dobodura. I know we were there for only a short time. My flight Form 5 shows that we flew on March 17, 18, & 29th, 1944 for 1:45, 2:05, & 4:00 daylight hours, respectively but none were listed as Combat Missions. I assume these were training flights out of Dobo. I know we flew a couple of skip bombing practice flights on a beached Jap ship in the Huron Gulf of the Solomon Sea where Dobo was located.

When we moved to Nadzab, I remember we loaded all of our belongings in our airplane, including our tents, and we flew up the coast to Nadzab. During the month of April 1944, we flew five Combat Missions for an average of about 11:15 hours each. At Nadzab, we lived East of the airstrip, in the foothills of the mountains forming the Markham Valley.

One of the first missions we flew out of Nadzab was north up to the Equator searching for enemy shipping. I remember, we flew through the waves of the equatorial weather front, weaving our way through the heavy clouds by radar. I remember it was a dark, rough, night of climbing, turning and descending that must have given Navigator Burhoe fits trying to plot our track.

THE BOMBARDIER'S PERSPECTIVE

Steve Perrone: A comment on how this retrospective came about. On my birthday, one of my daughters gave me a copy of News Anchor Tom Brokaw's World War II book titled "The Greatest Generation." I always thought the greatest generation was the generation that fought the War of Independence, and then went on to form a new nation. But he may have a point. In a sense, we fought a worldwide war of independence. I remember as a young teenager, Europe was being overrun by Hitler's panzers. American ships could not sail freely, German U-boats were sighted off our East Coast beaches; and on the other side of the world, Japan had invaded China, Manchuria, and French IndoChina. We always feared that we would have to get involved sooner or later. We did, and returned from a conflict that historians say consumed more than 50 million lives. That's a little of the big picture. What we put together is a personal perspective ... how we viewed this experience and how we felt about it at that time, as best as we can remember the events. Our military jobs in World War II were the most important jobs of our lives. That's why after 55 or more years, we still remember. Some of the details have faded, but we will continue to remember the effort and the friendships forged.

**Following are accounts of what we regarded as
one of our most successful missions:**

THE PILOT'S PERSPECTIVE

Kent Zimmerman: I think we all remember the night we found the Japanese convoy just northeast of Leyte Island. I especially remember that we were scheduled to take off at 0700 PM. During our pre-flight inspection, Rich discovered we had a cut in our left main tire and it was partially flat. We tried to jack up the left side of the aircraft, so we could change the tire, but it was loaded with 3,100 gallons of gas (about 18,800 pounds), four 500 and two 1,000 lbs. of bombs, and a full load of 50-caliber ammunition. It would be daylight before we could unload the aircraft, but the Wing Commander refused to cancel the mission. Therefore, we found a wing jack and tried to lift the left wing high enough to take off the tire. Our main concern was not to damage the left wing. We jacked up the left side of the airplane, but the left wing flexed about three feet at the tip, the landing gear strut extended it full length, and the tire wouldn't come off the ground. This forced us to lower the wing again, tie the strut with rope so it couldn't extend and jack up the left side of the wing again! Rich Howard and I were very concerned about

In Nadzab, New Guinea, the Skipper, Kent Zimmerman, gases up a jeep for a trip to Lae on the coast.

warping the wing, so we raised the tire enough to dig a hole under it and installed a new tire. We finally got airborne at 11:00 PM and luckily located the convoy about an hour later. We weren't sure if it was Japanese or ours. So we radioed 5th Bomber Command for permission to attack. While waiting for an answer to our message (which never came) we made a short search to the west of Ormoc and finally I made a decision to bomb the convoy. The rest of the story is told in the following Pilot's Narrative.

SUBJECT:
PILOT'S NARRATIVE OF MISSION FFO 341-C

TO: 63rd Intelligence

1. Staged out from Palau, landing at Tacloban at 1500/I/6. Took off Tacloban 2300/I/6, held on ground by red alert and night fighters landing. Mission was shipping recco from Manila Bay south and west. Sighted on radar two small targets at 0017/I off Bugtung Island, also 2 more small targets at 0020/I, moving south.

2. At 0030/I sighted 13 medium and large U/I ships coming out of Masbate, about 120 miles from Ormac. Possibly on a S.E. heading at about 10 knots. Radioed base for permission to bomb convoy, but never received confirmation to bomb. Returned and sighted supposedly same 13 ship convoy, at 0130/I off East Coast of Masbate Island 10 to 15 miles south of first position. Flew recco in Sibuyan Sea waiting for confirmation of bombing, but at 0400 returned to convoy and bombed closest target at 0630/I confirmed to be a 3000-ton Fox Tare Uncle. Bombs hit 3 x500 demos off port side, parallel to ship 20 to 25 feet. Water covered entire ship and caused it to roll considerably. No A/A encountered on this run. Shadowed convoy until 0540/I when another run was made on outside target, a DD or CL. Moderate A/A on run with 1st bomb approximately 150 feet short, 2nd bomb 75 feet short, and 3rd bomb on bow of ship followed by explosion and smoke.

3. In order to report damage and order of convoy, we flew another recco south of convoy and returned after daylight to visually check the composition. Checked visually 3 Fox Tare Charlie's, 3 DD's, 3 Tare Uncle's and 1 Fox Able. Stayed in area until dive bombing fighters arrived. At this time, the convoy was about 45 miles from Ormoc. Landed at Tacloban 0715/I/7.

For the Squadron Commander:

(Certified True Copy)

L. A. Zimmerman

1st LT., Air Corps Pilot

A Note From The Editor/Narrator: In May, 2000 I located the Air Force Historical Research Agency at Maxwell Air Force Base in Alabama. This is the agency where all military records are stored. World War II records are stored as microfilm and I ordered prints from the microfilm for the dates we spent with the 63rd Bomb Squadron, March 1944 to March 1945. I received 1287 pages (declassified) and from these pages I've culled information and events in which we participated more than 55 years ago. Because this information was compiled in various Southwest Pacific Islands by a rotating group of intelligence personnel and moved from island to island in tropical weather, and usually stored in rather primitive facilities, there are gaps in the material and many pages were not readable.

But listed below is the historical account of our December 7, 1944 mission:

Plane 041 got a late start because of a red alert at Tacloban but once off she did an excellent job, damaging a 3000-ton Fox Tare Charlie and sinking a 1700 ton destroyer. She caught a 13-ship convoy coming out of Masbate north of Leyte, and while waiting confirmation to bomb it, flew recco in Sibuyan Sea. She picked up the convoy again on the way back at 0400 and, choosing the closest target, let go 3x500-lb. demos. They struck parallel to the ship, a 3000-ton Fox Tare Charlie, about 20 feet off the port side. Water washed completely over her and she rolled violently. At 0540 the plane made a run on a destroyer on the outside of the convoy. Of the remaining three bombs, the first was 150 feet short, the second 75 feet short, and the last was a direct hit on the bow, followed by an explosion and heavy smoke. Slight ack-ack fire was encountered on this run. Making a visual check after daylight, the Fox Tare Charlie was found to be trailing oil slick and was obviously seriously damaged, while the destroyer was not seen and was claimed as sunk.

The same mission as recalled by Navigator George Burhoe:

THE NAVIGATOR'S PERSPECTIVE

George Burhoe: On takeoff, Kent Zimmerman, our pilot on intercom outlined the mission through the passages and straits north of Leyte to Manila. The Navy had spotted a convoy leaving Manila Harbor, heading south toward the north side of Leyte opposite the landing area. There were still enemy installations on the island and other nearby islands and it was thought the ships were trying to reinforce them with both supplies and troops. Several routes were possible and our job was to search, find, report and then destroy as many as we could.

The early hours were unproductive but about two-thirty or three o'clock, we spotted targets stretched out in single file close to Sibuyan Island. The pilot had been briefed about American ships north of Leyte but a quick check of our position ruled out any thought that they could be ours, so we lined up on the last ship in the line. Steve Perrone, the bombardier cranked up his LAB (Low Altitude Bombsight). George Burhoe, the navigator, set up a heading and we went in close enough for a bombing run. Perhaps the enemy did not have radar capable of locating us at our 900 to 1000 ft. altitude or maybe they thought firing would give away their position and type of ships.

The first run was very successful as at least one bomb hit the deck of a good-sized freighter and our crew reported it had rolled over in the water. For the next several hours, we simulated bomb runs on the convoy approaching within half a mile or closer. When daylight was getting close, we made the second business run with the second string of a five hundred, a thousand and a five hundred. The convoy had regrouped into battle formation with destroyers and destroyer escorts around the freighter/troop carrier ships. Again, our run was successful with a direct hit on the fantail or bow of a destroyer.

It was getting daylight by this time, and we were drawing anti-aircraft fire. Our mission was complete, so we executed that famous air corps maneu-ver. We got the HELL out of there.

Our briefing called for a clear code message when we spotted the convoy. That had been done and confirmation of its reception was a formation of P-47s heading for the area we had just left. A welcome sight indeed. The P-47s made short work of the rest of the enemy ships.

The Brass was waiting when we landed to congratulate us and to find out any more information we might have.

THE GUNNER'S PERSPECTIVE

Harold Donner: Evening of December 6, 1944: scheduled for a takeoff from Tacloban airfield, Leyte. As I recall the events, we were originally scheduled to fly to Clark and Nielson Fields near Manila and bomb and harass both airfields. Mission was changed to find, report, and bomb a forming convoy. I don't recall its location. Detained at takeoff by an arriving Navy Privateer that experienced a collapsed landing gear on the runway. Also delayed by American fighter planes coming back from daylight strikes.

By this time darkness had fallen — and then an incoming aircraft with running lights was coming in for a landing. Our anti-aircraft gun batteries at the end of the runway opened fire on the aircraft. We evacuated our airplane, which was sitting at the end of the runway waiting to takeoff. We ran and dove under a large earthmover. The plane was shot down right over the run-way. We learned the next day that the plane was carrying a platoon of Japanese Kamikaze soldiers seeking to destroy our armed and ready aircraft, pre-paring for a major December 7 strike.

Don't recall what time convoy was picked up on radar, but it was the early morning of December 7. The first bomb run was made through the center of the convoy. I was at the waist escape hatch with one or two crewmembers and assistant Engineer Charlie Nunez to help release the flares. In dropping the flare, we realized that the flare arming cord, which was at-tached to the aircraft, had become entangled with Charlie's foot or ankle and it was pulling him out of the hatch. One of the crew grabbed him and held on until the flare released. I wonder if Charlie remembers this incident. When the bombs detonated beside a merchant ship, a wall of water surged over the deck, washing crewmen over the side. The light of the flare made this very clear. To this day, I can see the Japanese crewmen tumbling. No enemy fire was encountered.

The second run was sometime later. We dropped the flare, but cannot recall where bombs hit. Remember hearing and seeing muzzle blasts and fire from guns on destroyer that was our target. Followed convoy until daylight. Destroyer was lagging far behind and very low at the stern.

Remember being told about the 50-plus enemy aircraft destroyed by P38s shortly after we left the convoy. Also, when the daylight attack planes got to the convoy only 11 ships were counted. Our crew got credit for sinking two ships.

THE BOMBARDIER'S PERSPECTIVE

Steve Perrone: At our briefing, we were ordered to locate a Japanese convoy (my recollection is that the Navy cats first picked up the convoy the previous day), shadow it all night, report positions of the convoy through the night, harass it by making bombing runs over it, and then come home to base the following morning.

This convoy, the last "Tokyo Express" dispatched by the Japanese to reinforce their troops on the backside of Leyte Island, was comprised of 13 vessels, six troop ships and seven destroyer escorts or maybe the opposite. It was moving by night seeking cover among the many islands that make up the Philippine Islands. We flew over the convoy all night and made several bombing runs. On two of the bombing runs, we hit ships in the convoy. As bombar-dier, I could not see the hits, but our waist gunner and assistant en-gineer (and possibly other crew members) reported that they saw the bomb hits in the light of the flares they dropped upon hearing my intercom call, "Bombs away!"

Again, if my memory serves me, when we finally did make a visual observation of the convoy just as daylight broke that morning, there were 11 ships closing in on the Leyte Coast. But, we didn't observe them very long because the convoy, now in battle formation, opened fire on us in daylight, although they had fired on us infrequently during the bombing runs. I recall very well that early morning sighting of the convoy very well from the underside glass of the Bombardier's compartment. We were on intercom and just a few thousand feet high when the pilot came on and said something like let's get a better look at them, and he started to turn towards the convoy and it was like 4th of July fireworks, USA. The entire convoy opened up on our aircraft probably in retaliation for our bombing runs and our observation runs over and around them, and the fact that they lost two ships. This only took a minute or so, but I was sure that every tracer was coming directly into the nose of the B-24 – and between each tracer there were four or five projectiles we couldn't see. Of course, every crewmember saw the tracers, including Pilot Kent Zimmerman who turned and put the four-engined bomber into a dive toward the water and we got the hell out of there, as I recall it. We landed at Tacloban right after the mission that morning and were met on the strip by a major general from General Kenney's staff (don't recall his name) and another staff officer. The general congratulated the crew on our successful mission and we found out later that the Japanese convoy picked up fighter cover from their base on Cebu Island (we probably just missed them) at daybreak. Our fighter-bombers (P-47s) sank all the ships in the convoy and our fighter cover that morning (P-38s) shot down over 50 Japanese fighters.

This was an important mission because our crew performance was in-strumental in the total destruction of the entire convoy. Had the convoy discharged its cargo of men and supplies at the Japanese-held base at Ormac, on the backside of Leyte, it is possible that the strengthened Japanese ground forces could have threatened our airfield at Tacloban. This would have been a major defeat because at that time, Tacloban was our only airstrip in the Philippines. The Japanese occupied most of the major islands including Luzon, Mindanao, Cebu, and many others. It would also have been a setback for US Pacific Command's Island hopping strategy, which had been very successful in the New Guinea Theater and other Pacific locations.

In retrospect, this mission deserved a decoration. I don't ever remember discussing decorations with our crewmembers in combat. Our goal was to help defeat the enemy and then get the hell home as soon as possible. Some 45 years later at one of our reunions, I did learn that our pilot, Kent Zimmerman, was recommended for a DFC for this mission. Kent said the Wing Commander told him back then that he cancelled the request because of a disagreement they had before takeoff that night. As it turns out several years later, at a reunion, we were informed that the DFC was turned down on a technicality by a warrant officer at some desk job away from the combat area.

We were sorry it was turned down because it was deserved. Several of us agreed that the DFC probably should have been recommended for the entire crew because it was a team effort. The pilots flew the airplane, the navigator got us there, the radar operator picked up the ships on his SCR717B radar which could detect ships at a distance of approximately 200 miles, the flight engineer managed our fuel consumption, the bombardier picked up the targets on his ten mile RC 17 Low Altitude Bomb sight and dropped the bombs, the assistant engineer and the gunners released the flares, the radio operator sent position locations to headquarters all through the night. But, when you think about it, we were just doing our jobs.

Now an aborted mission remembered by a few:

THE BOMBARDIER'S PERSPECTIVE

Steve Perrone: An aborted mission that several crew-members remember vividly while many others do not. The crewmembers who were busy on this mission remember it best. The mission was flown out of Tacloban strip in Leyte. It was during the typhoon season in the Philippines, probably in October 1944. As I recall, our destination was the Manila area in Luzon. It was a very dark night with extreme weather conditions all around us when we flew into a thunderhead or some type of weather disturbance which caused the aircraft to suddenly lose several thousand feet. We were being bounced around when the smell of leaking gasoline spread throughout the airplane. And in those days, most of us smoked, even in flight. The leak was in the bomb bays.

I was on intercom listening to the pilot and navigator conversing with John Ahern, our radar operator, who was trying to locate some clear weather on his long range radar. As soon as the gasoline leak became evident, the pilot ordered the bomb bay doors opened to dissipate the fumes. I don't recall who discovered that the top bomb in one of the front bomb bays was jammed against the underside of the wing because of a twisted bomb shackle, caused by the sudden loss of altitude. The wing is where most of the fuel in the aircraft is stored. The mission was aborted. We were near the Japanese island of Cebu as I recall. The pilot ordered me to defuze the bombs and get rid of them.

A standard operating procedure on our combat missions was as soon as we leveled off after takeoff, Assistant Engineer Charles Nunez would meet me in the bomb bays with a box of bomb fuzes. Each bomb took a nose and tail fuze and we usually carried six 500 pound bombs or four 500's and two 1000 bombs. The fuzed bombs were now a problem.

Nunez and I again met in the bomb bays. But this time we had to work with the bomb bays open because of gasoline fumes and because I had to release each bomb mechanically, moving from bay to bay. Charlie and I now had to hold on for our lives, standing on the suspended catwalk, probably no more than eight inches wide, with one arm around the struts connecting the catwalk to the top of the fuselage. The plane was pitching and yawing, the wind was roaring in from the open bomb bays, and there was nothing but blackness below. And while all this is going on, Rich Howard, our engineer was bouncing in and out of the bomb bays from the flight deck, trying to locate a fuel valve that would stop the leak.

It took awhile because of the conditions, but one by one, starting at the bottom bomb in each bay, I unscrewed the nose and tail fuses in each bomb, handed the fuses to Charlie, and then dropped the bombs out of the plane. As I remember it, the top bomb with the twisted shackle released itself when I unlocked the shackle hoops supporting the bomb. It just dropped free out of the bay.

Another reason I remember this mission so well is because it made necessary another mission when I returned home some six or seven months later. To explain this comment: Overseas, it was customary for servicemen to try and locate family, friends or other GIs from their hometowns. A relative of mine located me when I first arrived in New Guinea. By the time our crew had completed 15 or 20 missions, replacement crews were arriving to replace crews that completed their missions. A co-pilot from one of the replacement crews heard I was from Philadelphia, also his hometown. He came to visit me – I think we were in Leyte at that time. He was a handsome Irish kid from a newer section of Philadelphia called Mayfair, a working class area of well-kept homes, while I was from the oldest section of Philadelphia on the south end, not too far from the waterfront. He looked like a schoolboy but he was about 21; I was about 24 at that time. We were in the same tent area and we visited from time to time to exchange news from our hometown. When his crew flew 10 or so missions, they went on leave to Australia. When they returned, he visited our tent to show me a collection of souvenirs he had purchased for his family. Our crew had flown about 30 missions at that time and we were due to be sent home. He asked me to get them to his parents because he had learned that the GI mail did not work for packages coming or going.

I'll digress from the narrative for a paragraph or two because I've learned after 55 years that if you recollect a little something, write it down or it will fade away again. About the overseas GI mail: Very few packages from home arrived unscathed. Early on, I asked my mother and teen-aged brothers by letter to send me my camera. It was a bellows-type Kodak – a very nice camera in those days. It never arrived. My family sent me a carton of ciga-rettes from time to time. Don't recall getting them. This was also true for packages going the other way. At that time, many of us played small stakes poker as a pastime. At the games, I met a pilot from one of the other squadrons in our 43rd Bomb Group. The other three squadrons, the 64th, 65th and the 403rd flew daylight formation combat missions, with fighter escort when necessary, while our squadron, the 63rd, flew single airplane missions in black B-24's at night seeking enemy shipping or as a secondary target, an enemy airfield or shipping port. This particular pilot/poker player would kid me saying it was suicide flying at night alone. He advised me to transfer to his squadron and fly daylight missions. The unique thing about this pilot was that he carried a Japanese Samurai sword with him wherever he went. I don't recall how he acquired it, but he removed the tape and protective covering to show me the precious or semi-precious stones that covered the handle area. Back to the GI mail problem: He could not send it home. There was no safe storage in any area we moved to; all facilities were in tents including living quarters, mess halls, operations, administration, everything. So he carried the sword with him wherever he went: the latrine, the mess hall, combat missions, it was a part of him. I hope he got home with it.

Back to the narrative and the aborted mission flown during the typhoon season in the Philippines. The crew of the young Irish co-pilot from my hometown also flew a mission that stormy night, but they never came back. Because of circumstances beyond my control, I did not get back to the USA west coast until near the end of May, 1945; in fact, I celebrated my 25th birthday on the second or third day in San Francisco while I was getting my travel orders to go on leave. I did celebrate that night at the popular Top of the Mark bar with strangers, but servicemen were not treated like strangers at that time in most American cities.

In a day or two, I boarded a train for home per my orders. There were no commercial airlines to speak of in that period, especially during wartime. And the war with Japan had not ended. The train ride home took five or six days, trains during the war were crowded with GIs, with wives and small children traveling to or from Army or Navy Bases, luggage all over the aisles and people sitting or sleeping on pieces of luggage because all the seating was occupied. I did arrive in Philadelphia the first week in June and my family was ecstatic and so was I.

During the second week in June, I called the family of the missing-in-action co-pilot from the Mayfair section in Northeast Philadelphia. Unlike today, very few families owned automobiles in the '40s, and during the war years all the auto companies were converted to the manufacture of tanks and other defense materials. So I boarded a streetcar – we called them trolleys – and I arrived in Mayfair about an hour and a half later. I saw the star in their window and his parents met me at the door, in tears, but smiling at me. To them, I was the last person to see and converse with their son. I gave them the notes and souvenirs and they read and reread the notes, and passed the souvenirs back and forth, all the while asking me questions about their son, and whether downed airmen missing in action are sometimes rescued.

I responded that there were more than several hundred islands that made up the Philippines, and only the major islands were occupied by the Japanese. And if they came down onto one of the hundreds of unoccupied islands, the Filipinos would hide them from the enemy. (Did I really think this could happen on a night flight in terrible weather? No. But I certainly was not going to destroy the hope they were nursing for the eventual return of their son.) I was there for more than an hour and we had some coffee and cookies, after which I indicated that I would be leaving. They embraced me with tears in their eyes and I'm sorry that after 55 years, I've forgotten his name. But I'm certain his parents never forgot it, he was their only child.

Now we'll shift continents back to the aborted mission during the typhoon season.

THE ASSISTANT FLIGHT ENGINEER'S PERSPECTIVE

Charles Nunez: I recall the dumping of the 500-pound bombs that got jammed on the shackle in the bomb bays under the wing tanks. You had nerves of steel–cool and collected–while disarming those bombs and with the bomb bay doors open. Would you do it again? I remember hearing you on intercom during a bomb run–"Bombs away, let's get the hell out of here." I used to keep the tags removed from the fuses when the bombs were fused. I wrote the date and target on each fuze. But I can't remember what I did with all of them.

THE FLIGHT ENGINEER'S PERSPECTIVE

Richard Howard: As to this mission, I don't remember the date or where we were going. We apparently ran into a typhoon off the Philippine coast. I remember the gas leak, which was in the right bomb bay. As you know, the wing tanks of the B-24 were comprised of 18 fuel cells. My first thought was to transfer fuel from the leaking tank to the wing tanks, but we were still leaking fuel after the transfer. The fuel tank pump did not completely drain the tank. I finally found that the fuel tank line from the bomb bay tank to the transfer system was leaking. I fixed it with a screwdriver.

As to what you guys were doing with the bombs, I didn't know. You were thrashing around and talking but I was so damned upset with the fuel leak, I didn't pay much attention to what you guys did. It must have been okay as we all got back safe and sound.

A Comment From The Editor/Narrator: The WWII events we are dredging up from deep within our memory banks after more than 55 years have forced us to think back to specific events which were remembered dif-ferently by several of us or not remembered at all. First Pilot Kent Zimmerman, in one of his letters to me said he was sorry he did not keep all his Pilot's Narratives of every mission, the official mission report given to the Intelligence Officer. If so, we could have included an official record of each combat mission. But we weren't thinking of records or history at that time, we just wanted to win the war and go home. He only kept one narrative, which is included earlier in this Retrospective. I'll now include some combat missions remembered by some but not all.

THE BOMBARDIER'S PERSPECTIVE

Steve Perrone: I don't recall the date of the raid on Brunei Bay on the northern side of the huge island of Borneo, an oil producing port captured by the Japanese weeks after Pearl Harbor. We staged out of Morotai, a small godforsaken island just north of Halmahera and the Moluccas islands, all occupied by the Japanese. We staged out of Morotai many times and enemy aircraft bombed us every night we spent there, or so it seemed. Our missions averaged 12 to 13 hours and this was a long one. George had to navigate us around the Celebes islands, then along the eastern side of Borneo to Brunei Bay. It was a dark night when we entered the mouth of the bay and we could see docks and ships all lit up with all sorts of activity. And they paid no at-tention to us, possibly because they didn't expect our planes so deep into their territory. My recollection is that I talked to the pilot and navigator on intercom, and we decided to skip-bomb the docks and ships. I remember it clearly be-cause it was the only time we skip-bombed on a combat mission. The pilot dropped down to about 300 feet and we went in. It was one of the few times that I could see what we were bombing. I don't remember how many bombs I toggled out, but because of the low altitude, we could feel the detonations. We got out to the mouth of the bay and it seemed like the whole area was in flames. I went over to talk to intelligence a day or two after and was told that the Navy Catalinas reported the fires were still burning.

OTHER CREWMEMBERS' PERSPECTIVES

Assistant Engineer Charles Nunez: I do remember the "milk runs" to Balikpapan and Brunei Bay. I can still remember seeing the ships lit up early in the morning right on the docks. Anyway, it was the most exciting part of my life being a crewmember and part of a top-notch bunch of swell people.

First Pilot Kent Zimmerman: From Owi Island, we also staged out of Morotai, close to Halmahera Island, in order to search for shipping around the Celebes and to hit targets on Borneo Island. The Japanese had an oil refinery at Balikpapan on Borneo and several other ports that the 63d Squadron and the daylight squadrons bombed. We didn't have to stage at Morotai to hit Borneo but the staging gave us more time to search for shipping. I think we had one or two missions over Borneo.

I do remember a mission we flew out of Owi Island where we bombed the oil refinery (Balikpapan) on Borneo with 55-gallon barrels filled with Napalm. We carried nine barrels fused with phosphorus hand grenades clipped in clamps welded to the bungholes on the barrels. We had to bomb from 10,000 feet so the barrels would burst and the grenades would start a fire. It was reported later the next day that the fire was still burning.

Bombardier Steve Perrone: Kent refreshed my memory on this mission. This was a total squadron operation. I don't recall how many *Snoopers* we got into the air that night, but I recall that all planes were given a time and altitude over the target, all around 10,000 feet. The barrels were toggled out of the aircraft, because they had no trajectory. We dropped on the fires burning, and we worried that one of our planes flying just above us in the same time frame would release their bombs through us. Also, I believe we drew some anti-aircraft fire that night.

Flight Engineer Rich Howard's diary has entries of November 22-23 and 29-30, 1944 for Borneo Missions. **Nose Gunner Harold Donner** has a diary entry of November 22-23 with a Morotai island staging for a Borneo mission. In Donner's own words: Do you recall that the Japanese bombers would get over the strip before the RedAlert would sound? On that mission, previous to takeoff while Kent and Jim were pre-flighting the airplane on the end of the runway, I was sitting on the waist window ledge and looked up and saw these white things floating down. I nudged Kermit Crabtree and he looked up too. Recognizing the anti-aircraft bursts, we both immediately went out the escape hatch. Eventually, the entire crew evacuated the plane except for the pilot. Finally, Kent got out too. He cut the engines but the put-put was still running and the runway guys were yelling to cut the damn lights. Kent told Flight Engineer Rich to go back and shut off the put-put. Rich replied, Hell No, if you want it off, do it yourself.

After the air raid, we were back on the end of the strip waiting to takeoff, but still on the taxiway. Behind us was a plane from the 13th Air Force. The tower operator told Pilot Kent Zimmerman if you can get off in one minute go. Kent put on the brakes, throttled up, turned into the runway and let her go.

The next morning on our return from the Borneo mission, we learned that right after our takeoff the night before, a bomb hit behind us on the runway in front of the 13th Air Force plane following us. Both pilots were hit; one was killed and the other was wounded.

Steve Perrone: Most of us remember this pre-takeoff exercise because it was not the only time we were caught on the airstrip during an enemy bombing attack. As Donner recalls, we did abandon the aircraft during the middle of the raid, in search of a place to hide, a shelter of sorts, but not on the strip on Morotai Island. Several of us found a depression in the coral about 10 to 12 inches deep just off the runway about 30 or 40 yards from our B-24, parked on the end of the runway with over 3000 gallons of fuel and a full load of bombs. We certainly did not want to be too close to our airplane if a Japanese bomb scored a hit. It seemed like everytime we staged out of Morotai we were bombed on the airstrip or in the tent area. There was a large foxhole in the tent area, large enough for about a dozen people. But because coral is so hard and difficult to work with, the hole was no more than two feet deep. It was covered by several sheets of corrugated metal roofing. We theorized what would happen if it ever took a direct bomb hit.

To attempt to summarize the accomplishments of our *"Snooper"* Squadron during the period we served, a Squadron Memo from March 29, 1945 is inserted below. The original of this memo was barely readable.

63rd Bombardment Squadron
43rd Bombardment Group
AP074

March 29, 1945

Subject: Statistics.

To: The Squadron Commander, 63rd Bombardment Squadron.

1. In conjunction with the preparation of a Unit Presidential Citation for this squadron many facts and figures present themselves. Taken one by one these figures seem quite ordinary but when they are compiled together they present quite an imposing array. For the benefit of those who may be interested, the following facts concern the 63rd Bombardment Squadron's record for a period of 206 days beginning September 1, 1944 and terminating March 25, 1945.

2. Concerning Operations the 63rd Bombardment Squadron flew 8,249 combat hours on 572 individual sorties. That is an average of more than 1200 hours a month and individual sorties averaged 14 hours.

3. Concerning Ordnance the squadron dropped 4,809 bombs of all types for a tonnage of 508, or in pounds, 1,017,238 lbs.

4. Deeply concerning the Japanese Navy and Merchant Marine, the Squadron's shipping record speaks for itself. Shipping definitely sunk totaled twenty one for 65,800 tons. Shipping probably sunk totaled five for 17,600 tons. Shipping damaged totaled 16 for 80,750 tons. The total sunk, probably sunk and damaged is 42 ships totaling 164,150 tons or in astronomical figures, 328,300,000 pounds.

5. Some of the land targets attacked during this period included Ambon, Ceram, Haroekoe and Laha in New Guinea. Kendare, Menado, Sidate and Lambeh Straits in the Celebes. Balikpapan, Mangaar, Sandakan, Tarakan, Labuan and Brunei Bay in Borneo. Davao, Matina, Sassa, Wolfe Field, Puerta Princessa, Bacoleod, Nichols, Neilson and Clark Fields, Alicante, Laoag and Apparit in the Philippines. Takao, Heito, Okayama and Kagi in Formosa. Hio-How, Mako, Tien Ho and White Cloud Airdromes in China and Tainan Island.

6. In October of 1944 the Squadron set a record for operations, flying 1,693 combat hours on 131 individual sorties for and average of four planes out each night and 13 hours per sortie. The period from February 24, 1945 through March 25, 1945 saw the Squadron set a new shipping record since its formation as a radar bombing outfit. During that 30 day period 16 ships were definitely sunk totaling 48,000 tons and five were damaged for a total of 25,750 tons. Total sunk and damaged was 73,750 tons.

Editor's Note: Following is a section of a "Special Report on Bombardment Operations in the Pacific" issued by the Air Intelligence Contact Unit on April 19, 1945. The report was written by Major Dickran M. Sarkisian, a B-24 combat pilot who was awarded a Silver Star, a DFC, and an Air Medal. After his combat flying tour, he served as Assistant A-3 of the Fifth Bomber Command. I received the report from the Archives Branch at Maxwell AFB, Alabama.

NIGHT *SNOOPERS*

Much has been said about the radar equipped B-24s used as Night *Snoopers* by the 5th Bomber Command. Briefly, these *Snooper* missions consisted of individual sorties by the radar equipped aircraft. Bomber Command had one squadron comprised solely of such aircraft and this squadron operated primarily against enemy shipping from low altitudes. It was also employed in harassing attacks against enemy airfields and ground installations and as a source of weather information. This Squadron, which operated as a part of a heavy bombardment group, was usually stationed at one of our most forward bases to permit coverage of the most distant targets. They were invaluable in helping to maintain the air blockade of the Japanese on New Guinea.

These aircraft were equipped with one bomb bay fuel tank and carried a 3000-pound bomb load, consisting equally of 500-pound bombs nose- fused for 1/10th of a second's delay against shipping, and of 260-pound frag bombs fused for 4/5th of a second's delay against aircraft and airdromes. However, they sometimes carried a bomb load that consisted entirely of 23-pound fragmentation clusters. At least one, and sometimes two, of the *Snoopers* were always sent out over the route the main bomber strike force was to cover the next day, and in all likelihood would execute a night harassing attack upon this target. In the Philippines the *Snoopers* were used immediately prior to the Luzon landing for the purpose of harassing Manila and neighboring airdromes, and to cut the enemy's lines of communication and supply by strafing vehicles, trains, etc. I do not believe that the latter plan was a good one, as strafing at night in a B-24 is too dangerous. The risk to the aircraft and the danger of the enemy recovering enough of the extremely secret equipment carried aboard the aircraft to conduct a successful study of it did not justify the results achieved.

In regard to the staging of *Snooper* aircraft is not wise to stage them through strange bases prior to a mission, as the delicate radar equipment is often thrown out of commission by the shock of landing and the forward bases usually do not have the special technicians needed to repair the equipment.

Another fact which must be borne in mind regarding the use of these aircraft is that any shore targets against which they are sent should be topographically well defined, such targets as obvious peninsulas and small easily distinguishable islands being excellent. In every instance we endeavored to make the stay over land of these aircraft as brief as possible. The primary reason for this being security.

CREW RECOLLECTIONS

Editor's Note: In one of my letters to the crew I asked them to think back to our overseas experiences and try to recall some interesting items, not necessarily combat related, but recollections about our day-to-day activities in the Southwest Pacific Theater.

Flight Engineer Richard Howard: We staged out of Anguar Island in the Palau Group before moving up to Tacloban airstrip on Leyte Island because Tacloban in the early days after the Philippine landings was overcrowded with Army Air Corps planes, Marine fighter planes, and airplanes from Navy aircraft carriers.

One day Radar Operator John Ahern and I were sitting on a beautiful beach on Anguar watching a group of landing craft unload a large freighter in the harbor. Suddenly, right before our eyes, the freighter disappeared. Then we felt the force of the blast and the sound of the explosion. We found out later it was an ammunition ship.

Another incident at Anguar: We had an engine that was skipping and running rough. There was a crew chief with us but I don't remember if it was our regular crew chief, Charles Parker. This staging area lacked the maintenance facilities present at our regular bases, but the crew chief scrounged an ignition harness and we began replacing the old one when we noticed there were four loose spark plugs on the engine, which probably accounted for the rough running. I notified the skipper, Kent Zimmerman, and he decided to take the airplane up for a test flight.

There happened to be some Army Tank Corps soldiers nearby from an Army group on the island. They asked if they could take a ride in the airplane. The skipper said if they gave us a ride in one of their tanks they were invited for an airplane ride. We took a ride in the tank and it was very uncomfortable. They then accompanied the crew on the test flight. The engine was fine and then, at about five or six thousand feet, Kent throttled back, dropped the nose and the B-24 went into a dive. The crew chief who was standing behind the cockpit exclaimed that he had 33 months overseas and this was no way to go. The two Army tank guys in the waist were as white as sheets and later said they would stick to tanks.

There was also a mission where we had a prop governor malfunction early in the flight that forced us to return to Tacloban strip in the middle of the night. We contacted the tower but no landing lights came on and a hundred or so Navy ships in the harbor opened up on us. They were very itchy because the Japanese made nuisance bombing runs over the strip and the ships in the harbor almost every night. Anyhow, we tried again because it was an emergency. Again no response, no landing lights, but more anti-aircraft fire. We got out of there but again came back. This time in disgust Co-pilot Jim Watts responded by way of the command set using about four or five American curse words and behold, the lights came on and the Navy held their fire. They must have figured that with that sort of language it had to be an American aircraft.

Editor's Note: At the 43rd Bomb Group Reunion in San Antonio in 2000, Crew Chief Charles Parker, at a wine and cheese get-together in the Zimmermans' room, made us aware of an incident that he had buried in his memory for decades. He said Flight Engineer Rich Howard was also aware of the unexploded Japanese shell he removed from the wing tank of our aircraft.

Crew Chief Charles Parker: The shell was found in the left wing main gas tank. When it entered, the shell hit the main beam of the wing and went into the tank. This sheared the firing pin from the main charge in the shell, which is why it didn't explode. The shell was almost the size of our 20 mm shells. I placed the shell in a can of water and set it away from the aircraft. A Navy ordinance man came for it later. I believe it happened at Owi Island.

Bombardier Steve Perrone: The skipper, Pilot Kent Zimmerman, probably has the best recall of WWII happenings. His recollections sometimes help me to remember some incident long forgotten. In a recent letter, he recalled that his mother sent him a Christmas package while we were stationed on Leyte Island in the Philippines, and the package contained four large bottles of Lavoris mouthwash. He couldn't figure out why she would send him mouthwash but he put them on a shelf in the tent and sort of forgot about them. Then one morning he decided to rinse his mouth with the Lavoris, and he found out why his mother sent him the package. The Lavoris was whiskey, which made him very happy.

When I wrote back to him I asked how come I was not aware of the whiskey in the Lavoris bottles. All four of the crew officers shared the same tent on all the islands we inhabited. Kent said the package came while I was in the Army hospital with amoebic dysentery and the rest of the crew had left for the States. Here are some of his other recollections.

Pilot Kent Zimmerman: I remember I went to Sydney on leave in a B-24. I don't remember if it was our own aircraft #0037, but I do remember some of our crew were aboard. I don't remember if this was the trip when Jim Watts met the girl he later married and brought to the States. I do remember I bought a case of Australian beer and had it in the back of the aircraft when we landed in Townsville, to refuel on our way back to New Guinea. The base operations personnel inspected the aircraft and told us we could not take any alcohol up to New Guinea.

So I found Rich Howard and told him to hide the 48 bottles of beer somewhere in the airplane. He and the crew chief, I don't remember if it was Charlie Parker, but that evening they took the 48 beer bottles out of the case and hid some of them in the main wheel housings, disconnected the heater duct in the rear of the plane and stuffed the remaining bottles in the duct. As we approached Nadzab, everyone began to sweat because a hard landing might knock the bottles loose in the rear housing. When we unloaded the beer bottles, we found all of them except one of those in the heater duct. For all I know, it was still in the heater duct when the aircraft was stored at Biak.

I remember someone had told me that the other 43rd Bomb Group Squadrons were being hit hard by the Japanese ack-ack guns during daylight raids at Wewak, New Guinea. The gun emplacements were located in the swampy forest, in back of the Japanese base. In order to silence these guns, the Group Armament Section designed a new type of bomb. They cut steel building rods the same length as a 500-pound bomb and with a light steel cable bound them around it lengthwise. They loaded these bombs in each bomb bay and armed them with a 36-inch "daisy cutter" instant fuse.

The theory was that the bombs would explode before hitting the ground, causing the building rods to cut through the trees and brush and take out the Japanese gun crews and guns. After five or six raids with these bombs, the gun batteries were silenced. When the army took over the base, we were told the bombs had worked as planned. The trees and brush had been cut off as if mowed, and there were some gun barrels with building rods wrapped around them. I recall we flew one of these missions at night.

We hadn't been at Dobodura but a week or so when the group and the four squadrons were ordered to move up to Nadzab, New Guinea. We loaded our tent and all our belongings in the aircraft to fly up to this new base. When we went out to the airplane to take off, we found that someone in the 43rd Bomb Group had filled the back of our aircraft with a lot of lumber and other equipment. The plane was so loaded the tailskid was resting on the ramp and the nose wheel was up off the ramp. We cranked up the engines and the nose wheel came down, the tailskid came off the ground and we took off for Markam Valley. We sweated out both the takeoff and landing, but we made it okay.

I recall several incidents that occurred while we were in Nadzab.

First, it was here that co-Pilot Jim Watts whittled a big glider out of a balsam tree that had been cut down to make room for our tent. The glider had a wingspan and fuselage length of at least three feet. Watts did not want to damage it by trying to fly it, but it was so well made that we put it on display in our tent.

One night, when the wind was blowing harder than usual, we were awakened by lots of shouting and noise in the tent area around us. Large balsam trees had fallen on some of the other tents. Some of the crews, when setting up their tents, had cut away the vines that had supported the trees, so that at the first strong wind, the trees fell over. We all left our beds and helped the other crews to get out of their fallen tents and gather up their belongings.

We were walking down to the mess tent one day when we heard a big explosion down near the runway. We saw a column of smoke rising over our bomb storage area and, while we were wondering what had happened, we noticed that the air blast from the explosion was coming toward us, blowing the tall Kunai grass flat on the ground. Before we could take shelter the wind and dust blast hit us, almost knocking us down, and blew over some of the Operation Tents. We found out later that the bomb dump crew and a 6X6 Army truck were blown up by a new type of Torpex bomb. The explosive material in some of the bombs had crystallized, and they blew up when they were being unloaded off the truck! Torpex was not as stable as TNT.

OUR AIRCRAFT

Pilot Kent Zimmerman: When we took delivery of our B-24J aircraft (#0037) in Middleton, PA, it had logged only seven flight hours since it was built. We flew it down to Langley AAB and calibrated the compass and altitude instruments. Then we flew up to Mitchell AAF where they checked our secret orders and we left for Townsville, Australia, our final destination. We found out later that our aircraft had three major problems built into it.

One problem was the auxiliary fuel cap. When we were carrying a full load of fuel and cargo and the wing flexed about a foot or more on takeoff, the cap would flip off and the gas would siphon out of the left auxiliary tank, creating a fire hazard. This happened twice on our way to Australia: once when we took off at Las Vegas, NV, and again on takeoff at Nandi Field, Fiji Islands. When this occurred, we would have to burn off fuel to the maximum landing weight of 52,000 pounds, land again, refuel, replace the fuel cap on the tank, and take off again. The second time this happened I told Rich Howard to fix the damn cap so it would stay on. I don't know what he did, but it never happened again.

Another problem occurred when we had a very heavy rain. The Static and Ram Air vents would get water in their systems. This happened when we took off at Hickam AAB, Hawaii and started for Canton Island. I kept going, hoping my airspeed, rate of climb, and altitude instruments would come back into normal range, which they did this time. Then it happened again on a night takeoff from Nadzab, New Guinea for a normal search and destroy combat mission along the coast. This time we were carrying a normal load of bombs and gas and I didn't dare try to land back at Nadzab because other aircraft were taking off behind us. We had to salvo our bomb load as soon as we were over water and I continued to fly by power settings only to Finchafen Army Depot, the friendly airstrip closest to our position. I told Rich to clear up this problem, even it it meant installing a pet-cock in the lowest part of the Static and Ram Air System.

And finally, aircraft 0037 was a tail dragger. Normal procedure was to climb about 200 feet above the cruising level you desired, level off, let the airspeed build to cruising speed, and then descend to the cruising altitude. This procedure was called "getting on the step." The airplane would then hold to the step-speed. 0037 cruised about ten mph slower than normal and would not hold the step or cruising airspeed. I described this problem on the Aircraft Form 1 several times, and every time we landed I told the crew chief that the airspeed was low. The line chief finally got the message and they re-rigged the flight controls, solving the problem.

REMINISCENCES

Pilot Kent Zimmerman: We might have flown one combat mission from Dobodura to Western New Britain in the Bismarck Sea along the New Guinea coastline. However, the bulk of our combat missions were flown from Nadzab and Owi Island in the Schouten Islands group.

From Nadzab we flew up and down the north and northeastern New Guinea coastline looking for shipping targets and bombing Japanese ground installations at Mandang, Wewak, Wadke Island, and Hollandia as secondary targets. We also staged through Wadke Island after it was captured and flew missions throughout northern New Guinea. We roamed all through the Pacific Ocean almost to the Equator and penetrated the weather associated with the Equatorial Fronts. This was rough flying; we had to use our airborne radar to thread our way through the fronts. Also from Nadzab, we staged to an airstrip on Los Negros Island in the Admiralty Island Group. There we joined our sister 868 squadron (assigned to the 13th AF) to bomb Biak Island prior to its invasion. We had to abort this mission as number 3 engine started running rough and backfiring after our takeoff. We had to salvo our bombs, turn away from the aircraft following us, and return to Los Negros.

The engine had to be changed and then a test flight made to check out engine and systems. I invited four sailors to accompany us on the test flight. After the engine controls all checked out I gave these sailors a ride they will never forget. I put the landing gear down at 12,000 feet, lowered full wing flaps, and slowed the airspeed down to about 90 mph. Then I pointed the aircraft's nose down to almost vertical and pulled up the gear and wing flaps! When the airspeed built to 115 mph I started pulling the aircraft out of the dive. We dropped about 5,000 feet but did not exceed 130 mph and the aircraft was in level flight again. My crew-members in the rear of the plane said, "Those sailors floated up off the floor and turned white as sheets."

Our next base was on Owi Island. We flew most of the rest of our missions from there. The runway took up most of the available space on the island, and our squadron area was located on the southwest beach. It was a clean and beautiful spot. Across the beach road from our camp was a natural amphitheater in the coral where movies were projected and USO shows put on. We spent a lot of our free time swimming and playing in sea water behind the coral reef that protected the beach. Our fresh water came from a shallow well dug about three or four feet beneath the sand to where fresh water floated above the seawater. In fact, we built a community shower by mounting a P-47 wing fuel tank on a stand and using an aircraft fuel pump to fill it with fresh water.

We had several Japanese bombing alerts at Owi caused by a lone enemy aircraft. We didn't know where he came from and started calling him "Bed Check Charlie." Our ack-ack guns would fire three spaced shots to alert us, and we would head for our foxholes. These were very shallow holes because of the underlying water level! During an alert, all lights were turned off, and you had to be careful not to jump on someone already in the foxhole! We would hear the Japanese airplane go over us and then hear our night fighters take off after him. Sometimes we would hear a bomb explode and then things would get very quiet. Most of us gave up on the foxholes as you got wet and dirty using them! I think the night fighters finally got Bed Check Charlie.

While at Owi we roamed through the Moluccas, Celebes, and the Philippine Seas and around the Halmahera, Salawesi, Seram Crem, and Borneo Islands and along the northern coastline of New Guinea, searching for shipping targets. We flew two missions to Davao Bay on the Philippine island of Mindanao and on both of these missions we picked up on radar what we later believed to be a U.S. submarine sitting on the surface at the mouth of Davao Bay. We made bombing runs on the sub both times, but when we got within ten miles it "pulled the plug" and disappeared. On both of these missions we encountered searchlights over Davao City and on the second mission almost had a collision with a Japanese night fighter! He missed ramming us by only 200 feet. On these missions we could find no ships, so we bombed the Davao airfield both times.

It wasn't long after the Leyte landing that we started to stage out of Anguar Island in the Palau Island Group to the new airstrip of Tacloban on Leyte Island. On our first flight to Tacloban we counted 52 aircraft in the traffic pattern waiting to land. If an aircraft had an accident on landing, a bulldozer pushed it off the runway into Leyte Gulf. On one staging mission to Tacloban two Navy Corsairs joined us (one on each wing) and flew all the way with us. We couldn't contact them by radio, so I figured they were lost or their carrier had been sunk. They stayed with us for about 100 miles and when they saw the airstrip they wiggled their wings and left.

We flew several missions, staging out of Anguar with our bomb load aboard and after refueling at Tacloban, flew around Sibuyan, Mindoro and the Sulu Seas at night looking for shipping targets. Then we moved to Tacloban and started flying missions from there. The Army found a warehouse full of Jap-anese Philippine invasion money at Tacloban and gave it to us to drop over Manila. We flew missions over Manila, dropping a 100-pound bomb every hour to keep everyone awake. Also we harassed the highway between Lingayen Gulf (where the Army had landed) and Manila where the Japanese were. It was from Tacloban that we found the only Japanese convoy we ever bombed.

Our combat missions, for the most part, consisted of long hours just drilling holes in the sky. The drone of the engines, the long nights, and the waiting for something to happen was hypnotic. We felt we were disconnected from our friends, relatives, and the rest of the world. When something did happen, such as an engine backfiring, a target appearing on the radar scope, a flight system malfunctioning, or severe weather conditions, everyone was instantly alert.

It's hard to try to tell about our individual feelings. Personally, as the aircraft commander and oldest ranking member of the crew, I felt responsible for each crewmember aboard. I learned quickly that I could not depend fully on my own decisions. Several times during my night flying I experienced spatial disorientation, vertigo, caused by the loss of all outside references to our position.

During certain flight conditions this disorientation is inevitable. If you can't determine where the real horizon is relative to your actual position, you are experiencing vertigo and cannot determine if you are flying straight and level. You must force yourself to realize what you're experiencing, to accept it and use other means of orientation. The only other dependable indicators available to you are artificial sources. You must accept your compass, airspeed, rate of climb or descent, and artificial horizon instrumentation. It is very hard to accept this dependence on artificial means unless you totally believe in them.

I firmly believe this problem accounted for the loss of many first and second mission crews. The lack of outside navigation aids, such as Radio Homing Beacons and Radio Heading Guides Instructions added to the problem. The base could not transmit any navigation or emergency radio messages because the enemy would use these to find and bomb the installation. Therefore, if you lost your radar and its use as a navigation aid and if the navigator hadn't kept an accurate record of your position, you were truly lost.

OTHER REMINISCENCES

Bombardier Steve Perrone: Something I remember rather vividly because it was so spectacular is the night we were held up on Tacloban strip before a mission described earlier. We had to leave our plane loaded up at the end of the strip because of a Japanese air raid. Several crew-members and I took refuge behind a piece of earthmoving equipment parked just off the strip. Japanese planes were in the area and the several hundred Navy ships in the harbor and all the guns around the strip illuminated the night sky with anti-aircraft fire. Then a twin-engine Japanese plane, with wheels down as I recall, flew by us as if in slow motion and attempted to land. We were no more than 20 yards from the runway and an anti-aircraft gun position behind us shot him down. The plane skidded down the runway and crashed into at least a dozen parked planes. One of the Japanese plane's occupants, possibly a pilot – he was dressed in a flight suit – was lying face up on the runway. One of his arms was missing, probably torn off by a shell or the crash. I stared at him for a moment and noticed that he was a clean-shaven young airman not much different from our crew-members. Sometime later, during our long missions, I thought about him briefly. I knew his parents somewhere in Japan would never know what happened to their son.

Another incident I recall happened on one of our staging missions out of the Admiralty Islands. Our flight engineer, Rich Howard, reminded me of this incident and Pilot Kent Zimmerman mentioned it in his reminiscences as a mission that was aborted because we lost an engine on takeoff. I believe we flew several missions with our sister *Snooper* squadron, the 868th in the 13th Air Force. I think we were the only two anti-shipping *Snooper* squadrons in the Pacific Theater using B-24 aircraft with low altitude radar bombing equipment.

On this particular mission, prior to takeoff, it was determined that we were too heavy (with bombs and fuel) to get off the short strip. Pilot Zimmerman decided we should drop one of the bombs onto the coral strip before we took off. When I checked the loaded bombs I had noticed by the markings that they were Torpex bombs, not TNT. It was known that Torpex bombs had a tendency to crystallize, which made them very unstable. The ordinance people who loaded the bombs were long gone because our takeoffs were usually in the evenings, or later.

Our flight engineer, Rich Howard, now says that I asked him to get a screwdriver and release one of the bottom bombs from the shackle so it would fall to the ground, a drop of about four feet. I don't remember it but he said "no way" or words to that effect. By this time the entire crew had retreated about 20 or 30 yards away behind a coral embankment that surrounded the aircraft on three sides, and all because they heard me say the word "Torpex." At that point the skipper probably said, "You're the bombardier, drop the bomb." But he also did say, "I'll accompany you to the bomb bays," and into the open bomb bays we went. I picked up a screwdriver, took a deep breath and released the 500-pound bomb, which dropped (harmlessly) to the ground. From behind the bunkers the crew cheered us with the same enthusiasm that was probably expressed by the noble Romans at the games in the Coliseum. We rolled the bomb several feet away from the airplane.

Our best overseas base was Owi Island in the Schouten Islands Group, probably several hundred miles north of Biak Island and New Guinea. Owi had a sandy beach, a coral reef and palm trees. Our squadron area was about 20 or 30 yards from the beach. The island also had a natural amphitheater where I believe we welcomed the Bob Hope entourage. Owi was the sort of island paradise advertised in the travel sections of Sunday newspapers during vacation seasons, except there were no luxury hotels with cabanas and other amenities. But there was a beach and the weather was perfect for swimming and paddling around in several P-47 drop tanks that had been converted to kayaks.

The fuel drop tanks were about eight-to-ten feet long and shaped like a kayak. The top of the fuel tank was cut away to provide a seat for the occupant and we had several paddles either handmade or commandeered from the naval base on the other side of the island.

One P-47 drop tank was converted into a freshwater shower as described by Pilot Kent Zimmerman earlier in this narrative. Before the construction of the freshwater shower our daily showers were provided by Mother Nature. Every day between the hours of three and four in the afternoon a large rain cloud would form over the island and then it would rain hard for about 15 minutes. We were always ready for this daily shower. When it began to rain we would step out of our tents with a bar of soap in hand, lather up and shower off. Then we stepped back into our tents, dried off and got dressed. By this time the rain had stopped and the sun was out again.

At Owi many of the tents had a barrel or a large container open to the weather. The daily rain showers kept these containers full or nearly full; we used this water for shaving. We filled up our canteens or basins from the barrels and shaved at some sort of stand outside the tent. Then we rinsed off. It worked and at that time we thought it an improvement over our other island facilities.

On the beach, Owi Island, On the left, Burke A. Tracey, Pittsburgh, PA, an airman from another crew, who was five or six years older than most of us. Burke was married with several children and had a deferment because he was a railroad employee. But he wanted to fight the war so he volunteered to fly for the Army Air Corp. He flew about 20 missions but was hospitalized and sent home. On the right, author Steve Perrone. To the left and right are two P-47 fuel drop tanks which were converted to Pacific kayaks by cutting the tops of the tanks to provide seats for the occupants. We had several oars that were used to paddle us in the surf.

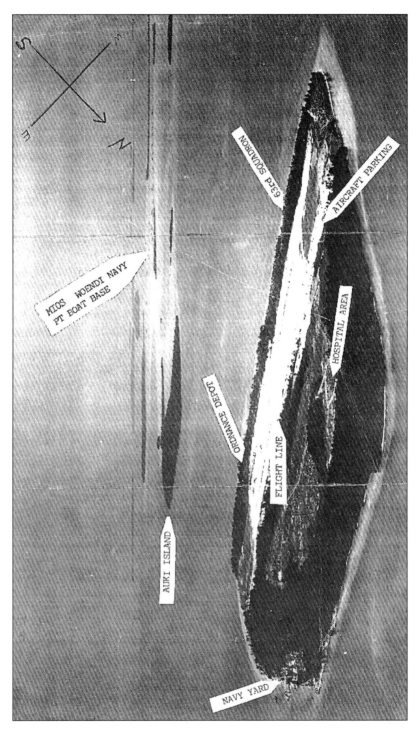

OWI ISLAND – VIEW SOUTH EAST — Summer of 1944

The 63rd Bomb Squadron logo depicted a seahawk in flight with a bomb in its talons. Our squadron was known as the Seahawks – a night-flying *Snooper* squadron with black-painted airplanes and low-altitude radar bombing equipment designed to locate and bomb enemy shipping under the cover of darkness. While stationed at Owi, I wrote a Seahawks squadron song – words and melody – although I could not write the music. One night at the Owi Officers Club, which contained an old upright piano, I met another officer who could read and write music. So over the span of one or two nights he wrote the music as I sang the verse and chorus (not well I'm sure).

He wrote the music to my lyrics on the back of a large Australian map of the Southwest Pacific. We cut the map into 11 x 15-inch sheets and I still have them. I don't remember his name and I don't know if he has attended any of our reunions.

Following is a sample of the lyrics.
>Japanese shipping off of Wadke
>>Airplanes are loaded, we'll have our spree
>We get the job done, just wait and see
>>Don't doubt my word and listen to me

Chorus You ought to fly for the Sixty-Third
>>Because the Seahawk's the best of the bird
>The Nipponese have reason to quail
>>Because on night strikes we never fail
>A pack of hotshots primed for the kill
>>Three hundred hours then over the hill
>So long lads, I'm Seahawk bound
>>With the boys from the Sixty-third
>>With the boys from the Sixty-Third.

As I recall we were the only 43rd Bomb Group squadron on Owi Island. Because we were a night-flying *Snooper* squadron employing single aircraft on search missions over a wide arc of the Pacific Ocean covering the Philippine Islands, the Indonesian Islands and parts of Malaysia, we were based closer to these areas, which included hundreds of major islands occupied by the Japanese. Our missions averaged about 13 hours, almost all over water, searching for enemy shipping. If we failed to locate shipping, we bombed an enemy airfield on one of the islands, depending on our location. Because of the length of the missions we covered over 1,000 miles of the Pacific Ocean on most of our missions.

From time to time our radioman, Cliff Grivous, would pick up Japanese disc jockey Tokyo Rose who played the very best American big band recordings, interspersed with Japanese propaganda about how our wives and girlfriends were having a good time with the 4-F civilians back in the States. On some nights Cliff picked up the music from the supper club bands in the San Francisco hotels. Flight Engineer Rich Howard says Cliff used something called "skip distance" for these radio pickups. Probably we were supposed to maintain radio silence on these missions but there was no way the Japanese could locate us in the middle of the Pacific.

On the long flights over water in the middle of the night the pilots took turns napping and watching the automatic pilot, nicknamed "George." The darkness and the drone of the four engines acted like a lullaby, making it very difficult to stay awake. There were many times when both pilots were asleep. If I awakened and all I heard was the drone of the engines and no intercom comments, I knew they were both asleep. I would click the intercom mike button and rouse them until I got a response. Although it seemed at times that the entire airplane crew was asleep, I knew there were several crewmembers who were usually awake: Flight Engineer Rich Howard was forever checking fuel consumption and transferring fuel; Navigator George Burhoe, with sextant in hand, would be checking the heavens to determine where we were and where we should be, and Radar Operator John Ahern in his compartment over the rear of the bomb bays would be checking his long range radar scope for navigational aids such as islands or looking for radar blips made by ships.

THE CREW RECALLS DECEMBER 7, 1941

Editor's Comment: Because December 7, 1941 was responsible for bringing us together, I asked each crew member, as best as each of them could remember, to tell me where they were on that day and their thoughts about that stunning event. I thought that "day" would provide a fitting closure for our Retrospective.

Flight Engineer Richard Howard, Hysham, Montana: Pearl Harbor Day as I remember it. Mildred and I were recently married and living on my father's ranch. You have to visualize rural Montana in the early Forties. We had no electricity, no telephone service, mail twice a week, sometimes; no local newspaper, and battery radios. We heard the news on the radio and because we knew that Mildred's parent's radio had dead batteries, Mildred decided to drive to their home some eight miles away. She jumped into an old Ford pickup we had and drove on a dirt road partly frozen and slick, and although she slid off the road once or twice, she got there and told them the news. But to us in that time and place, Pearl Harbor was in another world. I was drafted the next year and I joined the Army Air Corps.

Co-Pilot James Watts, Bluefield, West Virginia: I enlisted in the US Army Air Corps in September 1940 as a way to get out of West Virginia. I was sent to Air Mechanics school in Wichita Falls, Texas, followed by duty at

Valdosta, Georgia. As well as I can remember, I was home on leave on Pearl Harbor Day, sitting on the front steps. I was aware that the Japanese were causing problems in the Pacific Area and it was clear that they wanted to dominate this area just as Germany had demonstrated in Europe.

I had applied for pilot training and was accepted and shipped to Santa Ana, California. I completed single engine training in Primary, Basic, and Advanced. But it was a shock when I was ordered to report to El Paso, Texas for training in four-engined B-24's. I arrived in Pueblo, Colorado where I met the crew. I feel lucky to have been with the best crew the Air Force had, and it was a hell of a blast.

Nose Gunner Harold Donner, Tonawanda, New York: When we entered the war in December 1941, I was a 17-year old high school senior. In the spring of 1942, before graduating, I tried to enlist in the Navy and was rejected because of flat feet (so they claimed). In October after June graduation I attempted to join the Navy again. This time they said something was wrong with my back. Not wanting to slog through mud with a 50-pound pack on my back, I enlisted in the Army Air Corps.

I don't think at that time I really did any deep thinking about the war except we were in it and I would be involved one way or another. As it turned out, I was glad for the experiences, the travel and the many events that probably would never have happened to me otherwise. Of course, the most to be thankful for was that I came through it. (Someone up there had to be watching over me.) We all had some narrow escapes in training, on the way over and while there.

First Pilot Kent Zimmerman, Woodward, Oklahoma: I was living on the family ranch northwest of Woodward on Sunday December 7, 1941. It was just another day for mom and I, the only ones living on the ranch at that time. I have forgotten if I had received my draft classification before December 7th. But I had been given a draft rating of A-3 by the County Draft Board. But since my mother and I were in partnership of the ranch, and had just purchased a hundred head of steers to feed through the winter and grass-fatten the next spring and summer for sale, I might have gotten my draft classification changed or dropped, considering my rancher status.

My mother had lost a son, my half brother, in World War I, but she left the decision to me about volunteering or sweating out the draft. Mother was not a dependent of mine or of my brother, Pete, as she was teaching school. My brother wanted the chance to operate the ranch. I had grown up with war stories about World War I, and I did not want to wait and possibly be drafted into the infantry. I waited until Christmas 1941 and found out through our County Recruiter that the Army was looking for men to train as pilots. I went to Oklahoma City, passed the Pilot physical, was sworn in as an aviation

At a Bomb Group Reunion in San Antonio, Texas, in the late eighties or early nineties, the crew. Back row from the left, the tallest head is the Skipper, Kent Zimmerman, then Richard Howard, John Ahern, and George Burhoe, with the white mustache and goatee. Front row from the left to right, Jim Watts, in the dark blue shirt; Cliff Grivois, Charlie Nunez, and seated on the bed, Steve Perrone. Harold Donner did not attend this reunion. (John Ahern died July 12, 1994 and Kent Zimmerman died on April 27, 2001.)

cadet, and sent home on leave to wait for the next pilot class. In the summer of 1942, I was called back to Oklahoma City, put in charge of 10 other cadets and sent by train to Kelly AAB, in San Antonio, Texas.

I was 27-1/2 years of age when I enlisted in the Army Air Corps, so I was older than most of my classmates. As a result, I had a better chance of getting my wings and commission. In fact, I never received a test flight to prove my flying proficiency all through my pilot training.

Assistant Flight Engineer Charles Nunez, Brooklyn, New York: As for that "Day of Infamy" December 7, 1941, I was dancing at a friend's house. We all used to dance on Saturday night – and then continue on to Sunday afternoons. I didn't even know "what or where" was Pearl Harbor, although I knew where the Hawaiian Islands were. Ten months later, I volunteered and joined the Army Air Corps. I stayed in after World War II and served during the Berlin Airlift and finally the Vietnam conflict. There are so many memories of events that took place 55 years ago. Being a crewmember and part of a top-notch group of swell people was the most exciting part of my life. What else can I say! The only sad part was that Crabtree didn't come back with us.

Armorer Kermit Crabtree, Bowling Green, Kentucky: Sadly, we do not have Kermit's recollections. On January 9th, 1945, as the war was closing in on Luzon, the 63rd lost its commanding officer and 13 other officers and enlisted men in a fatal crack-up at Owi Island. Plane 425 was scheduled to bring the men to Leyte; she took off shortly past 0100, crashed 100 yards from the northeast end of the runway, just short of the coral bank, and burned. None of the 16 men survived. It has been impossible to reconstruct the accident. It is known only that the ship had been airborne and suddenly failed. As she struck the ground she plowed into a tree stump four feet high and two and a half feet in diameter which ripped through the plane from nose to tail.

In addition to Major Merrill F. Sargent, CO, the plane carried five other officers and eight enlisted men of the squadron.

From our crew; Sergeant Kermit C. Crabtree, 24, married, returning from sick leave. With the 63rd since March, 1944.

Navigator George Burhoe, Boston, Massachusetts: (As George remembers it and in his own words). Sunday, December 7, 1941– Radio Station WEEI, Boston. We interrupt this program to bring you a news bulletin:

Pearl Harbor in Hawaii has been attacked by Japanese bombers and the place is in shambles. Navy ships have been sunk in the harbor and the ground installations are on fire. Many of the ground crew are either dead or injured. The attack took place at daylight on Sunday morning when the Navy was still in bed from their Saturday night revelry. The planes came from the north over the mountains and caught everyone by surprise. There was little time to respond to the raid and most American planes were destroyed on the ground and many of the ships in the harbor were sunk where they lay at anchor.

Monday, December 8, 1941 – All radio stations. "Yesterday, a day that will live in infamy"– President Franklin D. Roosevelt. We were in the "Brigade Room," the social center and fire brigade meeting room in a small paper mill in eastern Massachusetts, listening to FDR's report to the nation after the December 7 attack on Pearl Harbor.

The "eligible" (under 26) members of the accounting department group were Bob, Larry, Bill and myself. Bob's father was dead and he was supporting his mother so he had a deferment. Larry had married the previous fall and he was exempt. (He was drafted later in the war.) I was also supporting my mother and had a medium high number so service was not imminent. Bill's number was coming up and he was 1A. All this led us to much speculation as to Who, If and When. I had pretty much decided to wait and see what happened. Then on Friday, at the supper table, my mother said, "I got a job today!" My only reaction was "why?" Her response, "No son of mine is going to have to shirk his duty to his country because of me!"

On Monday, I related the Friday conversation to Bill and we considered the options. There were two that appealed to both of us. The Air Forces and the Cee Bees. Our bosses gave us full authority to take all the time off we needed to pursue the options and said our pay would not be docked. Boston was about 25 miles away and that was the closest point to both CB's and AAF's recruiting centers.

Both branches gave a mental and physical exam. I lost out on the CB's because they required a strong 20/20 eye result. Other physical problems not so demanding. Bill lost to a physical problem at the AAF exam. He passed the CB's with flying colors and went in a month later.

It was winter in New England, the cold season, and it took four trips to Boston before my blood pressure got low enough to pass their requirements. My eye exam was also marginal and the eye doctor took me aside and said he would approve only after telling me I might not pass the exam at the classification center and I would become an enlisted man instead of getting flight training. My reaction was "Go for it."

Actual call to duty was something else. I had completed all the preliminaries in March. By June, I expected to be called at any time so I gave notice at the paper mill for July 1. No call so I became a counselor at the Boy Scout camp at the shore 50 miles away. Surely the call would come in August! No call, so after camp I took a job on the steamship dock where the Island Ferry went to Martha's Vineyard and Nantucket. Finally, in December "Report to Camp Devens" and a long train ride on "Land Grant" railroads to San Antonio classification center. The eye doctor's warning in Boston was justified because when they dilated my pupils, the best I could see was 20/30. Fortunately, my aptitude tests came on strong for navigator and no waiver was required for navigation school. Off to Houston, then Hondo, Texas to be a navigator.

Bombardier Stephen Perrone, Philadelphia, Pennsylvania: On Sunday, December 7, 1941, now known as Pearl Harbor Day, several of us returned to our barracks from lunch at a PX coffee shop on base at Chanute AAB, flopped on our bunks and turned on a radio. The news that came over the air was shocking, unbelievable, like something out of an Orson Welles Invasion from Mars documentary. As Americans we certainly were not prepared for it. Over the years, we had been led to believe that the Japanese were small yellow-skinned males with thick lenses in their eyeglasses living in a nation that could only produce cheap toys and inferior copies of German cameras. Certainly, our military intelligence must have known that the Japanese had a large Navy and a well-trained naval air force. But maybe our battleship admirals preferred to believe the same media and propaganda that was gospel at that time.

Because it was such a traumatic event, I'll never forget my thoughts and feelings on that date. I reasoned that I was already in the service; it would take four or five years to turn it around and defeat the enemy but I could not envision my making it through the long war to come. Most of us believed we would win even if we doubted that we could live through it.

How did I get to Chanute Field, Illinois? In 1940, I was working for a textile firm with some defense contracts. After attending school for one year, I dropped out of a private business college because I realized my parents could not afford it. In response to the depressing news from the war in   Europe and other world events, the United States enacted a Selective Service Military Draft. I don't think I registered in 1940 because of my age, but I applied for entrance into the Aviation Cadet Program at a traveling Cadet Board that was in Philadelphia at that time. I passed the written exam but was rejected in the physical exam because of a deviated right septum. They said I had a 70% obstruction in my right nostril which would affect my ability to perform at high altitudes. (When I was 15 or 16, I broke my nose playing sandlot football.) In early 1941, I read that the traveling Aviation Cadet Board was in Baltimore. I went through the same procedure and a different group of doctors gave the same diagnosis.

On October 23, 1941, I was inducted into the United States Army. I was asked if I wanted to serve my two years as a draftee or did I want to volunteer for a three-year term in one of the other services. I volunteered for the Army Air Corps and that's how I got to Chanute Field. In late December, 1941 one of the traveling Aviation Cadet Boards visited Chanute Field and advertised for applicants. I applied for the third time: I was given the written test – I passed. I went through the physical and when it was over, the medical officer in charge, a major, stamped my form, shook my hand and said something like you're accepted into the Aviation Cadet Program–Congratulations! In an aside, after I received all my signed paperwork, I asked him if I had a deviated septum. He said, "Yes, does it bother you?" I said, "No." He said, "You'll be fine." The difference was there was a war to be won and they needed more Aviation Cadets. But I was happy. In March 1942, I received orders to proceed to Santa Ana, California for preflight training as an aviation cadet.

In Closing: A Note to the Crew

Steve Perrone: It happened in Leyte, I don't remember the date but probably early in 1945. I recall I had 31 or 32 combat missions with the crew and 400 combat hours and we all were looking forward to a return home. I came down with amoebic dysentery and our flight surgeon shipped me to a tent hospital in the interior of Leyte, closer to the ground troops fighting the Japanese troops at Ormoc. I was confined there for about three weeks and I was weak and sick. My recollection is that Kent visited me but I'm not sure. During my stay there, I made friends and talked with many of the other patients. As I recall, most if not all of them were combat-wounded ground troops. When I began to feel better, I became somewhat ashamed to be hospitalized for a stomach bug while these guys were bleeding from bullet or shrapnel wounds. Then I was released and shipped back to our 63rd squadron area and I was shocked to find the tent I shared with Kent, Jim and George was empty, except for my cot and air mattress. I had had no news in the hospital as to what was going on in the 63rd, but I found out my crew was sent home and Kent was checking out B-32's. No information on location.

It was strange being alone, after getting accustomed to functioning as a crewmember. It was lonely because all the crews we came overseas with were also gone. I knew some of the guys in the replacement crews but not real well. I met with our CO at that time, Major Brownfield, someone I knew very well. In fact, Brownie and Doctor Frederick Mott were the most familiar faces remaining. During our meeting, Brownie said my promotion was lost somewhere between Brisbane and the Philippines, but it would catch up to me in a week or two or three. Or if I wanted my leave orders first, my promotion would catch up to me a month or so later in the states. He suggested I recuperate a week or so in the squadron area until my promotion came through and then he would make up my leave orders. It was my choice. He also suggested that I should consider a service career after the war because I had a reserve commission. I said I wasn't sure about that, but I decided to wait for my promotion. Not long after, the 63rd Squadron was moved to Mindoro Island, about halfway to Luzon. I don't remember Major Brownfield moving to Mindoro; but several weeks later or less, I was informed that I would have to go back on flying status. The reason given was there was a major push to end the war in Europe and more replacement crews were being sent there. I wasn't happy but it had been my choice to remain. Also, I was nervous about flying with pilots and navigators I didn't know.

I may have flown one or two missions out of Mindoro but I don't recall them. Our next move was to Clark Field on the island of Luzon, not too far from Manila. I shared a tent with our weather officer, a friendly redhead probably known to Kent and George, and an ordinance captain from New York. Our tent was on the edge of a revetment, about 20 feet from a stripped Japanese Zero. I only flew when needed so sometimes I didn't fly for weeks. From time to time I went to the airstrip with the captain in his jeep, as he performed his duties. Once or twice we rode into Manila. It turns out that Kent was at Clark the same time I was but we never ran into each other.

I flew two missions with a Captain Butts; I'm sure his name is familiar to Kent. I also flew my last mission with Butts, a 15-1/2 hour mission from Clark Field to Shanghai Harbor to find and bomb a Japanese carrier converted from a cruise ship. It was a long flight; we got into the harbor in the middle of the night and our radar picked up hundreds, probably thousands of blips – Chinese fishing junks which also served as homes for the families. Hundreds stacked along the shores and hundreds more probably fishing in the open waters. Finally, we decided to pick out the largest blip or blips and bombs away, because we had a long flight back to Clark Field. After we dropped the bombs, I told Butts on the intercom – we probably killed some poor Chinese fishing families trying to catch their meal for the next day. In the early morning on the way back, we passed too close to Formosa (now Taiwan) and the Japanese anti-aircraft opened up on us, but Butts got out of there quickly. We landed at Clark and when I climbed out of the B-24, I kissed the ground. I knew it was my last mission. I believe it was mid-March 1945. On April 3rd, I received my promotion and my Leave Orders and I still have them. They read: 37 combat missions and 495 hours, 10 minutes/Total combat hours this theater.

That accounts for the time I was separated from the crew overseas. It was 35 years before Kent's letter in *Air Force Magazine* asking if anyone recognized my name, and my first reunion in Washington, DC. Now once a year we become a crew again.

63rd Bomb Squadron Headquarters at Tacloban.
Photo provided by Fred Peters

Thomas B. Bonney

Previously printed in the April 2000 *Snooper News*.

SPLASH – ONE MISSION TOO MANY!
Story and Photos by Thomas B. Bonney

The day of June 11, 1944 was an uncomfortable one for Lt. Wagner and his crew. That evening they were scheduled for a mission over the heavily defended Japanese base at Truk. By no means could they be considered a battle-hardened crew, having only four daylight milk-run missions behind them, but the main cause of their uneasiness was not their inexperience. During the two previous nights two *Snooper* crews left Mokerang Airfield on Los Negros Island for the same target and failed to return – with no clue as to what happened to them. Fear of the unknown was gnawing at Wagner's crew.

It was quite natural then that they talked about survival procedures. Tales about the beheading of aircrew members who had bailed out over the Truk atoll convinced them that a very high priority was to keep themselves out of enemy hands. Bailing out over the ocean wasn't a much better alternative. Although a Mae West provides good flotation, it offers the wearer lim-

Rear Row, L. to R.: S/Sgt. Rokos, S/Sgt. Dotterer, S/Sgt. Musey, Cpl. Davis, Sgt. Wolfsberger, Sgt. Whitmore. *Front Row:* Lt. Goerke, Lt. Bonney, Lt. Pickering, Lt. Wagner.

ited survival time, the real risk of becoming shark bait and a diminished probability of being sighted in the water. For these reasons they decided, in the event of an emergency, to stay with the aircraft if at all possible and attempt a ditching – in spite of the B-24's lousy reputation for such a procedure. And, with a little bit of luck, life rafts could be pulled from the ditched aircraft to give them increased protection from the sea and its predators, and greater visibility to sea searchers. Although these decisions did not require too much intellect it was fortuitous that they were made prior to the mission and did not have to be made under the stressful conditions to be encountered later that night.

The crew's slim hope for the mission being scrubbed was not fulfilled. With two full auxiliary gas tanks and nine 250-pound bombs in the bomb bay the crew took off from Mokerang Airfield at 1931 hrs, headed for Dublon Town in the Truk atoll, some 600 miles away. It was a beautiful night for flying, clear skies, a half-moon and a large selection of bright navigational stars to help us find our way. As navigator, my responsibility that night was not only to find the target, but also to determine when and where the bombs were to be dropped. The mission's objective was purely harassment, which did not require the bombing accuracy that the bombardier normally provides. As such, the bombardier was a passenger on a trip that, I'm sure, he would just as soon have passed up. I was to be the bombardier and to drop our bombs on the target with whatever degree of precision a 1944-radar scope would permit. With the scope I was certainly able to distinguish land from water.

Near midnight as we approached the target, Lt. Wagner desynchronized the engines to confound the Japanese range detectors, which purportedly relied on audible signals to detect us (we were assured the islands' defenders had no radar). At 0017 hrs, 12,000 feet altitude, a heading of 270 degrees and with our engines emitting a god-awful wow wow wow wow, we began our bombing run on Dublon Town. Suddenly, a bluish searchlight appeared and immediately found us. Within seconds some 12-14 conventional white searchlights appeared, unerringly intersecting the blue light at our altitude. (So much for the absence of Japanese radar controls.) In our small section of the sky it was literally and disconcertingly like daylight. Anti-aircraft guns immediately put up a barrage of extremely accurate fire. In short order our aircraft sustained considerable damage, the least of which was the loss of our radar spinner. With that the image on my scope disappeared, terminating my brief career as bombardier and leaving me with little to do but to observe and to shake. Lt. Wagner now had the added responsibility of bombardiering. At 0018 hrs it was bombs away.

At about the same time a series of explosions walked across the wings of our already battered craft. Weeks later, upon debriefing, it was inferred that these came from 20mm guns of a Japanese Irving night fighter flying below us in our blind spot. The dimensions of the holes in the wings were characteristic of this caliber weapon. Intelligence was aware that Irvings were operating in the area. Regardless of causation, air to air or ground to air fire, our aircraft was seriously damaged. Lt. Wagner made a diving turn to the left and was successful in getting out of the searchlights and (unknown to us) evading the fighter, which diminished the probability of further damage.

Our plane was all over the sky, but at least, it was still in it. Having no immediate responsibilities because of the aircraft's unnatural and untraceable course, I stepped behind the pilot and copilot to observe their progress in controlling the wounded bird. Always the navigator, I could not ignore the compass heading. Although erratic, our course was obviously to the north – and the only friendly territory was south. Alarmed at this, I felt obliged to inform the pilot and shouted, "South, South, South!" The response from the flight deck was immediate as well as unprintable. Roughly translated, Lt. Wagner stated that he appreciated my concern and would be happy to point the nose of the plane in any direction I chose once he could determine if he could keep it in the air. Appropriately chastised, I kept any further useful suggestions to myself.

With no small effort, Lts. Wagner and copilot Pickering managed to bring the unwieldy craft under control and, to my relief, began flying in a southerly direction, albeit not for long. It was time to assess the damages and determine our next course of action. Two engines out. No. 3 feathered and No. 1 windmilling. All controls shot out except for rudder. Fortunately, the automatic pilot controls were functional – *except* for rudder. Gas cells were shot full of holes, compliments of Irving. The radar spinner was down and the bomb bay doors were open, and with a non-existent hydraulic system, they would remain so. And, if this wasn't enough, there were still a few 250-lb. bombs in the bomb bay that were hung up in the racks. There was no question that we would have to ditch. The only question was how soon, and how soon depended on how much fuel we had.

Lt. Wagner directed Sgt. Dotterer, the flight engineer, to read the gas gauges. Sgt. Dotterer found it impossible to obtain anything resembling an accurate reading since the levels continued to drop precipitously as he watched. Under these circumstances there was no need for accuracy. The continuing rapid loss of fuel convinced Lt. Wagner that if we had any chance of a power-assisted landing we had best ditch as soon as possible. He ordered the crew to throw out everything not tied down in order to lighten the craft, extend our range and minimize the possibility of objects becoming missiles upon impact. Of greatest immediate concern was the presence of bombs still hung up in the racks. With considerable effort and, after what seemed to be an agonizingly long time, Sgts. Dotterer and Wolfsberger finally managed to drop them into the Pacific.

The decision to ditch immediately was a double-edged sword. Although it enhanced the possibility of successfully ditching the B-24, it did not give me the needed time to determine our exact position. This prevented any possible rendezvous with an American submarine in the area that was responsible for picking up strays such as we. The same time constraint prevented Sgt. Rokos, the radio operator, from making contact with the submarine, or anyone else who might be able to increase our chances for survival subsequent to a successful ditching. In possession of my best guess about our position, Sgt. Rokos was ordered to send out a distress signal. He made the first keystroke with hesitation and apprehension – the odor of high-octane fuel was strong on the flight deck. With no undesirable consequences resulting from the initial electrical contact, he completed the brief and futile SOS. Now it was time for those not needed on the flight deck to move to the rear of the bomber.

I stuffed the pockets of my flight suit with the E6B computer, charts, a plotter and whatever articles I thought would be useful for nautical navigation. I never saw them again! Jumping down from the flight deck to cross the catwalk across the bomb bay I was not prepared for the next challenge. Hydraulic fluid and gasoline covered the catwalk, the bomb bay doors were open, our flight path was erratic, there was no rope railing for support, and to put icing on the cake, the door into the rear section was closed. I waited for a brief period of straight and level flight, took a deep breath, did a rapid ballet dance across the narrow passage, unlatched the door and fell into the rear compartment. Oblivious to everything except my own sense of extreme gratitude for a successful transit, I unwittingly let the door slam shut. In doing this I had given Lt. Goerke, who was immediately behind me, the opportunity to experience the same thrill as I did. He did not neglect to mention this to me.

Those of us in the rear of the aircraft would brace ourselves, as well as we could, against the radar spinner assembly. Prior to taking my position I stood by the waist window so as to monitor our descent and advise the others when impact was imminent. Lt. Wagner turned on the landing lights and began a "normal" approach down this long, wide, soft, wet and undulating runway. In order to keep landing speed to a minimum it was his intent to make a dead stick landing, having the craft stall out exactly at sea level. Even under these worst of circumstances, this was actually accomplished with unbelievable precision. It is appropriate here to give recognition to the high level of skills that these two pilots demonstrated. Making a survivable water landing in a B-24, even under ideal conditions, is an awfully dicey procedure. It is astounding that Lts. Wagner and Pickering accomplished this in a four-engine bomber having only two functioning engines, open bomb bay doors and without flaps, and by maneuvering the aircraft by kicking rudder and twisting dials on the automatic pilot.

When contact with the water became imminent I joined the others clustered around the spinner. Within seconds the tail of the aircraft made contact with the first wave top, then a second, a third and a fourth. With that, the B-24 stalled out, plunging its nose into the ocean. The noise and the force of deceleration were incredible. I had the feeling of bouncing off the bulkheads (which was probably close to reality), to the accompaniment of flashing white lights (which undoubtedly originated within my battered head). Then all was blackness and silence. Gradually, I became aware that I had survived the ditching and was lying in a foot or so of water. My surroundings were in almost total darkness. I did, however, see a faint glimmer of light that I eventually determined came through the open waist window. One of the flight crew was sitting in it, guiding the crew out of the plane and into the water. I needed no invitation.

Jumping into the sea, inflating my Mae West and floating alongside of my crew mates, I experienced a brief period of relief, but suddenly the awareness hit me that our situation was not too much improved, and I wondered, "What next?" A very welcome response to my query was not long in coming. Lt. Wagner and Sgt. Dotterer managed to climb out of the hatch over the flight deck, jumped onto the wing and pulled the two four-man life rafts out of their storage place in the fuselage. They shouted the good news to those of us in the water, giving us a considerable lift. It was still too dark to determine the number or identity of those of us in the water, so Lt. Wagner called the roll. It was then that we realized Lt. Pickering, the copilot, and Sgt. Wolfsberger, the assistant engineer, did not survive the crash. Exactly what happened to them, no one knew. They were with us at one moment and, in the next, they simply disappeared into the darkness. I'm certain that most of the crew were surprised, as I, that our losses were not greater.

Lt. Wagner and Sgt. Dotterer launched the two rafts from the trailing edge of the wing and began pulling the rest of the crew out of the water. They also retrieved a first aid kit that almost miraculously found its way from the flight deck to the water alongside the rafts. It contained the only medicines we had and was badly needed. Most of us either had broken bones, bruises, abrasions, lacerations, shrapnel wounds or a combination thereof, some of them severe. Therefore, the threat of infection was real and we were fortunate and relieved to have the sulfa powder that was in the first aid kit. Furthermore, Lt. Wagner had a very painful shoulder dislocation that he managed to pop back into place with the aid of morphine, also found in the kit. Although each one of us had good reason to moan and groan, for the most part, we did not. I attribute this, in large part, to a very courageous airman, Sgt. Whitmore, the most seriously wounded member of the crew who set the tone. Even with a deep and painful gash down the length of his back, he maintained his disposition and resolve with never a complaint. He was a tough act to follow.

Most of us spent the first few hours at sea that night trying to adjust ourselves to the circumstances with which we were confronted. We soon had physical adjustments to make, as most of us became violently ill. I suspect that our illness was more the result of what we had experienced than of the ocean's movement. Mercifully the malady was brief and never bothered any of us again for the duration of our journey. With this illness behind us we soon came out of our stress-induced shells and again began communicating with one another. In retrospect, I find our first discussions intriguing yet illustrative of the strong bonds that develop within the military. Here we were, in as difficult a position as one could imagine, yet each of us felt it necessary to express a deep and sincere concern about the other *Snooper* crew that was scheduled to follow us and attack Truk later that night. Soon, however, we were confronted with other more immediate and personal concerns that captured our undivided attention – sharks!

The entire crew regarded sharks as terrifying, carnivorous creatures that represented a threat to our survival. Our singular desire was to have them go away, no one had any idea of how to fulfill this desire. We did, however, find a pamphlet in the rafts' survival equipment that gave us two tips on how to get rid of sharks. The first stated that sharks have sensitive hearing and by firing a gun you will drive them away. Although we had a 45 on board, it did not seem to be a very good idea to fire it since we still could be uncomfortably close to enemy-held islands. The second bit of information stated that sharks have very sensitive noses and if you ram their snouts with an oar they, very likely, will seek a less hostile environment. Unfortunately, I was on the shark side of the raft and was assigned the duty. With considerable skepticism my eyes went back and forth between the pamphlet and the nearest shark. However, since I knew zilch about sharks and had an apparently authoritative military document at hand, I said to myself, "What the hell!" and drove the oar home. It was a bull's eye – or a shark's nose, if you will. It also was apparent that the shark did not like this treatment, and by inference one might conclude it had a sensitive nose – but it didn't go away. Instead the shark dove and immediately resurfaced, contacting the underside of the raft, threatening to dump us into the briny with him. From that point on we maintained a live-and-let-live existence with these undesirable neighbors who were never very far away. I often wonder if the author of the survival pamphlet ever saw a shark, save in *National Geographic*.

In the morning we were relieved to find that we were out of sight of land. Without nausea, having had a little rest and with the shark issue resolved, we found our spirits to be vastly improved. However, this in no way caused us to underestimate the gravity of our situation. We deemed it essential to evaluate our options and to promptly make those decisions that we believed would enhance the possibility of our survival. The first item of business was to take inventory of our resources, most of which came to us by way of the survival equipment packaged with the life rafts. We had four boxes of K-rations, four quarts of water, a tin of hard candy, fishing tackle (fishhooks, line and pork rind bait), a flashlight and a small compass. There were many items that should have been included with the survival kits that simply weren't there. It was immediately apparent that our provisions were pathetically deficient. One glaring deficiency was the absence of any signaling device such as a signal mirror or flare pistol. With either, our journey would have been considerably shortened.

Since there was no replenishment of our supplies in the foreseeable future, rationing was instituted immediately. Lt. Wagner undertook the duty of ration officer. If we were to get any additional food we would have to fish for it, and this we did, almost immediately. Water was another matter. Although we could be prepared to collect and store it, there was nothing we could do to generate it. We were ready to collect rainwater with the sails that came with the rafts and store it in several Mae Wests that were saved for the purpose. Parenthetically, I must state that, unless one has tried it, he cannot possibly imagine the flavor that a warm rubberized Mae West imparts to water that has been stored in it. Using the flotation device as a reservoir for drinking water encourages drinking in moderation.

The question arose as to whether we should sail our rafts individually or tie them together. We could conceive of no benefit of separate sailing. On the contrary, we felt that the two rafts tied together would be more easily sighted. The major question raised was "Where do we go from here?" The more precise question should have been "Where do we *try* to go from here?" The answer to that was quite obvious – southward toward our departure point of Los Negros in the Admiralty Islands some 600 miles away. And if we missed them (which was more likely than not) we would have a big land mass, New Guinea, as a back-up. Although Japanese were in some portions of it, they didn't occupy all of it as they did the area where we were. In any other direction there was no friendly land that we could conceivably reach.

A liferaft is a survival vessel, not a sailing craft. Especially without a rudder, tacking is not one of its strong points. In general it goes where the wind blows. But it was what we had and we'd have to do our best to persuade it to go in the desired direction. With a friendly wind out of the north, we headed south. Suddenly, we heard the sound of an aircraft engine! In seconds we pulled down the sails and, with the blue side showing, covered the rafts and ourselves with them. The source of the sound, a Japanese Oscar, soon appeared flying at an altitude no higher than 500 feet and heading almost directly for us. From under our cover we followed the aircraft's course with apprehension and, at the same time, cursed the person who designed the sails to be shorter than the rafts. When the Oscar came abeam of our fleet he was no more than 100 yards distance. To our extreme relief the pilot maintained his course and the plane was soon out of sight.

Although we saw a number of Japanese aircraft over the next four or five days, none of these came close enough to cause us concern as did the Oscar. Generally they were seen just prior to the appearance of the 13th's daylight bombers en route to Truk. Apparently the Japanese did not want their aircraft to be caught on the ground during an air raid. For two days we observed the B-24s, and were still close enough to their target to observe the flak they encountered. Although the daylight bombers knew of missing aircraft and looked for possible survivors, they could offer us no help. We were too close to their target and by the time they dropped down to search altitude they were well beyond us. During the latter half of our journey we must have seen a half dozen Catalina flying boats. Some were heart-breakingly close but we had no means of signaling them. It was just happenstance and extremely good fortune that one of them ultimately spotted us.

Since our rafts' departure point at Truk was north of the equator, I could estimate our latitude by observing Polaris, the northstar. Nightly observations of the star unerringly determined if we were traveling in a southerly direction toward our objective. At the start of our journey we were fortunate in having several days of wind out of the north. In the course of a week I was almost ecstatic as I observed Polaris slowly, but definitely, move toward the horizon. Subsequently the ecstasy turned to despair when the star showed no further movement, remaining in a fixed position above the horizon. This did not mean that we were no longer moving. On the contrary, we were moving with the prevailing ocean current, which was westerly and also being propelled (with or without benefit of sails) by the wind, which also happened to be westerly. After the first week of travel we made no further progress south. With the passage of each day it became more and more apparent that reaching friendly territory on our own was not to be.

Afloat in equatorial waters one can expect high temperatures during the day. The crew tolerated the heat quite well. We were young, healthy and had been in the tropics long enough to become acclimatized to the environment. Furthermore, if we became uncomfortably warm we could always go over the side, sharks permitting. Sunburn was not a problem. I was the only one with fair skin but I protected myself by fashioning a hood from excess clothing. Our greatest discomfort was from the cold rather than the heat. This occurred on a single stormy night during which waves from the rough sea persistently broke over the rafts, thoroughly soaking us all. Here again we cursed the designer of the sails that failed to provide us adequate cover. The night was a long and miserable one that gave us a better appreciation of the hot days.

Our daily existence was one of monotony and loneliness – and toward the end of our journey, despair. There was little activity to occupy our time, save occasional fishing or managing the sails. Nights were worse, at which time we were left to our own thoughts and prayers. Conversation largely concerned our families and loved ones and food. The latter was maddening since we were already starving and didn't need to be reminded about what we were missing. In spite of everything we managed to keep our sanity throughout.

By the third day at sea our K-Rations were consumed, leaving us with a modest supply of candies similar to Lifesavers. Thereafter, we were subsisting on a piece of candy and a gulp or two of water each day. This continued for a week to ten days at which time our supply of candy and water was almost completely consumed. Although we fished daily we could not land anything. It was devastating to watch the fish in the clear blue water as they examined our offering and then swam away.

The circumstances under which we caught our first fish were bizarre. On this momentous day we observed a distant area of the sea to be white instead of its usual blue. As we drifted toward this strange area, some 50 to 100 yards in diameter, it appeared that the sea within it was boiling. Getting even closer we finally understood what we were seeing. It was a school of frantic fish churning up the water. Although we did not see them, we assumed that our constant companions, the sharks, were having their lunch in the school.

Unable to avoid it, we soon found ourselves in the middle of this turmoil and shared the panic of the small fish, expecting to join them at any moment. Although the ride was rocky our rafts were stable and we soon found ourselves outside the circle, but with an additional passenger. In the midst of the frenzy a small shark, perhaps 12-15 inches long, flew into one of the rafts. We welcomed the company. On the other hand, in 1944, raw fish was unheard of as a component of the American diet. In spite of our starvation it took all the courage of a combat veteran to take the first bite. The shark was a bit chewy, but all things considered, not bad. After this initiation we could handle any other fish that came along, with relish and without reservation.

The "flying fish" not only fed us but its inedible portion also gave us bait. With the new bait we were able to catch other fish. Although the supply was not bountiful, it was a vast improvement over what we had in the preceding days. Any short-term surplus was dried out in the tropical sun and saved for another day. Our water supply improved at about the same time when we experienced the stormy night described above. The accompanying rain enabled us to fill our Mae West reservoirs with the much-needed water. Having food and water we were now able to extend our anticipated survival time.

Toward the end of the journey our attitude was one of despair. By now most of us had some doubts that we would make it. Our spirits picked up somewhat on the night prior to our rescue when we spotted a light in the distance. The overwhelming majority of the crew was in favor of trying to make contact – knowing full well that the source of the light might just as well be enemy as friendly. Regardless of our desires, the flashlight battery by now was capable of producing a light that could barely be seen in the adjacent

raft. We had no means of signaling. Later we learned that there was a Japanese submarine operating in the area.

On each of the four days preceding our rescue we sighted navy Dumbos that could not hear our whistling and yelling. On the day of rescue, our 19th day at sea, the expected flying boat arrived early. The pilot was avoiding a local thunderstorm resulting in an earlier arrival time and, more importantly, a closer proximity to us. We expected it to fly by, as did so many others. Suddenly the Catalina's starboard wing dipped and immediately we knew we had been sighted. There is no adequate way to describe our feelings at this moment. Suffice to say we were one happy group of airmen.

After an agonizingly long time of circling over us (the pilot was requesting permission to make his first open sea landing) the Dumbo finally landed. As the plane taxied toward us, one of the navy gunners eyed the suntanned and skinny survivors and yelled, "They're Japs!" With that he swung his 50-caliber toward us. Fortunately, one of the Catalina's engines was between his gun and our rafts. Lt. Wagner saw what was happening and let loose with a string of GI invectives that no one aboard the navy craft could mistake for Japanese. With our identity firmly established, the navy crew became almost as excited as we were. They dangled beefsteaks before us,

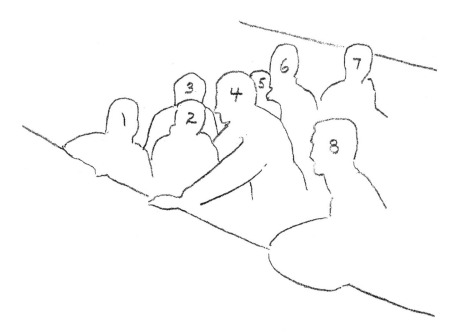

Sgt. Musey. 2. Lt. Goerke. 3. Lt. Bonney. 4. Lt. Wagner. 5. Sgt. Dotterer. 6. Cpl. Davis. 7. Sgt. Whitmore. 8. Sgt. Rokos.

intending them for our inaugural meal. We had some crazy idea that, following our starvation diets, we should resume eating gradually and in moderation and gratefully refused, accepting bread and jelly instead. Ironically, in the hospital that evening, the first meal given us was corned beef hash!

Our stay in the hospital was a short one and we recovered rapidly from our physical wounds. However, the ordeal resulted in wounds to the spirit as well, and recovery from these was slow. It would be many months before we could again experience the euphoria that most flyers feel when they "... have slipped the surly bonds of Earth and danced the skies on laughter-silvered wings..."

LT. WAGNER'S CREW		
2nd Lt.	Jack L. Wagner	Pilot
2nd Lt.	*Russell W. Pickering, Jr.	Copilot
2nd Lt.	Thomas B. Bonney	Navigator
2nd Lt.	Charles L. Goerke	Bombardier
S/Sgt.	Harold R. Dotterer	Engineer
S/Sgt.	Jerome J. Rokos	Radio Operator
S/Sgt.	Merle R. Musey	Radar Operator
Sgt.	Charles E. Whitmore	Gunner
Sgt.	*Clarence F. Wolfsberger	Asst. Eng.
Cpl.	Leonard M. Davis	Gunner
	*Missing in Action	

Note: At 1931 hours on the evening of June 11, 1944, the Lt. Jack Wagner crew took off from Mokerang Field, Los Negros in the Admiralty Islands for a bombing mission of the Truk atoll some 600 miles away. During their bombing run they were picked up by searchlights and then damaged by accurate anti-aircraft fire. They dropped their bombs at 0018 hours and were jumped by a Japanese Irving nightfighter that inflicted further damage which crippled the 868 Squadron, 13th Air Force B-24. The Japanese pilot was Warrant Officer Yoshimasa Nakagawa.

On the evening of September 4, 1944, Lt. Roland Fisher and crew from the 63rd Bomb Squadron, 5th Air Force took off from Owi Island for a mission to search for shipping in Davao Gulf, Mindanao Island, Philippines. His secondary target was Matina airstrip. Finding no shipping, Fisher decided to attack the airstrip. The airplane was caught by six or seven searchlights and after some inaccurate anti-aircraft fire, a Japanese nightfighter, later determined to be an Irving, made several passes and then rammed the B-24. The Japanese pilot was Warrant Officer Yoshimasa Nakagawa again.

Some 20 years later Roland Fisher and Yoshimasa Nakagawa met in New York City on the Dick Cavett Show.

Roland
T.
Fisher

SMOKIE ONE
WITH THE 63rd BOMB SQUADRON
Story and Photos by Roland Fisher

Introduction

I joined the 63rd Bomb Squadron, 43rd Group just after Christmas, 1943, at Dobodura, New Guinea and left the Group from Clark Field, Luzon, Philippines in May 1945. In those 17 months, I had compressed a near-life-time of experiences that, today, nearly 60 years later, are still fresh and vivid in my memory.

Before relating them, I think it in order that I describe some of my background that led to my life in the 43rd Bomb Group.

Growing up in Depression-crippled Denver in the 1930s, my dreams were focused on flying airplanes and the men who did so. I read every book I could find about aviation, (remember – no TV and movies cost a whole nickel, which was really hard to come by). In my imagination, I got to know every aviation pioneer and war hero first hand. I knew the Spads and Fokkers, the Curtis Hawks and Boeing P-12s, the clumsy Ford Trimotors and the Douglas B-18s, and I built models of them all. I worshipped Rickenbacker, Lindbergh and Doolittle and the brave army airmen who set endurance and altitude records. I wanted to be one of them.

So, it was proper that, after high school, when I was old enough to join the Army Flying Cadet program, I applied. Since I had not been able to afford the two years of college required, I petitioned for and took the alternative written examination that was allowed, passed it, and on my 19th birthday was called by the Army Reserve office to take my physical exam. The flight surgeon noted that I was in superb physical condition, as he checked my heart, reflexes, etc. I could see like an eagle and run like a deer.

Then, near the end of the exam, one of the nurses brought out a little book of about ten pages with a title, "Ishihara Vision Test." Each page had a printed disk full of colored dots. She asked me to read the number that showed in the disk. I did. She suddenly looked very concerned, called the other nurse over and asked me to read the next number. I did. She looked concerned and called the doctor. He showed me another page and asked me to read the number. I did. They all looked at each other and the doctor had me finish reading the rest of the pages.

When I finished, the doctor closed the book, put his arm over my shoulder and said very gently, "Son, I'm sorry. I cannot pass you. You will never be allowed to fly. You are color-blind." My shiny world and my high hopes shattered and crashed in little pieces around me. I was absolutely crushed.

What happened then is a story in itself that I shall tell another time. But I will summarize, as that story is significant in that it led me to being, perhaps, the only color-blind pilot in the 63rd Bomb Squadron, maybe in the whole 5th Air Force, a fact that remained my deep, personal secret throughout the war.

When I recovered from my shock, I went to a medical school library and studied everything I could find about color vision. I learned only males are afflicted, about 15 percent of all in the world. It is genetic, females are the carriers and they pass it to male offspring. I borrowed a copy of the test book and with my mother's guidance, I memorized each page as a normal person sees it, so thoroughly that I could read the pages correctly, even if upside down. From that time, I could "pass" the color vision test though I could not see colors as do most folks. To this day, I can't see the numbers in the book the same as seen by normal eyes. But I KNOW what is there!

This was in 1940. That fall I hitchhiked to Los Angeles where I got a job for $.75 an hour (BIG MONEY!) and began private flying lessons. I lived most frugally and put every dime I could into flying. I soloed in eight hours, got my private license in 35 hours, in February 1941, and began cramming to build up hours. I went to work at 3 a.m., so I could get off at noon and go to the airfield.

An organization, The Clayton Knight Committee, was recruiting pilots for combat with the British Royal Air Force. Minimum time required was 85 hours. I got to about 65, padded my logbook for the rest, passed a flight test in an AT-6, (the biggest plane I had flown till then was an 85 HP Supercub), and in June, 1941, I was accepted. I was sent, as a civilian, to the Spartan Flying School in Tulsa, Oklahoma, where I got day and night training in AT-6's, instrument time in a Link and navigation in a Spartan Executive (a plane ahead of its time). At the close of this program, I was checked out by an RAF Squadron Leader, Greaves, a veteran of the 1940 Battle of Britain who ranked me head of the class and offered me a commission in the RAF in combat. Most of my comrades were made Sergeant Pilots.

Still a civilian, I was given money and directions to travel to England via Halifax, Nova Scotia. On the way I had to check with the British Consul in Ottawa, where there occurred an event of human empathy that will be one of my fondest memories as long as I live.

While I was in Canada, the Japanese attacked Pearl Harbor, leaving me in doubt as to whether I should proceed. The American Consul advised me to continue, saying that would best serve the Allied cause and that I would be given a chance to join American forces later. I went on to Halifax, boarded a motor ship, The Dominion Monarch, and, with one companion vessel, crossed the North Atlantic in under five days. The companion vessel was torpedoed three days out and sank.

My ship continued at full speed to Liverpool where I took a train to London, to an RAF office and, with an American Embassy representative present, I was commissioned Pilot Officer, serial No. 116959 in the RAF Volunteer Reserve. To avoid risking my American citizenship, I did not swear allegiance to the Crown as did British subjects. Rather, I gave my oath as a gentleman that I would "obey my commanding officer, whomever he may be." Then I was given a uniform allowance as an advance on my future salary of 14 shillings, sixpence per day, ($83. U.S. per month, which included flight and combat pay), was directed to Saville Row for a custom-fit uniform that the tailors made up that day, opened a checking account at Barclays Bank, and reported to The Air Ministry for orders.

This was followed by a few weeks of military protocol schooling, some months in an Advanced Flying Unit for twin-engine training, then to Scotland for training in airborne-radar equipped night fighters in an ultra-secret environment. (No one used the word "radar" then.) Here is where I first used the call name, "SMOKIE ONE" that I continued throughout the war. I flew operations until the end of 1942 when I was ordered to London to transfer to the US 8th AF. As a reward for my service, while still in the RAF, I got to go through a complete six-week class at an Operations Training Unit on Spitfires simply because I asked if I could fly one. At graduation I went to London, was commissioned a Second Lieutenant and was posted as a pilot in 8th AAF Fighter Command.

An American major, Winston Kratz, an aide to General Hap Arnold, was in England through much of 1942, observing the British Night Fighter program. General Arnold felt the USAF badly lacked night fighting capability and ordered Kratz to build a program modeled on the British techniques. There were 32 of us Americans, scattered throughout the British night fighter squadrons, and as we transferred to the USAAF, Kratz pulled us all together, and sent us to Orlando, Florida where we became instructors in a new night fighter training school set up in February, 1943. Our planes were P-70s, which were A-20s modified to carry radar and 20mm cannon. It was a great low-level attack plane but worthless as a night fighter.

In October '43 the 418th, Night Fighter Squadron, the first to come from the Orlando school, with me as Operations Officer, was deployed to New Guinea. We arrived at Dobodura and were made to feel unwanted from the start. Fifth Fighter Command stated, as night fighters we were a waste of pilots and planes. Unlike that in Europe, the theater lacked effective ground radar. Our P-70s were old and worn, carried very crude radar and could not cope with the faster, more nimble Japanese planes. Until the superior P-61, Black Widows arrived eight months later, night fighters were not able to be of value to the 5th Air Force.

In January 1944, I was called to fly over to Port Moresby to report to 5th Bomber Command who apparently had learned I had previous experience using airborne radar. There I was interviewed and ordered to report to the 63rd Bomb Squadron. So I flew my P-70 back to Dobodura, said goodbye to my 418th comrades and got a jeep ride to the Dobodura airstrip where the 63rd was located. Thus began my career with the 43rd Bomb Group.

I was made to feel most welcome by the Squadron CO, Herbert Derr, and was assigned to a tent where I met my tent mate, Lt. John W. Kingston who was Squadron Meteorology Officer (The Weatherman!). John and I bunked, (or tented) together for the next 15 months at five bases even after I was assigned to Group Headquarters at Leyte. We stayed in touch after the war until he died. Two other new pilots, transferees from a P-40 outfit, Les Hackler and Don Hopperstadt, lived with us in that tent.

On February 2nd, Harry Park took me up for two hours transition time, my first ride in a B-24. He had me do some takeoffs and landings. Apparently, I did OK because the next day, the CO, Herb Derr, had me ride co-pilot on a supply flight to Milne Bay and return. He had me land the plane at Milne Bay where we loaded some sacks of cement. On the return to Dobodura, he landed and literally slammed the plane onto the runway – the hardest landing I have ever been in short of a crash. Afterward, I heard crewmen talking about how he was the worst B-24 pilot in the squadron, that he had most of his time in B-17s and never could adjust to a B-24, especially landing them. Derr always blamed the B-24 as "too hard to fly."

That week, Park gave me a final check to qualify me in B-24s and I was ready for missions. My first mission Feb. 8/9 was with Lt. Gregg to Rabaul. We found no ships so dropped on one of the airstrips. We were at about 5000 feet, so there was a lot of small ack ack, but the searchlights missed us and we received no hits. A few days later, Steve Ring's copilot did not want to fly anymore, so I was assigned to Steve's crew. Major Joe Kinsel, Squadron Navigator, was Steve's navigator, and a good one. February, March and April, I flew with Steve. He was a good pilot, but somewhat nervous when on instruments and I was very good on instruments, so we were a good match and Steve had me do most of the flying in the night.

Following are detailed accounts of my recollections of the bases from which we flew, accounts of my most significant missions and an abstract from my log book of all missions I flew.

MEMORABLE MISSIONS AND ADVENTURES
Mission To Palau

In London in 1942, while I was a night fighter pilot in the RAF, I met an American from Portland, Oregon, who flew Spitfires in an RAF squadron. We became very close friends and as often as we could, we met in Lon-

Roland Fisher and *Out of the Night II,* B-24 at Clark Field.

don on leave. Johnny Yerby was blond-headed, had a powerful build and always wore a butch cut. He had been a top football player at the University of Oregon. In late 1942, his entire squadron was posted to the North Afri- can Desert and I lost track of him.

Two years later I am a B-24 pilot flying out of Nadzab, New Guinea, and I was assigned a bombing mission to Palau. It was too far to reach from Nadzab so we staged from Nadzab to Wakde Island where we fueled and loaded bombs, then took off for Palau in the evening

We approached Palau, found no vessels so lined up on the airstrip at Pelelieu. We climbed to 1000 feet and ran right down the strip. The damn bombs hung up! We did a 180 and made another pass and they still hung up. The Japanese threw a lot of automatic fire at us but never hit us.

Two more passes – and we still had our bombs! Howard Hammett, my bombardier, just about came unglued. On the fifth pass, they dropped and we turned out of the ack-ack. That night I won the hearts and confidence of my new crew because they said I flew the plane as cool as a summer breeze. In truth I sat still and flew the plane smoothly on five consecutive passes because I was so scared I could hardly move.

In the morning we approached Wakde. We were really low on gas and I was having some prop trouble, so I told the tower I needed to come straight in. They cleared me for a priority landing. On our final, a P-38 came in from somewhere underneath me and got right in ahead of me. The tower kept waving him off, but he really had his head way up his rectum. He landed, with me right behind him and I had to slam into the strip and ride brakes hard to keep from overrunning him. I was furious! As soon as I parked, I stormed out of the plane over to the P-38 revetments and found the pilot still by his plane. I grabbed him by the shirt and was about to deck him when someone from my crew held me back. I could have killed him but I just pushed him a little.

We had the plane serviced, then went over to get some breakfast. We drove by some P-47s that were getting ready for a mission and I saw a pilot standing, bareheaded, with his back to me. Incredibly, I saw a sight I had last seen in London two years before: A bull neck with blond hair and a crew cut. It was my good friend Johnny Yerby, just climbing into a P-47 to fly a ground support mission across the strait against Sarmi on the mainland.

We hugged and pounded each other and in the few minutes we had before he took off he told me he had been sent from North Africa to Australia where he had transferred from the RAF to the 340th Fighter Squadron and been sent New Guinea. He had to take off and I had to get back to Nadzab so we agreed we would stay in touch and try to meet in Sydney.

Back at Nadzab a day later I came down, really sick, with dengue fever and while in the hospital I wrote Johnny. The letter came back "Deceased."

How utterly ironic that, in an incredible coincidence, I would find my friend on the opposite side of the world from where I last saw him and lose him so quickly. I still struggle with why it happened that way.

On a later staging mission out of Wakde, I learned from his squadron mates that his plane caught fire just after takeoff and he rolled over and plunged into the sea. They found the cockpit of the wreck but all they ever found of Johnny was his .45 pistol in its holster.

Here in Portland, every Easter, a beautiful lily plant is placed by the altar in a church I attend. It is dedicated to John Yerby. His sister puts it there.

The Souvenir Adventure

A constant goal of everyone was to get good souvenirs of the war. The most sought-after was a Japanese personal flag. These were very colorful, usually of silk, with a Rising Sun in the center and inscriptions in writing around the edges.

We, in the Air Force, were at a disadvantage. We met the enemy in battle but did not make direct contact like foot soldiers until long after. The result was they got all the good mementos and we rarely found anything worthwhile after a battle on the ground. Sometimes the Aussies and our ground troops would try to sell things to us. A lot of it was phony, especially from the Aussies.

Nadzab, New Guinea, June 1944	Portland, Oregon, Oct. 1999
Roland T. Fisher	Same Guy
Smokie One	Same Flag

Bob "Red" Walters and I were close friends. While we were at Nadzab, we talked about this matter and decided we would go out on our own and find some things. We knew the landings at Hollandia had just taken place and that our ground troops had landed at Humboldt Bay and driven inland to secure all three airfields so there was a perimeter around them with the Japanese on the outside. We decided that was a good place to look. Eino Walden, a bombardier, heard us talking and said he would go with us.

We went to a cargo squadron and hitchhiked a ride on a C-47. The pilot had to land at Finschhafen on the way and when we landed, he told us to wait on the ground as he had to take an engineer pilot up for a brief test hop. On takeoff, he lost his right engine, veered off line, caught a tree with his wing and crashed onto his nose. We ran over to help but both pilots were in bad shape and had to be pried from the wreckage by medics. One died. We lucked out there.

We caught another C-47 headed for Hollandia. It had an extra gas tank lashed in the cargo bay hooked up to the engine feed lines. On the way, the tank relief valve flipped open and saturated the interior with 100 octane gas. We got it plugged with tape but we were a flying bomb and did not dare use any radio or other electrical equipment for a couple hours until we cleared the ship of fumes. Once again, we really lucked out and finally made it to Sentani strip, Hollandia.

At Hollandia, we approached some infantry on perimeter guard duty, who were living in pup tents and asked them where to find some battle souvenirs. Three infantry guys agreed to go outside the defense lines with us. The six of us, they with rifles and we with pistols, entered a dense rainforest as we walked along a streambed coming down the slopes of Mt. Cyclops.

In about a mile, the ground rose steeply and we climbed up the streambed to a kind of ledge. The light was very dim under the thick forest canopy. As we climbed up onto the ledge I heard a loud scream and there, 20 feet ahead, was a bearded Japanese in front of a rude hut holding his hands in the air. Another man came running from the hut with a long gun and others appeared to be behind him. I think we all shot at the one with the gun at once. He fell down the ledge into the streambed, the others all screamed and held up their arms.

I was so scared, I was shaking so, that I still don't know how I did what I did next. I bolstered my .45 Colt, rested my camera on the top of a big boulder to hold it steady and took a picture of the fallen man. Then I hollered "Let's get out of here!" We grabbed the arms of the two Japanese holding up their hands and shoved them ahead of us and literally ran down the slippery, rocky streambed. I expected an army to start shooting at us any minute.

We got back to the defense perimeter line OK, drenched in sweat from fear and humidity. We took some pictures of us with the prisoners (about a dozen infantry guys horned in), then took them to the POW camp.

They looked starved. We gave them some food and kept telling them we were not going to hurt them. I think they were completely resigned to being killed until we got them to the POW camp and a translator talked to them. When he said they would not be hurt, and they saw other Japanese in the compound, safe and well, one of them came over to me, dropped to the ground, hugged my ankles and bawled like a baby. He pulled out his wallet and body pouch from under his shirt, pulled off his watch and pushed them in my hands. I gave him back the watch but kept the wallet and body pouch that had two beautiful personal flags. (Just what I came after! I still have them today.) The wallet had a picture of a Japanese aviator in flying suit that I took to be a friend or relative of our prisoner, a pay book and a roll of money.

While we were still with the translator, he brought out a young prisoner who, he said, was a navy Zero pilot. We had a hanger-talk, bull session with the pilot through the translator. He said he had shot down three "Curtis's" (P-40's, I guess). He loved flying and was quite open when we talked about it. But when I asked about how American POWs were treated, he got evasive.

Later we looked around and sat in some of the Japanese planes on the airstrip. There were mostly Oscar and Tony fighters and scads of Helens,

Nells, Dinahs and a few Bettys. It rained nearly all the time we were there and we really were soaked. That afternoon we caught a transport back to Nadzab, and this time had no scares or close calls.

When we got back to Nadzab, Col. Pettus called me in and chewed me up one side and down the other for this caper. Then he said he wouldn't have been so mad if we had asked him to go along.

St. Elmo's Fire Mission

In August 1944, on Owi Island, scrub typhus devastated the 63rd squadron. My engineer, co-pilot. radio operator and a gunner came down. From then on, I used fill-in replacements; some of them brand-new pilots.

On the evening of August 22nd with a Lt. Patton, a new guy as co-pilot, we departed Owi to search south of Davao. We had orders not to bomb a vessel unless we could visually identify it. (Apparently, an American sub had complained that it had been attacked when some of our planes were in the area.)

We went into Davao Gulf at 500 ft. and got a blip. No IFF so we dropped a flare to see it. We got horrendous flak and on two passes we could not see the target. It might have been making smoke.

It did not respond to IFF but we never could get a visual so we went on to a secondary target.

In the mouth of the gulf, we climbed to about 8000 ft. and ran into some mild turbulence. The radar showed dense clouds about 40 miles ahead, over the target. Just then my nose gunner, Bowling, called over the intercom, "Hey lieutenant – my guns are on fire." His gun barrels were glowing with a blue fluorescent light. Then the prop tips began to glow, then turned into four, solid blue-light discs. Every projection from the plane, antennae posts, wires, pitot tube, was glowing with a brilliant blue light. The blue light came into the cockpit. The throttle knobs, pitch control handles, all glowing with a blue aura. My skin felt prickly and everything in the plane looked like a blue neon light fantasy.

Then we hit very rough turbulence and there began an unbelievable display of lightning. The flashes came closer and closer together until they were almost continuous. The engines began cutting out, then catching and the props would surge, run away for a few seconds, then an engine would cut out again. The wings were flapping, the ship was jerking about in every way, the bombs were banging against the stanchions, and outside was solid, brilliant light.

My instruments spilled. With the constant wracking of the plane, the surging engines and the lightning, I lost orientation completely. My airspeed built up and I knew we were diving. I finally gained control at quite some lower altitude and the turbulence decreased. The airplane was handling very poorly but we took up a heading through the storm and dropped our bombs dead reckoning, then turned out and headed home.

I could barely maintain trim going home. The engines ran OK but the plane felt like it was trying to do everything but fly. But it did. After inspecting the plane at base, Engineering told me the insulation on the magnetos was literally fried and that it was a miracle the engines had gotten us back. The plane was badly wrinkled and bent up and I don't think it continued in service.

The Kamikaze Event

On September 4, 1944 with Lt. Louis Bryant, a brand-new replacement as my co-pilot, we started our takeoff from Owi at about 20:00 (dark night), briefed to search for shipping in the Davao area. Going down the runway, our AA fired a red alert, indicating we were under attack by Japanese bombers. I was halfway down the runway when my #2 prop ran away and I tapped the toggle switch control "back" to bring the prop speed down to normal takeoff r.p.m. The damn switch stuck "back," bringing the prop speed abruptly to very slow r.p.m. with the engine at full boost. I was just lifting off when the #2 supercharger let out a big bang and shot a gust of blue flame clear to the ground. Just then one of our own A.A. guns fired a big burst of tracers that cut right across our top. I thought the bastards were shooting at us! Everything was happening at once!

I got the r.p.m. toggle back to full forward but No. 2 engine was surging up and down so I cut the supercharger out entirely. The engine then ran smoothly but at reduced power output. With three good and one "half-ass" engine and our heavy load, I struggled out from Owi just barely able to climb. I think our low altitude saved us from being shot with our own A.A. because back in the dark, all hell had broken loose with guns firing from all over Owi and Biak.

After a few minutes I found the No. 2 engine ran OK at half power if I left off the turbo. So, with the mess going on at base, I decided to go on with the mission. What followed the rest of the night was well reported by Steve Birdsall on page 210 in his book, *Flying Buccaneers,* so I will let him tell that part of my story.

> **Author's Note:** The following section titled "Night Flight to Davao" was printed in the book titled *Flying Buccaneers* (pages 210 to 213) by Steve Birdsall and published by Doubleday & Company, Inc. in 1977. Copyright in 1977 by Steve Birdsall.

Night Flight to Davao

"Meanwhile the 63rd Squadron was still flying its missions to Davao from Owi and on the night of September 4, at about eight o'clock. Lieutenant Roland Fisher lifted the B-24D "Miss Liberty" off the runway. Fisher and his crew had been briefed to search for shipping south of the Philippines and in Davao Gulf, with Matina airstrip as their secondary target. By midnight they had found no shipping, and Fisher decided to attack the airstrip."

"It was a very bright, moonlit night, which the 63rd crews disliked intensely, but there was no apparent opposition as Miss Liberty began her bomb run at 5000 feet. They were approaching the coast and the bombardier, Lieutenant Howard Hammett, was taking control for the bomb run when the B-24 was caught perfectly in six or seven searchlight beams. Anti-aircraft fire followed, but it was fairly inaccurate. Fisher felt the plane bounce as the bombs dropped and he turned hard to the left and dived to shake off the lights. He had just rolled out of the turn and picked up speed to about 175 when he saw small flashes in the shadow of his plane, straight ahead. Miss Liberty was still nailed in the searchlights but they were coming from behind, and what Fisher was looking at was a Japanese plane coming in head on, shooting.

"Fisher saw the gun muzzles blinking and caught the outline of a plane. I started to call a warning to my crew when my senses told me that plane was going to take me head on. I reflexed and rolled the aircraft hard to the left and pulled back on the yoke. The fighter flashed by, clearly visible, and passed directly under my right engines. His wingtip missed the lower right part of my fuselage by inches. I could see his aircraft very clearly in the bright lights and I saw his head, flying cap and goggles through the canopy as he went by. The plane was a Nick. (I reported it as a Nick but later learned it was an Irving – very similar appearance.)

"I was still hollering on the intercom at the crew that we were under fighter attack and I rolled the plane back to horizontal and stuck the nose down hard to get some speed. I think I was hitting about 200 and maybe at 4000 feet when I heard some pop-pop sounds and there was a terrific, muffled bump and I went into an even steeper dive. I remember hearing the top turret swiveling but nobody said anything and I was trying to sort out just what was going on and read the instruments when the radar operator came on and said his radar was gone. By then we were down perhaps to 2000 feet and I remember my air speed was pretty well over 200 and I decided to ease it back and discovered I had no pressure on my elevators. Again reflexively I snapped "on" my master switch on the auto pilot and began to feel for control over the elevators with the elevator knob. There was a brief response, I thought, but it did not last and I was still in a steep dive, still picking up speed. I could see the surf on the beach on the south end of Samal Island very clearly. It felt as if I was looking straight down.

"I remember then thinking 'Jesus, we are going to hit – I should push the bailout bell, but nobody could make it anyway.' While I was thinking this, I started rolling the trim tab back. The damn thing worked and we sailed out of our dive. I don't know how much altitude we had left, but I will never forget being able to see those damned waves in the moonlight. At any rate I left my power on and got her reasonably level using the trim tab and we sailed out of Davao Gulf and took up a heading for Owi.

"We lucked out going home. Those Pratt and Whitneys ran perfectly all the way and the weather was calm. The flight engineers assessed the damage and reported huge, gaping holes, that our main elevator control cables had been cut, that we had no hydraulic pressure because of severed lines, and the electrical system was erratic because of torn wires and conduit. We had three crewmen wounded, with masses of fragments of metal in their backs. From this we thought that we had been struck by a large shell causing the big holes in the bottom of the aircraft, just in back of the bomb bay keel between the two waist windows, and also throwing fragments through the sides tearing out the cables, longerons, and tearing a hole in the top. Actually it was cannon fire that cut the cables on the sides and blew the top out as well as wounding the men.

"It was all hard to figure out and we were more concerned with helping the wounded men than trying to repair the cables. The engineers worked hard with pliers and spare wire trying to splice the cables, but whenever I put pressure on the yoke the splices would part. We decided I should continue to fly home on the trim tab and that we would try to disturb the trim of the aircraft as little as possible by all sitting still. This is why we lucked out on the weather because I'm convinced I never could have made it if we had hit turbulence.

"When we approached Owi, control told me that they might request that I ditch because they had the entire day strike almost ready to line up for takeoff and they didn't want to take a chance of my crashing and blocking the runway. I reported to them that I did not have good elevator control and did not think I could ditch it, and we had wounded men aboard. So they agreed I could take a crack at landing. I swung the old lady down south of the island in a big gradual turn and got her headed north on a long slow final approach. We figured if we could get fluid back into the hydraulic system we would have enough to operate the brakes with maybe one shot if we cranked everything else down by hand. So we collected fluids in the customary manner of shot-up bomber crews . . . grapefruit juice, coffee and water from canteens, urine and spit.

"On the approach we cranked the wheels down, but I did use hydraulic power to put down about 20 degrees of flap and lock them. I just kept on easy power and played the trim tab over the fence and made the best goddamn landing I ever made in my life. Right at the end of the strip I popped on the brakes. They lasted for a second or two and then went out so I ground looped it right in front of the palm stumps."

Everybody was excited and kept looking at the plane. The two sides of the rear of the fuselage were intact but the top had a hole blown just above the waist windows and the bottom was shredded."

"Inspecting the torn condition of the bottom we found strange pieces of metal and glass sticking in it and only then realized that we had been struck by another aircraft. This was when I remembered a big orange boom I had seen off in the night and I felt satisfied that the twin engine fighter I had seen in the searchlights had attacked us from the rear, collided with us and crashed. So we reported the mission as such.

On the ground at Davao a Japanese night fighter squadron was congratulating Warrant Officer Yoshimasa Nakagawa and his observer for destroying an American intruder. They had taken off to intercept Miss Liberty and were closing in when the cannon jammed and it seemed that the enemy would escape. The Japanese pilot decided he would ram, and his propeller slashed into the bomber's fuselage. Nakagawa reported that the big American aircraft started to fall immediately. His plane, its canopy smashed, kept flying. His eye had been gashed by flying glass and the wind buffeting his face forced him to turn sideways in his seat, but he managed to control the battered plane. When the bomber started to level off again Nakagawa was about to repeat the attack, but the American plane reportedly faltered and plunged into the water. The damaged Japanese fighter landed safely back at its base."

General Kenny called me in one day, gave me the D.F.C. for getting everyone down OK, and "for batting a Japanese fighter from the sky." And for not crashing and blocking the runway. He also said he had written General Arnold a letter about the incident because of the humorous remarks we had radioed to base when we were trying to get home. I never saw the letter although years later while in the Reserve, personnel officers would mention they had seen it in my 201 file.

Postscript To Kamikaze Event

In 1962 I read in a book co-authored by Roger Pineau about a Japanese night fighter who claimed a B-24 victory by ramming over Davao. Immediately recognized this as my experience and I wrote Pineau. After about two years he was able to locate a man in Japan with the same name but the fellow would not confirm that he was the pilot. Pineau suggested I write to him, which I did and started a warm correspondence. This led to a reunion in Japan, an article in *Life* magazine and a joint appearance on the Dick Cavett show in New York.

Visit To MacArthur Headquarters

A few days after the Kamikaze Mission, I was ordered to fly down to Hollandia to be on a radio program. I rode down in the back of a B-25 and was nearly deaf from prop chatter when we landed. That had to be the noisiest plane in the Air Force.

General Douglas MacArthur
and Colonel Ramey

I was taken to MacArthur's compound in a clearing on a ridge on the side of Mt. Cyclops. Wow! It was like being back in civilization. MacArthur lived in a beautiful, newly built, ranch-style house, painted white. There were several other, smaller, new frame buildings nearby. These were mostly living quarters for all the war correspondents and were really plush inside. One building was set up as a lounge, complete with bar and chairs and tables.

I was assigned to bunk with Spencer David of Associated Press and a famous Hollywood writer (I can't remember his name). A Second Lieutenant, who said he had been MacArthur's orderly in the Philippines before the Japanese took them, was also there, to be on the same program. I can't remember his name either. He was a mild little guy. He told about his days serving MacArthur.

The program, called "Thanks To The Yanks," was sponsored by R. J. Reynolds Tobacco Co. and was broadcast nationally. I was given a copy of the script, which said that Reynolds was sending 400,000 Camel cigarettes to us, free, in my honor. I wonder how much lung cancer that caused in the Fifth Air Force?

MacArthur really took care of the war correspondents. I was there four days and really lived high on the hog! All meals included fresh eggs, fresh vegetables and fresh meat – steaks, chops, and (WOW!) fresh refrigerated milk, all flown in from Australia, daily. And every night the correspondents gathered in the bar and started a party. There was every kind of booze, with enlisted men in white s mocks serving. One night, the Hollywood writer got drunk and read a poem he had written. It was a parody of Shakespeare and I remember the beginning words. "Hollywood, mewling and puking, with your whores and harlots, flinging money . . ." The correspondents all got a huge laugh from it. The writer threw the poem away and, in years to come, I often wished I had picked it up. It would be worth quite a bit. After four days of being a well-fed hero, I got on a B-25 and went back to the real world at Owi.

The Suicide Paratroopers

In early November we moved to Tacloban, Leyte, P.I. The weather was almost steady rain. The whole place was soupy, deep mud and was jammed with men and equipment. Tacloban airstrip was on a swampy finger of land stuck out into the bay. The navy had pumped sand onto it to build up the level and the engineers laid down metal matting. The whole strip kept sinking and became crammed with planes. Army, Navy, Marines, so many that when we landed B-24's (almost always in a strong crosswind) our wing tips just cleared noses of planes parked on the edge of the strip.

General George C. Kenney
and Colonel Ramey

To top it off, the Japanese bombed us almost every minute. It was the only operational strip we had on Leyte and they did everything they could to immobilize it. The place was a nightmare, and a "daymare!"

By this time I had lost all my crew members to illness or rotation. Col. Pettus had assigned me to Group Operations, although I still flew with the 63rd with make-up crews, usually flying a Ferret ship.

One morning Jim Pettus and I were standing on the strip just after a bad air raid. A taxiing B-25 got a wheel stuck in a hole and could not get out with its engines. Men were dashing about and planes were burning from the air raid when Jim turned to me and said "Fisher–go help that guy in the B-25, then I want you to run this airstrip and keep it operational!" This was a tough assignment because there was something crashing, exploding or breaking (especially runway-light wires) every minute, and the congestion was fierce.

My command post was a jeep with a radio on tower frequency. My tools were tractors, bulldozers (to push wrecked planes from the strip into the surf), crowbar and pliers, and tape and chewing gum to patch the runway light wires.

One evening we were alerted that the Japanese might try a paratroop attack. Some of our infantry came down to the strip and dispersed around its edges. Their C.O. was a Lt. Rector. Just at dusk a Navy B-24 landed with a damaged wheel and could not taxi off the runway. I jumped on a cleatrack, hooked onto the tailskid and towed the B-24 over to the edge of the strip. I left the cleatrack on the beach behind the Navy plane. By then it was dark and a bunch of Marine Corsairs came in, got into the pattern, some shot up with injured pilots, and began to holler for landing clearance and strip lights. I radioed from my jeep to turn on the strip lights. The wires for these lay loose along the edge of the matting and were frequently broken by wheels passing over them.

Two or three of the Corsairs had landed and pulled over onto the beach along the strip when the lights on the beach side went out. I knew it was wire break, so I walked out in front of the B-24 I had just pulled off, found the broken wires, twisted them together, and got a hell of an electric shock. I got them partially on, kind of flickering.

The Corsairs in the air kept circling in the dark with their navigation lights on when all hell broke loose out in the bay. There must have been 500 ships off the beach and they all started shooting.

I have never, in four years of combat duty, seen and heard such a concentration of ack-ack tracers and shell bursts. The stuff went in every direction including right over the strip in sheets. I thought sure it would hit some of our planes in the pattern but it didn't. The air literally fried with the noise up above.

By now, it was quite dark. I saw the navigation lights on a plane pass downwind of the strip, very low, and turn into the landing pattern on the downwind leg. Some 40mm fire went at it from the landside of the strip and somehow I knew, as dark as it was, this was not a Corsair but a Japanese bomber. The plane completed its downwind leg, turned onto base and lined up with the strip on a perfect final approach. I thought sure it was going to lay a stick of bombs down the runway and I ran to the cleatrack and ducked behind the treads. I watched its lights approach the end of the strip in horror, because I thought it would drop bombs right in front of me. It was just over the end of the strip when a 40mm fired a short burst and I saw a bright flash on the wing of the approaching plane. It veered to the right, then straightened out and came scooting down the beach on its belly, right at me.

I thought sure its bombs would go off and in desperation I ran and dived into the surf. Right behind me the plunging plane hit the cleatrack and exploded with gasoline but no bombs. I ran back onto the beach and saw men screaming and running around in the light of the burning plane. Right in front of me a man, his clothes on fire, ran toward me howling and pulling a gun from his holster. I knocked him down or pushed him and grabbed the gun from him. It was so hot it scorched my hands although I didn't feel it at the time. He thrashed around. I think I hit or pushed him again. Then I backed away again to the water because my own clothes were hot from the fire. He never got up again and I ran to some of the others who were flopping around. Some were Americans and some were Japanese. Everybody was covered with sand and blood and smoke and it was an unbelievable mess. Lt. Rector came up, and soon some medical corpsmen came, and we spent the rest of the night sorting out injured people and bodies and trying to put out burning airplanes. Some of the Japanese, who we now realized were paratroopers, were horribly mangled. I don't know how many there were or whether any came through it alive and sneaked off.

When dawn came a photographer took pictures of the carnage. I realized I still had the gun I had taken from the running Japanese stuck in my belt. I went back to the spot and found his body (it had burned quite badly) and got the holster but it was burned so it was useless. (I still have the gun and the burned holster.)

My burns were minor but I sure was sore for a couple of weeks. I think what saved me from serious burns was my jumping in the surf just before the Japanese plane hit the tractor and blew up, and being all wet when I struggled with the man on fire. I think he was the pilot and didn't have the murderous equipment the troopers had. Whatever, whoever, I was lucky and he wasn't.

During the night, we carried off more than 30 dead or wounded Americans, mostly marines who were with their Corsairs that were lined up on the edge of the strip when the Japanese plane had slid right down the line of them, chopping them up. In the morning, we counted the bodies of about a dozen Japanese paratroopers, most badly mangled. They were carrying grenades, small machine guns and firebombs. Intelligence found papers that showed they had planned to belly-land on the strip, let the men out in the dark, and immobilize the strip for as long as they could.

Roland Fisher and debris on strip.

Recollections

Lt. Col. Edward W. Scott and the first 12 B-24 anti-shipping radar-equipped airplanes arrived at Jackson (Seven Mile Strip) out of Port Moresby on October 16, 1943. They flew several combat missions out of Jackson until Dobodura was taken. On November 1st, the Scott Project Group moved to Dobodura. There were several airstrips here in a flat swampy area back from the beach with jagged mountains, rising abruptly, about 10 miles from the coast. When we returned from an all-night mission, low on fuel, the flat area with the airstrips often would have a blanket of fog covering everything. We had no blind landing aids or ILS in those days. However, off the beach was an old Japanese freighter, partly submerged. When the strip was covered with fog, we would come in from the sea at about 100 feet altitude, line up with the freighter on a given heading, head inland for three minutes after passing over the ship, then descend into the fog. If we did not see the strip in one minute we had to apply power and do a hard turn to the left or hit a mountain.

On one mission, when I was co-pilot to H. Gregg, we had to follow this procedure and he was just hitting the throttles to go around because the one minute was up when I barely glimpsed the strip through the fog out my side, chopped the throttle and dived the plane down and to the right and lined up on the strip. Gregg leveled off and made a perfect landing. Then he said I flew like I was in a Spitfire. I told him that was the only way I knew how to fly.

We had a good movie amphitheater here and one of our sergeants (I can't remember his name) who had a great announcing voice and a stage personality, handled the movies and told stories over the PR system. One memory that really sticks is the night he announced that Lt. McGehee's plane had crashed at Cape Gloucester and McGehee was killed. Usually the audience was talkative and noisy, but when they heard that, there was utter quiet.

John Kingston and I scrounged some lumber from some shipping crates and built ourselves wood bunks (which beat the hell out of army cots) and some desks and chairs. The wood bunks made it a lot easier to hang our mosquito bars under which we slept. But we still had a dirt floor.

Once, out in the jungle, I found a banana tree with a full bunch of fruit. John and I ate lots of bananas for several days.

Most of the time at Dobodura, it was hot, humid and rainy with every kind of insect there is. Some of the grasshoppers and praying mantises were longer than my hand. The praying mantises were voracious insect eaters, and we kept them on our writing table because they would attack insects attracted by the candle we used when we wrote letters. Even with their help, letters I sealed up often were full of insect bodies, and people I wrote to, wrote back about the insects I "shipped" them.

One day, driving a jeep through the forest road where it was low light, I ran the front wheels over what felt like a log. I stopped before the rear wheels went over and the "log" started thrashing under the jeep. The jeep really bounced. I backed up slowly and saw the log was a giant constrictor type snake. I got out, shot it in the head with my .45 and loaded it a section at a time in the rear of the jeep. It filled the entire rear.

We had some native laborers there who agreed to skin it if they could have the meat. They tied it by the tail, hoisted it up to a tree limb, and had one of their kids climb up with a knife in his mouth, then start down it peeling off the skin. He was slimy with blood and oil but he got the skin off and gave it to me. I tried to dry and keep the skin but it rotted and Kingston threw it away because of the stench.

One of the 418th Squad P-70s crashed in the water near the Japanese ship derelict off the coast. The pilot was a good friend of mine. The 418th CO came over and asked me if I would help find the plane. I went down to the beach and asked the Navy Beachmaster, a Lt. named Wally Weems, for Navy help. He was very kind and gave me the services of a barge, a diver and crew. We went out on the barge to the Japanese wreck and the diver located the P-70. The three airmen were still in it and we brought up the bodies. That was my first experience with men who had been in a warm, tropical sea for a couple days. They were horribly bloated and the stench was beyond description.

When I saw my friend, I cried and gagged at the same time. Wally was very kind, told me to stand back and had his crew put the bodies in rubber bags. We went back to shore and Wally took me out to a huge supply vessel, one of the fleet standing offshore. They made me stay overnight and I ate in the ship's mess. Wow! I had fresh steaks, fresh frozen vegetables, mashed potatoes, fresh milk and ice cream for dinner, and fresh eggs and bacon for breakfast. I stayed there two days and lived high on the hog. What a contrast between Navy food and the bullybeef and dehydrated crap we lived on back at Dobodura.

I went back to shore where Wally lived in a prefabricated house and as I was leaving, I noticed Wally had some huge iron kettles over fire, boiling something. They were Japanese skulls that he had taken from bodies left out in the swamps from the Battle of Buna. He said he boiled and dried them, then sent them to people in the states that he thought were not doing their part in the war effort. Macabre!!

I was afraid I would be chewed out for being gone so long but Derr said that Navy Commander Freddy Smith had called the 43rd Headquarters and said they needed me for a couple days to help with the bodies. Wally thought of everything.

Nadzab

We moved to Nadzab sometime in March, '44. It was the dry season and it was hot and dusty. The Markham valley was pretty flat, a sea of Kunai grass that was tall, tough and sharp. Clearing it with a machete was hard work and we got lots of cuts on our arms from the sharp grass blades.

Here we had some hard surface runways. Between our strip and the sea, about 10 miles away lay a mountain. When we took off at night we were always pointing right at the damn mountain and, just as soon as our wheels were up, we had to start a three degree turn to the right, fly for five minutes, then turn to the left to miss it. Lae was on the gulf side of the mountain on the coast. A big volcano blew up while we were at Nadzab and it was dark for three days. It probably was Mt. Wilhelm.

While here, my tent mate was still John Kingston but we got a new guy, John Landt, a bombardier from the Third Attack, who had put .50 caliber guns in their B-25's noses and didn't need their bombardiers anymore. Landt and I became fast friends and he flew several missions with me. We still are close friends and I talk to him frequently.

Although we rarely had any booze, we always built a beautiful "Officers Club" out of palm thatch and drop chutes. We had a very nice one at Nadzab. Between it and our sleeping tents lay an uncleared patch of jungle about a large city block in size.

One week, we got some booze somewhere and had a party. After quite a few drinks, John Landt left the "club" at dark to go back to our tent. Somehow he stepped into the jungle. The next morning he burst out of the thicket with his clothes in shreds and his skin bleeding from a hundred scratches. He had become lost in it and thrashed about all night. We still laugh about that.

One memory I have is of a day when Chuck Quinette and I went up to do some radar calibration. I landed and as I was taxiing down the taxiway, I used just my rudder to steer the B-24. Chuck said he had never seen that before and I explained it was a habit I got from flying British planes. They all had such poor brakes that faded easily, so we always taxied with rudder and used the brakes just to stop.

One of my fondest memories is seeing my first P-61, Black Widow, night fighter. John Myers, young factory representative from Northrop, flew it in to train the night fighter pilots in it. Charles Lindbergh was at Nadzab then teaching fuel management to the P-38 pilots, and I watched as Myers gave Lindbergh some cockpit drill and they took off. They came back that afternoon loaded with fresh vegetables. They had flown up to Mt. Hagen and got the produce from the native gardens.

I had a great reminiscence about that with John Myers three years ago at the North Atlantic Air Museum in Pennsylvania where they are rebuilding a P-61 that we brought back from New Guinea. It is expected to fly again.

Coming back from a mission to Palau, about an hour out, I started to ache all over. When I landed, I could barely move, I hurt so much. Doc Mott sent me to a tent hospital where they said I had dengue fever. For a week I was really sick. There is no medication for it. All they could do was bathe me in rubbing alcohol three or four times a day to reduce the fever. A pretty nurse did it and I was not even interested in her. I finally got well and went back to flying. But there is another memory I will always have.

That spring some replacement crews came in. Among them was one with Tom Watkins as pilot. Quinette took Watkins out on a "break-in" mission. Then Watkins and the new crew were sent out on their first mission. I don't know that they ran into any problems, but when they came back the next morning, Watkins walked in and told the CO that he was not going to fly anymore, and he was grounded.

Capt. McIntosh came into my tent and said, "Fish, you have a crew." And I did. Initially, they all were sullen and suspicious of me. That was understandable, because their leader had quit on them. Why should they trust anyone?

But on our first mission, staging through Wakde Isle to bomb Palau, we made five runs over the target at low level before the damn bombs would release. On each run, I was scared stiff, and flew the plane with very slow movements on the controls. The crew thought I was really cool in moments of stress and, on the way home, Navigator Murray came up, put his arm around me and said. "We'll fly with you anytime." Everyone chimed in.

Of that original crew, Murray, Hammett and Bowling stayed with me most of the time, and were with me the night we were rammed by the kamikaze.

Owi

We moved to Owi in July. The brass picked it because the Japanese were hanging tough on Biak and keeping our troops off the airstrips there. The natives said Owi was "Taboo." The Japs had started a strip there but never finished it. We found out why! It was loaded with a deadly disease, tsutsugamushi fever, scrub typhus! It knocked out 25% of our guys in three weeks. Luckily, it was not as fatal a strain as in other places, but it was much more prevalent and easily caught. However, those that got it had some terrible things happen: loss of hearing, loss of visual acuity, joint problems. They knew it was carried by a tiny mite so we were all doused regularly with DDT!! Wow! How did any of us make it??

The 63rd was given a spot right on the beach to build our camp. Except for the heat, humidity, insects and the scrub typhus, it was a beautiful place with white coral sand beach, right off our tent door. Since our rations were so lousy we fished a lot, tossing weighted sticks of dynamite off the reef and picking up the stunned fish. We fried them in our mess kits in issue tropical butter that had a wax base, and they were delicious.

I was made assistant operations officer to McIntosh, and started briefing crews. Sometime in August a new crew with Lt. Tom Savage as pilot came in. Tom was the scion of the Savage Arms Co. family. He was a handsome young man, a good pilot and really eager. He begged me to let him go on a mission with his own crew; said he was ready and could do it. I had him ride with us, first, on a mission as a second copilot to give him a feel for things. Then I assigned him a mission. His nose gunner was sick so Bowling, my nose gunner, went. They never returned. Bowling was about 19, a little guy from the mountains of West Virginia. I still hear his soft hillbilly drawl and see the fuzz on his chin. Savage's plane was found on a mountain in Mindanao after we retook the Philippines.

Kingston, Landt, Hopperstadt and I tented together here. We dug a well in the soft coral sand, built a great shower using a Lister bag and lived in pure cleanliness until our water started smelling like sewage. The engineers had dug the squadron slit trench about 50 yards up grade from our camp and all sewage moved in the water table to our wells in about a month.

The Japanese bombed us a lot here, often using a small anti-personnel bomb that looked like a big black cigar and was sprayed out in clusters. One morning after a raid, one of our enlisted men found one a few feet from Doc Mott's tent. He picked it up, shook it and it exploded, killing him. I thought Doc Mott was going to need a doctor himself, he was so upset. He had a tough time.

One night, Bob Walters caught his wingtip on a parked plane during takeoff and aborted. The plane caught fire and burned. The guys aboard thought all were out but one of the crewmen, who had been in the nose, was not accounted for in the dark and died in the fire. That just about finished off Doc Mott.

Allen Clatworthy scrounged some lumber somewhere and made himself a one-man hut next to Doc Mott. Doc's tent had the only refrigerator, for medicine, and Clatworthy used to sneak a bottle of water into the fridge, then sneak it out for a cool drink. Doc never caught him.

Several times I had a ringside seat on the beach and watched Japanese bombers get shot down by my former buddies in the 418th and 421 Night Fighter squadrons. Two of them, "Pappy" Harper and "Blackie" Blackman, Pilot and R.O. from the 421st Night Fighter, landed at Owi with a bottle of booze one day to celebrate my escape from the Jap kamikaze at Davao. They both were in the RAF with me in 1941-2. They were teamed as pilot and R.Q. by the RAF in 1941 and were kept together as a team. They crashed together in Manila Bay in 1945 and their P-61 was found just a few years ago. I visited their memorial on the edge of Manila Bay in 1975. We could see Biak across the water and watched the land battles, tracers and artillery, day and night, as the infantry tried to drive the Japs from the airstrips. It was quite visual.

Bob Hope, with Jerry Colona and Francis Langford, entertained us and while we were watching them, the Japs raided us. When the red alert went off (three shots), people were diving for foxholes. Hope ran off the stage, stood out in the open and hollered, "Get the sonuva bitch – get the sonuva bitch!" He was a hell of a guy.

Our food, canned bully beef, was so awful we did all kinds of things to break the monotony of it. Johnny Landt found out that they served canned turkey at the hospital on the other side of the island. So we swiped a couple hospital robes, got in the chow line with ambulatory patients, and got servings of canned turkey. It was cooked in patties, the way our cooks served bully beef, but it looked so much like beef patties, we could not eat it.

I think what saved our sanity from the horrible food was the fresh fish we got with the dynamite sticks and the fresh bread the cooks baked every morning at 4 a.m. That was delicious! And the coffee was good. The coffee was boiled in huge kettles and we dipped it up with our mess cups. After most of it had been dipped out, there was a thick, syrupy liquid left over the grounds. I made a practice of filling my canteen with this super-coffee to take on my missions. It helped keep me awake when I had to fight sleep after hours in the air. One time, as I was dipping up some, pushing the grounds aside to get liquid, I exposed a yellow arm and claw. I pulled on it. Out came a 15-inch iguana that had fallen into the pot.

Leyte

Leyte was a hellhole; mud, rain, constant bombing and our strip at Tacloban was the ONLY strip we had operational in the Philippines. We jammed it with planes. Army, Navy and Marine, many from U.S. carriers that had been sunk by the Japanese. The Japs did everything they could to keep us from using it.

This was the toughest job I had in the war when Jim Pettus assigned me to run the strip. I think I went over two weeks without changing my clothes and with very little sleep.

I saw a lot of guys buy the farm during the war and always felt sadness for those I knew. But the time that we lost Hugh Noonan, 63rd Engineering Officer, probably hit me the most. I was working on the strip one evening. Hugh (we called him Knobby) was working in a B-24 that was parked nose to the strip when a P-38 taking off, veered and plowed right through the B-24. There was a huge explosion of fuel and Hugh came running out on fire. We doused him with seawater and sand and got the fire out, but he was horribly burned. We lay him on a stretcher, on the sand by the surf. I bent over him. He saw my face and said, "Don't worry Fish, I don't hurt." HE was worried about ME! He died about two hours in a field hospital tent.

One of the nurses said that just before he died he said, "What a lousy way to die." He was 19 years old.

One night Jim Pettus and I were on the Tacloban strip during a raid, standing beside a palm log bomb shelter. (These were built like igloos of heavy logs above ground because you could not dig a hole in the soupy Leyte mud without it filling up with water.) We heard the engine of a Jap start to howl in a dive aimed for us and Jim ordered, "Get in there Fisher." Because of courtesy training from my mother, I said, "You first, Col.," Jim hollered "Get your ass in there Fisher!" and I dropped down on my knees and crawled into the shelter with Jim right behind. The bombs went off and I began to choke for air. In the blackness, in the shelter it looked like a thousand fireflies glowing and the air was foul from cigarette smoke from a mob of guys smoking. I was STRANGLING! I crawled right back out. The hell with Japs, bombs and the Group Commander's orders.

Our group camp was about a half-mile from the end of the Tacloban strip in heavy trees and a 90mm AA battery was about 100 feet away. Because there were so many vessels in the harbor with so many guns, the Japs would make their bomb runs from land toward the strip to avoid going over all the ship flak. This put them right over our heads on their run. If they were high, the 90mm would go off and the noise would nearly break our skulls. But most of the time, they made low-level runs, and as they would pass over us, our light flak would start to shred them and their tail gunner would shoot back. One night I watched a Betty, 50 feet above me, turn into a torch and the tracers from his tail guns sprayed all through our camp.

Near the end of Tacloban Strip lay a fuel and ammo dump. When I was in charge of running the strip, I often went to the dump to get something we needed. A black engineer contingent handled stuff at the dump and I got well acquainted with a black sergeant who had a huge smile and was always ready to help with what we needed. I enjoyed knowing him. One evening the entire dump went up and fuel burned all night. The next day, we could not find a trace of the sergeant or any of his troops. I never learned his name but I will always remember his smile.

Clark Field

We moved to Clark in early March, ' 45. Col. Pettus and I flew up there from Leyte to lay out our camp and drop some supplies. I flew left seat back to Leyte and on my final approach I could see there was a severe crosswind from the right, which made it bad to land between the planes lining the sides of the strip. I set up my approach by angling in from the left so just as I flared, I straightened out and centered perfectly down the middle with no side stress on the gear. Jim said, "You fly this like a Spitfire." I had heard that before.

Jim and I had both started the war flying for the British, he with the RCAF and I with the RAF. Although he was a Bird Colonel and I, then, only a Captain, we shared a lot of feelings in common and were good friends during and long after the war until he died.

Clark was a different environment. We were back in civilization although the Japanese had really wrecked Manila and all the pre-war buildings at Fort Stotsenberg and Clark Field. And the Japanese hung tough. For several weeks after we moved in, they hid in the fields and crept in to sabotage planes. Several times, Air Force guys shot Japanese that were trying to kill us or do damage.

More than once, I saw General Kenney, in shirtsleeves, with a tool like a shovel, helping with some difficult problem setting up our bases. He was right there with his "kids" taking the same risks. I heard some Japs were flushed out of the brush and shot quite near him. I believe it.

Bill Jones, a 63rd pilot, and I found a wrecked L-3 (Piper Cub) and scrounged stuff to repair it. We worked on it for several weeks and finally got it ready. I had soloed in a J-3 Cub four years before, so I test hopped it. It flew great. Jones then took it up and totaled it when he "landed." He was not hurt, but I could have killed him.

Jones and I flew a Ferret ship on a mission to the China coast to check out Japanese radar. We were in the air 18 hours 35 minutes, from liftoff to touchdown. When we returned we had only about an hour of fuel and a damn storm socked in the field. I was flying and just squeaked in.

A lot of Japanese planes were captured here and put into flying order. I saw lots of new types, Franks, Jacks, etc. Tech units then tested them. Afterward they were destroyed. What a shame, but no one thought they would have any value. Tell it to The Confederate Air Force!

I went down toward Manila to get something for the group. I went into a transient camp to get some lunch and while standing in the chow line, a PFC in front of me turned around and there was a high school classmate. We had quite a reunion. Later, that day, I walked by another camp and, incredibly, there, another PFC, was one of my high school teachers. Again, we had a reunion. He was a very religious man, was a conscientious objector and had been assigned to a Chaplain Unit. I really liked him and we had a long talk. He took me inside the chapel and introduced me to one of his colleagues, another Chaplain's Assistant; a third coincidence for the day! The guy was Lew Ayres, a famous movie actor (Dr. Kildare). Ayres was also a conscientious objector and a most humane person. Both men have my deep admiration.

At Clark, the 63rd began to get the first black-painted planes. One was called, "OUT OF THE NIGHT." I had my picture taken by this plane.

I was really getting tired by now. Col. Pettus shipped me off to Australia for some leave, and I really got sick while I was there. When I got better,

I went back to Clark but the Doc would not let me fly. I did get a chance to check out in a P-61 with one of my night fighter buddies.

In May the Doc called me in, said Pettus had written orders for me to go home and I was to go ASAP. I traded my only two bottles of booze to a transport officer for a seat on a C-54 and went Clark-Guam-Honolulu-Hamilton Field- D&RG RR-Denver, and was home in a week.

I came down with a vicious malaria, spent most of the summer in and out of an army hospital and left the service December, 1945.

It was all a long time ago. But I never will quit living those times.

Manila Bay
Japanese Ships under attack – B-24s
Photo provided by Roland Fisher

Roland Fisher and John Kingston with Owi island fish catch.
Photo provided by R. Fisher

REMINISCENCES

In 1941, the Southwest Pacific was one of the worst places in the world just to live. And fighting a war there added to the general misery. Life, especially in the tropics of New Guinea and north to the Philippines, involved constant threat to health and hours of discomfort and boredom, punctuated by moments of choking fear with your heart in your throat and a band around your chest as you made an attack on the enemy.

Still, we were young, eternally optimistic about surviving it all and quite innovative at finding humor in the miserable environment.

1941 New Guinea was a raw world hugging the equator. It was a huge island of contrasts: the world's largest swamps ridden with disease; hundreds of square miles of mountains rising to 16,000 feet, some active volcanoes; a blanket of a rain forest of an incredible variety of old growth, giant trees on the higher lands; a mass of jungle so thick you could not see into it over the swamps, and on the drier flatlands, hundreds of acres ofkunai grass, taller than a man and made of tough blades sharper than a razor. It would rain for weeks on end then quit and we would cook in heat and humidity that was like steam.

Scores of our planes with their crews disappeared in that savage world. Sixty years later, loggers, miners and native hunters are still finding their remains and reporting them to U S Graves Registration forensic specialists who identify them and bring them home.

In all that savage environment, if one looked, there were beautiful and wondrous things to see. The structure of a giant rain forest tree fascinated me. The ten-foot wide trunk grew hundreds of feet upward before leafing out in a top that joined its neighbors, forming a canopy that shut out the light to a twilight on the floor. The soil was very thin so a tree stood on a base of wide spreading roots each with a high ridge. Every guy in the group had been issued a machete and some, being really just kids with new knives, had a habit of hacking on the tops of the roots. Enough cutting weakened the roots and, after some giants toppled in a wind and wiped out a few tents, Command issued orders for no more root hacking.

Around Dobodura, especially toward Buna, the wild life was fantastic: brilliantly colored birds, wallabies, huge insects, snakes of every size and color, and wild hogs. We were told the hogs were not realty wild; that they belonged to the natives and we were not to shoot them. But we had boiled pork a couple of times when one mess sergeant took his .45 and broke the rules. He claimed it came into his tent and "attacked" him.

Aside the risks we took on combat missions there were dozens of ways to die. Every now and then, some one would be missing from the daily activity and we would learn he had come down with a "fever". It seldom was malaria; that was understood and, because quinine was very scarce, it was suppressed with atabrine. That kept us from malaria but we all looked like we had been dipped in a yellow dye and we lived with rumors that we all would go nuts or some other gruesome end because no one knew the long term effects of atabrine.

But there were other insect transmitted illnesses for which our medics had no cure or prevention. There was a little known disease named, "Tsut-sugamushi" fever, commonly called scrub typhus. It was not common but was invariably fatal. A Fifth Air Force Flight Surgeon of another group died of it and that shook our Docs to the core. At Owi, we had many cases of it. For the first time, it was only about ten percent fatal but it made a mess out of those who got it.

There was Dengue, sometimes called "break bone fever". I, personally, can explain that name. When I came down with it at Nadzab, for three days I had severe muscle convulsions that made me feel as though my bones were breaking. For the rest of the week, I could only lie in the heat of the tent hospital, so weak I could barely move. While there, the medics brought in an airman who had been hit between the eyes with a sharp piece of shrapnel, and put him right beside me. The piece was still in there as they were afraid to operate to remove it. Every day, the docs would come and review x-rays and discuss what they should do, then decide to do nothing. He was semiconscious and would talk to me but had a really tough time. He was still there when I was discharged and I went back to see him after and was told they had flown him to Australia for brain surgery. I think of him often.

Then, there was the ever present "jungle rot**, fungi that loved to gobble all the skin from anywhere on our bodies. When some of our guys in the 63rd got bad cases on their feet and Doc Mott could not do much to help them, I decided I just did not want the stuff. So I improvised my own prevention. We all had been issued olive drab colored cans of foot powder and we could buy ankle socks from the quartermaster made of soft, white, Aussie wool. They cost 25 cents a pair. Every day, after my shower, I dumped foot powder in a new pair of socks and pulled them on my feet then put on those ugly but well fitting GI shoes. Each new day, I threw away the socks and put on a fresh pair. It cost me two bits a day and some effort but I came home from the war with perfect feet. I did get a little fungus on my scalp and still have itchy spots there. But some of the guys came home with feet that looked liked they had been badly burned.

There were other odd things that happened, that came within a few inches from putting us on the KIA list. One day, Kingston and I were sitting on our bunks facing each other in our tent at Nadzab. He had something he wanted to show me more closely so we stood up and moved toward each other. As our heads were a foot apart, a loud "THWACK" sounded in the tent wall beside us, the air between us went "PSST" and there was another "WHACK" in the wall on the other side of the tent. In each wall of the tent where the "WHACK" had sounded was a 1/4 inch hole. A single .50 slug had passed between us. We never learned where it came from.

On one mission I was briefed to fly north in the dark toward Leyte, arrive at dawn at 12,000 feet over Leyte Gulf and loiter for a short time to see what reaction we might get. It was a clear but very black night on the way up. As we approached land, in the blackness I kept seeing a faint light dead ahead and I asked the navigator what the radar showed. He said it showed land off to port. But the faint light ahead grew more visible and seemed closer. The radar still showed land off to the left but much closer. Finally, I felt so uncomfortable, I banked to the right and, in the darkness, I barely saw a large mountain top move under my left wing. We finally figured out that the radar had some how rotated 90 degrees and everything dead ahead showed 90 degrees off to the left on the scope. We finished the mission OK after that But my old color-blind, superior night vision sure kept us from splattering onto a lonely mountain top that night.

One morning, as I returned to Owi from a mission, I called Bayleaf tower for approach consent, put my engines and props in landing readiness and turned onto the base leg at about 500 feet altitude. Just as I was about to turn onto final, in my side vision, (my wonderful peripheral vision) I saw a prop spinner coming right at me. In a time span far less than I take to describe it here I pushed my nose *down* hard and looked left. In that split second a P-47 pulled *up* hard, banked left and his prop tips missed my windscreen by inches. Then I had to pull up hard to keep from diving into the water. Both my waist gunners nearly went out the side windows from the abrupt motion. Had I *not pushed down as the P-47 pulled up,* there would have been a giant fireball in the sky over Owi that morning.

There were funny things also. At Owi we were right on the beach and learned how to supplement our lousy GI food with fresh fish we stunned with explosives. John Flis, our ordnance officer, rigged up bombs for us by tying a couple sticks of dynamite to a rock with a measured fuse. When the tide was out we would light the fuse, toss them over the edge of the reef and as they sank there would be a "WHUMP" and fish of all sizes and colors would float to the surface. They were just stunned and soon would recover and dive under the water. At first we would rake in just a few before they dived back down. A Melanesian native, hired on a work crew, watched us and came over. His name was Cos. He showed us that if we dived in after a bomb went off, we could pick up far more fish because most were floating under the surface. We got so many that way, we let him take all he wanted when he left for the day.

One day we were fishing and Cos was there helping. We had just exploded a bomb and had dived in. Cos was a terrific swimmer and was way down ahead of me when suddenly he streaked past me for the surface and behind him I glimpsed a huge white body and what looked like the worlds largest jaws. I was not very far behind Cos as we went to the safety of the reef top. Cos took his fish, shook his head like "no-no" and left. That pretty much crimped our fresh fish diet.

I went on leave to Australia, from Owi with Jim Pettus and Art Mulligan. We flew down in a worn out B-25 to bring back liquor and other goodies. We crossed Geelvink Bay south over the narrow part of Western New Guinea that is like the neck of the bird and down along its breast to refuel at Merauke. The scenery was spectacular: Huge waterfalls cascading from the 15,000 high mountains into the Fty River Swamp. As we landed, a young 2nd Lt. ran out to receive us shouting, "Welcome to Merauke!" He was lonely and hungry for news and just wanted us to stay and talk. He epitomized the ennui of war being stuck in a backwater where nothing happened except the people passing through. I heard he was assigned there for over two years.

While in Australia, it was rainy and I bought a beautiful soft fabric raincoat. I liked it so much I intended to keep it for civilian use after the war. It was truly beautiful. Just before I returned to Owi, I ran into one of my night fighter buddies with whom I had flown with in England. He liked my raincoat so much he borrowed it so he could get one just like it. Time came for me to leave. He had not returned my coat and I called him at the dormitory. He said he had not had a chance to get to the clothiers but promised he would bring it to Owi in a couple days when he returned. This was OK by me as his squadron was also based at Owi, so I caught my plane. A week later I learned the plane he was returning on had crashed landed in dense swampland on the Geelvink Peninsula. After a horrendous struggle through the swamp and jungle for six weeks he and his comrades were flown back in a Catalina. Upon his return he handed me a pile of what looked like shredded rags: my raincoat. He said it had kept him alive.

When we got to Leyte, after months of living in primitive New Guinea, it was back to civilization! The villages looked like cities and the girls looked great! And wonder of wonders – out in the rice paddies there were flocks of wild ducks just like those back home where I had loved to hunt them. When we who had grown up hunting saw them, nothing held us back. We got out the squadron shotguns, put on some old GI shoes and shorts and waded out into the rice paddies. The fact that the water was bobbing with rotting Jap corpses did not hold us back. The ducks were plentiful and hunting was good. After we each had strung up a bunch of ducks we headed to camp to clean them and feast on roast duck.

As we walked in, Doc Carp and the other "medics came unglued! He started hollering, "Don't you know what you catch in those swamps? – Liver flukes! – Shistosomiasis!". We all had to disrobe while the docs went over us with with magnifying glasses and tweezers. From all the hollering I learned that a deadly parasite lurks in the swamps and waits to pounce on you. It penetrates your skin, invades your blood stream and ends up in your liver where it proceeds to devour it. I also learned that if the 'flukes have penetrated your skin you are well on your way to liverwurst. So far, 60 years later, the only damage I have had to my liver is from the bad booze I imbibe.

Bob Hope Troupe, August 1944, Owi island.
Photo provided by Roland Fisher

Trevor Bevan

"Second Battle of the Bismarck Sea"
Trevor Bevan

My crew was formed at Davis Monthan AAF, Tucson, Arizona, in March 1943. We received our training there and at two other bases in California until September 1943. We were then selected for further training at Langley AAF in the First Sea Search Attack Group. The training was in low-altitude bombing in preparation for search missions for enemy shipping and navy ships protecting them.

Crewmembers are as follows:

Capt. Trevor Bevan, Pilot, Illinois
Lt. Jack Evans, Co-Pilot, Illinois
Lt. Casey Shamey, Navigator, Pennsylvania
Lt. Steven Pazar, Bombardier, New York City (Bronx)
Sgt. John Schlitz, Flight Engineer, Milwaukee
Sgt. Ken Daugherty, Asst. Flight Engineer, Ohio
Sgt. R. Conley, Radio Operator
Sgt. David Cohen, Radar Operator, New York City
Sgt. G. Hatton, Waist Gunner, Oklahoma
Sgt. Grady, Waist Gunner, Unknown Address

Near San Francisco, California, 1944. Feeling no pain are Trevor Bevan and C. Shamey. *Photo provided by Trevor Bevan.*

Upon completion of training at Langley in January 1944, we departed for Mitchell AAF where we picked up our B-24D Bomber. We departed for the West Coast in early February 1944, and arrived at Hamilton AAF three days later. We then departed the U.S.A. for Hickam AAF Hawaii. While we were in Hawaii we saw some of the carnage the enemy did to Pearl Harbor and Hickam AAF. I thought to myself that my crew was going to get some revenge on the Japanese when we start bombing their ships. After leaving Hickam in February, we made five stops before arriving at Dobodura, New Guinea and joining the 63rd Bomb Squadron.

At Dobodura, we made several training flights before the operations officer, Capt. Craig McIntosh, said we were ready to go on combat missions. After three combat missions where we searched for enemy shipping, we ended up each time dropping our bomb load on the selected Japanese targets and returning to our base. The crew and I wondered at that time when we were going to see any enemy ships.

On March 18, we received our mission briefing from Capt. Moss, our Intelligence Officer, and departed from Dobodura at 7 p.m. on our fourth search mission. Everything was uneventful for the next few hours until we passed into the combat zone. A bright moon was shining while we cruised along at 4000 ft. when Cohen, the radar operator, called me on the intercom and said he spotted some unidentified targets, maybe 30 or 40 miles ahead. I talked to navigator Shamey and told him to get with Cohen to figure out if the targets could be shipping and if so how many and what size if possible. I took preparations to circle the targets and Shamey finally notified me that the target blobs had broken up into two large objects and three small ones. I then told the crew to prepare for attack and for bombardier Pazar to arm the bombs.

I instructed Conley, the radio operator, to make a report back to the base, which Shamey would prepare for him. I then descended the plane to 1500 ft. and circled around the target so that we could make our bombing run into the moon and make it more difficult for the ships to spot us. I told the crew we were headed for the targets and for the bombardier to pick out the largest ship. We were less that a mile from the target when numerous lights came on and, within 30 seconds, anti-aircraft fire began. As we got closer, it seemed like all hell broke loose like skyrockets on a July 4th night. Each shell from the guns seemed like it was between me and the number two engine. When the bombardier shouted, "Bombs away!" I began taking evasive action to get out of that area. When we were finally safely away from the targets, I again began circling the bomber at a safe distance from the targets. At that time an unknown member of the crew said over the intercom, "Sir, do we have to go back over those ships again?" I didn't want to, but I told the crew that we had half of our bomb load left, and we had to make another run. We did make another run, and I told the bombardier to pick a smaller target, which he did. This time we made the bomb run safely with some lights and anti-aircraft fire as before.

Note: *The onboard United Press Correspondent, Ralph Teatsorth, revealed it was Bevan who discovered the convoy originally, thereby setting the stage for the "second battle of the Bismark Sea." According to the news story in the Champaign (Illinois) News Gazette of that battle, Allied bombers and submarines destroyed 28 Japanese ships.*

ALLIES DESTROY 28 JAP SHIPS IN PACIFIC

Champaign Fliers Play Leading Roles When MacArthur Men Smash Convoy

By LLOYD HIPPENSTEELE
News-Gazette Telegraph Editor

Japan's precarious ocean supply lines throughout her mushroom empire in the Pacific dwindled away Tuesday by at least another 28 ships as Allied naval power took a heavy toll throughout the Pacific war zone.

Twenty-two of the ships were sunk by submarines – both British and American – while another five were wiped out by General MacArthur's air forces and the final one of the 28 by Admiral Nimitz' air arm in the Marshalls.

Two Champaign fliers played leading roles in the battle – Lieutenant Trevor G. Bevan, Jr., son of Mr. and Mrs. Trevor G. Bevan, 611 West Clark street, and Captain Max H. Mortensen, son of Mr. And Mrs. Henry Mortenson, 905 South Locust street.

Leads Rough Raiders

For Mortensen, it was just another battle. Time and again, he has led his "Rough Raiders" unit of Mitchell bombers into battles against such convoys as this one, wreaking havoc among Japanese supply lines.

This time, his Rough Raiders blew a corvette out of the water with a direct hit.

For Lieutenant Bevan, it made the first time he has won mention in the dispatches reaching The News-Gazette from the Southwest Pacific.

But when he *finally* broke into the cables, he did it in a big way. Because a dispatch from United Press Correspondent Ralph Teatsorth revealed it was Bevan who discovered the convoy originally, thereby setting the stage for the "second battle of Bismarck sea."

Beven Sights Convoy

"The battle started late Saturday night in a bright moonlight," Teatsorth wrote, "when Lieutenant Bevan, piloting the Liberator "Miss Liberator," located the convoy steaming from Hollandia and blasted one large merchantman, which was left sinking."

The Associated Press added that Bevan smashed the freighter with A 1000-pound bomb and navy Catalina pilots believed they had finished the ship off later during the night.

The dispatches did not wholly explain the sinking of this freighter – the official communique from General MacArthur mentioned only troop transport. It could mean the day's announced bag of Jap ships would be raised to 29.

Captain Mortensen described to Reporter Teatsorth "one of the strangest incidents of the engagement," telling how, while he was flying over the scene of another sinking – apart from the corvette his Rough Raiders had bagged – about 25 Japanese, clinging to bits of debris or bobbing on life lifejackets, started firing their pistols in a futile attempt to hit his plane.

Mortensen said the sky literally was filled with Mitchells and Bostons attacking the ships in crisscross fashion, with wave after wave roaring in just above the top of the masts, each trying to outdo the other units in a race for the targets.

"We raced another outfit for a ship and got there first," he explained. "We strafed them and then feinted to get the ship position for other Mitchells.

Dobodura, New Guinea, 1944. Relaxing in our tent – T. Bevan, S. Pazar and J. Evans

On the return flight to our base I don't remember much crew conversation, but I did tell them all that they did an excellent job, and to think about what they observed so we could make a good debriefing when we returned. It was early morning when we landed at our base in Dobodura. The first place we checked with was the Flight Surgeons office for our shot of old "overalls" as we called Old Overholt rye whiskey. Several of the crewmembers didn't like rye whiskey so they gave me their ration voluntarily, I noted. Then we were de-briefed by Capt. Moss and turned over as a group to be interviewed by reporters from Associated Press and United Press. They took our picture and made us feel like celebrities.

The next day the crew members came to my tent and relayed to me the information that the check of our B-24 revealed an unexploded 20-caliber shell had stuck in the floor beneath the radio operator's seat. Needless to say, we were all shocked and very happy to have returned safely to home base. Of course, the radio operator, Conley, was the most happy "fella" of all, but I wonder now if that might of foretold of his tragic end in the aircraft accident at Owi Island when he took the flight to make up for lost time when he was on sick leave.

We made other combat missions where we made contact with the enemy and received return fire, but the alternate targets that were hot spots for my crew were in Palau Island and especially Manila, Nichols Field in the Philippines. We came cruising into Nichols Field after midnight at 5000 ft. and received lights galore, and it seemed like the whole city was firing at us. I wanted to get out of that area and never return. I learned from that attack that there were no milk runs or easy targets.

After my crew and I completed our combat missions and we were waiting on returning to the USA, I was notified by Capt. Albert Brownfield CO, 63rd Bomb SQD. that I was going TDY back to Nadzab, New Guinea, to help train Australian pilots to fly the B-24. It was more or less a favor to the CO and I didn't complain too much then. It developed that I was at Nadzab for almost two months. The Aussie pilots were nice guys, but they didn't like to follow procedures like using checklists and radio communications terminology. When they were ready to solo, I got out of the aircraft. I was told one day by Operations to pretend the flight was a combat mission for the Aussies. All went well in our flight to the target at Rabaul, a former hot spot months previously, when I happened to look out the side window and saw puffs of smoke. Well, I knew what that was and took evasive action to get out of there. Hell, I was finished with combat.

I took immediate action to get a flight back to Clark Field. I did get to fly a P-47 for one hour at Nadzab. I was scared to death, but my aviation cadet buddy was the operations officer and shamed me into it. On my return, I was requested to share a tent with Capt. Brownfield and Capt. Larry Kottal. At that time there was no sign of a C-54 on the horizon to return to the USA. Capt. Brownfield said he needed a pilot for a secret mission to fly 10 P-38 fighter pilots to Hickam, pick up P-38's and to escort them back to Clark AAF.

This was to prove that it would get the P-38's back to combat areas faster than they had been coming by boats. Larry Kottal was waiting on a flight so he volunteered to be the co-pilot with me and Lt. Nelson came along as navigator. The first stop was Guam, then Johnston Island and on to Hickam. We were there over a week until the P-38's were ready, and then we took off for Canton Island. Boy, the fighter jocks in the new P-38's really gave us, in the B-24, buzz jobs. They stayed with us a while until they were receiving radio compass signals and then took off for Canton Island. The rest of the ferry flight was into Tarawa Island, Palau Island and then Clark AAF in the Philippines. All told this ferry mission, in my memory, took approximately 17 days.

I finally got on a C-54 transport for a return to the good ole USA sometime in late March 1945. When I arrived back in Champaign, one of the war mementos my mother gave to me was the local newspaper clipping of my crew's combat mission of March 19, 1944, as reported by a United Press correspondent. My mother also gave me a letter she received on August 6, 1944, from General George C. Kenney, about that combat mission.

December 7, 1941

I had finished my freshman and part of my sophomore year at the University of Illinois when, at the urging of my best friend who was being drafted, I enlisted in the U.S. Army Air Corps on May 20, 1941. As luck would have it, my friend was sent to Chanute AAF, Illinois for aircraft mechanic training, and I was sent to Scott AAF, Illinois for radio communications training. Chanute is close to my home town of Champaign, Illinois. The communications course was for eight and a half months, and while I was there I also decided that I would rather be an officer and become a pilot. I then made an application for flight training and was accepted and told that I would hear at a later date when I would enter training.

I graduated from radio operator training on December 5, 1941, and went home to Champaign on two weeks leave. My orders assigned me to the 1st observation group located at Candler Field at Atlanta, Georgia. On Sunday, December 7, I was having noonday lunch with my parents and also listening to news on the radio when an announcer broke in saying that Japanese warplanes were attacking Pearl Harbor. My parents and I were absolutely stunned at this news, and they were now unhappy because I was going into flight training because they felt I would be safer as a radio operator in a war. They eventually calmed down and said they were happy for me. Now my problem was wondering what to do and whether I should report to my new assignment in Georgia or complete my leave time at home and then depart. I finally decided to wait; the air corps knew where I was and would call me if I was needed.

I reported in to my new assignment on December 21, just in time to be put on guard duty. No one seemed worried that I could be called at any time to report for pre-flight cadet training. The next day everyone was told to pack their bags and be ready for departure to God knows where. We were all loaded on a train on December 22 and we arrived on December 24 in New Orleans. We were bunked at Camp Jackson until the following week. While there I decided to check in with the camp commander. I told him my story, and he said that the powers that be would notify me when they were ready.

The next day we were all loaded on a troop transport ship, and I believe it was approximately a week later that we docked on the Pacific side of the Panama Canal Zone.

Our group was assigned to Howard Field in Panama. In May my orders arrived assigning me to Maxwell AAF for pre-flight cadet training. I was finally on my way and graduated from training as an officer and was assigned to B-24 bomber training at Davis-Monthan AAF in February 1943.

B-24 artwork, Clark Field, 1945.
Photo provided by Fred Peters

Frank
C.
Kotouch

A Voice From Out of the Past
Frank C. Kotouch

On a pleasant Sunday evening this summer, June 22, 1969 to be exact, I was relaxing at home about 9 p.m. when I received an unusual phone call. The caller asked if he was talking to Frank Kotouch, and after I assured him that he had the right party, he identified himself as Robert (Bob) Allen of Victoria, Australia. I was somewhat confused, as I knew no one in Australia. He then asked me if I recalled a day in July, 1945, in the South Pacific. I told him I surely did remember certain events that took place 24 years ago.

To tell the story properly, I must turn back the pages of time to the summer of 1945. I was a S/Sgt. with a B-24 Bomber Squadron called 868th *Snoopers*. Some of you old timers will recall we were one of two bomb squadrons equipped with radar for night bombing at that time. You may also recall that all of our dozen or so planes were painted a dull black with "S" on the tail. The black color was to help us evade enemy searchlights during our night bombing raids.

One of my regular crew members and I had missed a regular mission, so we had signed the extra list for a make-up mission. This was to enable us to complete the same number of missions as our regular crew so that we would end our tour of duty the same time as they did. This particular flight we were chosen for was of a routine nature, but long in terms of distance and flying time. Being a "Good Joe," our regular pilot Eugene "Gus" Maggioncalda came to the briefing with us, and when he heard the flight plan, he jokingly said, "You'll never make it, I'll be out looking for you guys in the morning."

Our take off time was late afternoon of July 24, 1945, and as we were boarding the truck to take us to the flight line the co-pilot of this crew spotted me and said, "It looks like this will be a rough one, here comes my jinx." He and I were not the best of friends, mainly because during baseball games we couldn't ever agree on any of the rules. The co-pilot, Jack Counts (Bluefield, W. Va) was a little hot tempered and so was I, so many times we were at each other's throats over a called strike, safe on base, etc. Anyway, I didn't choose his crew, it was just that they needed two men to complete the crew, so "Ace" Kupperman (Omaha) and I were it.

This mission was mainly to harrass the Imperial Japanese Forces, keep them awake, and wear down their resistance so that the Australian Forces could have it a little easier during the coming invasion of the Island of Borneo in the Celebes Sea. We carried small 100 lb. bombs and were supposed to drop one every half hour, coming from different directions to confuse the enemy. During one of those passes, we lost our #4 outboard engine, either from malfunction or small arms fire, no one knows for sure. This created a problem as we still had bombs to drop and the fuel mixture would have to be changed to enable the remaining three engines to operate correctly. The officers of the crew decided to complete the bombing on the next run and release the remaining few bombs and head for our base (Moratai) which was a long way off.

Due to the increased fuel consumption, we began to run out of gas far short of home base. Around 2 a.m. July 25th the #1 engine quit due to lack of fuel, so we had two inboards left for a short time. The radio operator sent the May Day signal and our position. The crew decided to "ditch" the plane into the ocean until a weather report said there were 8-10 ft. swells and without full power we would break up on impact. Therefore it was decided to abandon the aircraft by parachute at 2:30 a.m. It was dark and by moonlight it was observed by some of us that all 11 of the personnel on the plane got out and their chutes opened. Incidentally, none of us had ever had a parachute jump; not even a simulated one, let alone one over the water at 2:30 a.m.

Although at the time it was nightmarish, looking back now, some things almost seem humorous. We all had our life jackets and individual seat pack rafts with the parachutes. I had my 45 cal. revolver in a shoulder holster but neglected to tie it down. When my chute opened, the 45 struck me in the jaw and almost knocked me out. The coolness of the Pacific quickly revived me as I hit the water. I immediately inflated the "Mae West" life jacket, and then I inflated the life raft. I attempted to climb aboard but could not. Visualize what it is like trying to stand up in a hammock. Well, after numerous attempts and near misses, plus lungs full of dirty green Pacific, I finally managed to get into the raft, and then I became violently ill. Seasick is the word, I believe. While I was recuperating from shock and swallowing water, I heard cries for help and then the sound of a shot. I paddled towards the sounds in the darkness, but to no avail, just water and darkness.

I just rested and floated until dawn, then I saw a yellow speck off to my right. It would disappear and then reappear due to the swell of the waves. I began paddling with my hands towards the object. After what seemed like hours, I got within shouting distance and began to be encouraged. A little while later I was able to recognize the occupant of the other raft. Guess who it was? Jack, from Bluefield, West Virginia, my friendly enemy, and me his "Jinx" together in the middle of the big Pacific. We decided to bury the hatchet, (not in each other's heads). We took turns keeping watch and kept up each other's spirits during times when we thought rescue was not possible. While drifting along, we spotted a motor launch heading our way. Our hopes were up and rescue seemed sure. It turned out to be a Japanese launch and for some unknown reason it abruptly made a sharp turn away from us and disappeared over the horizon.

Numerous planes were spotted all that day, because we were on the invasion route to Borneo, but we must have drifted off the direct course, and and the planes didn't see us or did not get a reflection from our signal kit. Nighttime was hectic, due to the fact it got chilly and the spray from the waves didn't make it any too cozy. Jack and I took turns napping during the night and held the hand rings of each other's rafts to make sure we didn't drift apart. The following day, the 26th of July, was a repeat of the days before, more planes sighted, more disappointment when they didn't see us. It was getting on in the afternoon when we spotted a plane low on the horizon in front of us. At first we thought it was of Japanese origin the way it was coming in low and straight on. We thought, "This is it, we're going to be strafed like animals, so we both held hands and said our prayers. At the last moment the plane veered off in a gentle upswing, showing the Royal Australian Air Force marking, and the pilot was signaling the Universal OK with his fingers. We were overjoyed to the point of tears when he signaled that help was on the way. Shortly, one of our Navy's PBY Patrol Planes appeared, circled and attempted to land. But, because of high seas, and the danger of the plane breaking up in a water landing, they signaled that a surface craft was on its way, having been diverted from the invasion route to Borneo. We found out later that U.S. Navy and Air Force were supporting the Australian Invasion Forces.

Later that afternoon, between 4 and 6 p.m. we saw a whiff of smoke on the horizon. It turned out to be the destroyer USS Bailey. As it apporoached us, we could see the deck lined with sailors, and one of them yelled with a megaphone that they would toss ropes to us and not to reach for them for fear of falling out of the rafts, but to wait till one or more fell across our rafts. Sure enough, many of them landed on us and we were pulled to the side of the ship. Sailors galore were at the water level on boarding nets to snatch us from the rafts and hoist us hand over hand to the swaying deck. Being an Air Force land lubber and cramped in that raft for approximately 40 hours, I didn't have my sea legs and promptly fell to the deck when left alone for a second.

They gathered us up, helped us to their Officer's Quarters where we had a shower. They laundered our clothes and fed us a soft diet during a brief interrogation. We learned there were five survivors of the 11 on board the plane. "Ace" was not one of them. After being shown about the ship and treated to a practice Evasive Action Display and gunnery practice, we were transferred by boatswain chair to an L.S.T. This was another first for us and it was scary as well as a new experience. We slept overnight on the L.S.T. until sometime the next day when we arrived at our base and were immediately hospitalized for three days for exposure and shock.

Ironically enough, the statements of my regular pilot "Gus" commenting that he would come looking for us almost happened except that our Commanding officer wouldn't release our crew because of other commitments. Later, our forces searched for weeks, maybe months, but to no avail and the other six crew members were given up as lost.

Now back to the present time. Yes, this distinctly British-type voice on the phone was that of Robert (Bob) Allen, the pilot of the Australian Spitfire that spotted us in the Pacific so many years ago. He said he had wondered on many occasions whatever became of the "blokes" he had sighted that day? He said he wanted to look us up if he ever came to the United States. However, he had only made it as far as Canada on business so he contacted the War Department in Washington, D.C. giving them the time, date and place of rescue. They in turn, gave him the names of the five survivors. He said he was unable to contact the others. He was glad to hear that I was alive and well. He gave me his address in Australia and I have written to him about all the facts before and after and up to the present date.

As I am preparing this report, it is November 11, 1969, my 44th birthday. Fate works in strange ways. Here I am owing 24 years of my life to a man I saw for a brief moment. I often ask myself where would I be if this unknown man had not taken the time to investigate and relay an SOS. I will be grateful to him for the rest of my life.

The Rest of the Story

It is 24 more years later. It is now Veterans Day, November 11, 1993. I read this story at our Coffee Hour at Francis One Mobile Estates in Sebring, Florida, where we spend six months a year since I retired. I still say the Good Lord must have had a place for me in this life. My wife Dorothy and I together have five children, 15 grandchildren, and six great-grandchildren. All because this voice from the past made it possible to bring this all together for the future.

Frank C. Kotouch, Sr.

As I am writing this little memo, America is celebrating the 50th anniversary of the ending of World War II and the victory in Europe and victory over Japan. This year, July 25, 1995 is the anniversary of my little story and tale of my contribution to that war in the Southwest Pacific. I hope you will read it, understand it, and pass it on to your sons, (daughters also if they would like), I wrote it many years ago and have updated the ending until now I shall say – "The End of the Story."

We World War II folks, men and women, were born during the roaring 20s, endured the great depression, learned the value of honest hard work, and took to heart the blessings of living in a free nation. We gave up the joys of youth for the sake of our country, trading the comforts of home for the horrors of the battlefields. We left the peaceful civilian life for a dangerous, uncertain future in uniform. In the Old Testament, Genesis 6:4 says in part, "There were giants in the earth in those days . . . mighty men which were of old men of renown." When the time came for service, and the day called for courage and the hour required sacrifice, a generation of Americans – chosen of God or fate, stepped forward to save our country and the other free nations of the world. So, always remember the Americans who gave their lives so that you and I may continue to live in peace and freedom, for those are indeed, "Giants in the Earth."

So I say to you now . . . "Nobody Lives Forever." That's what makes us so special. We are temporary. Our lives are on loan to us. Just for awhile, and nobody knows how long each life will be. That's why we have to take care of each other, and remember every day, to appreciate the ones we love.

Your Dad, Grandfather and Great-Grandfather,

Frank C. Kotouch, Sr.

Kneeling front row: Sherl Hendricks (Red)*, Lawrence (Wally) Wallatka, Frank Kotouch, Sr.*, Don Callison*.*Standing:* Kupperman ("Ace"), Cleve Stout, Bob Stephey, Earl Helms, Douglas Dean*, Jack Counts*. *Engineeer in picture, name unknown.* Gestalser not pictured. Mission incomplete – bailed out 2:30 am July 25, 1945.

*Rescued. Balance M.I.A.

Photo provided by Frank Kotouch.

Edward G. Harris

Not Yet 18 on December 7
Edward G. Harris

I was born and attended elementary and high schools in the small East Tennessee town of Morristown. At the age of 17, I entered the University of Tennessee in Knoxville in the fall term of 1941. I majored in Electrical Engineering. In December of my freshman year our country entered the war. I finished my freshman year and worked during the spring and fall quarters as a co-op student at the Aluminum Company of America in Alcoa, TN. Between the summer and fall quarters at the university I hitchhiked to Corsicana, Texas to see my brother who was an Aviation Cadet. Then I continued on to visit another friend in the Air Force at Midland, Texas. My brother became a pilot in the Troop Carrier Command of the Fifth Air Force. Later we had a chance to see each other at Nadzab and Biak in 1944.

On December 8, 1942, about a year after we entered the war, I went to the army recruiting office in Knoxville and enlisted; I was 18 at the time. On December 11, I was put on a train for Camp Forrest in Tullahoma, TN, and my three-year military career had begun.

I clearly remember Sunday, December 7, 1941. I was home for the weekend visiting my family in Morristown when we heard on the radio the news of the bombing of Pearl Harbor. I rode back to the university that afternoon with one of my few friends who owned a car. Between news reports on the car radio we talked about the war and how it would affect us. We agreed that it was a very foolish thing that the Japanese had done. We knew that the Japanese were weak little guys who lived on fish heads and couldn't shoot straight. We thought the war would be over in a few months. Only later did we learn of our terrible losses at Pearl Harbor. One of our friends was to die in the Philippines.

Our Crew

I was assigned to a crew at Langley Field, Virginia. The members were:

Brownfield, Albert W.	Pilot
Koglin, Melvin E.	Co-pilot
Kriete, Richard A.	Bombardier
Bloch, Ira J.	Navigator
Bickford, Henry K. Jr.	Engineer
Edw. G. Harris	Radar Operator
Sedilko, Alex	Radio operator
Clausen, William H.	Armorer, waist gunner
Sloan, Robert T.	Waist gunner
Simon, Paul R.	Tail gunner

There was a tenth member of the crew named Musica who was an assistant radio operator and (I think) ball turret gunner. The ball turret was replaced by the radar antenna on the planes we flew. Musica was removed from the crew and I, the radar operator, replaced him. Our crew was more experienced than most. Both the pilot and bombardier had been instructors and held the rank of Captain. The engineer had also been an instructor and held the rank of Tech-Sgt. The radio operator had already completed a tour of duty flying in the south Pacific, returned to the U.S. where he served as an instructor and was now going back for a second tour; he was a Tech-Sgt. The co-pilot and navigator were 2nd Lts., and Clausen, Sloan, Simon and myself were Sgts. I had forgotten the first names of most of the crew, but after the first version of this chapter was written, I heard from a pilot I had flown with and he had the names. We always addressed each other by last names. The final member of the crew was a small female dog of uncertain parentage named Dingy. We got her as a puppy at Langley and she stayed with us until run over by a truck on the island of Angaur. When we were flying, Dingy often rode inside my leather jacket with her nose sticking out.

We were being trained for low altitude (between one and two thousand feet) night bombing of shipping by radar. We flew in four-engine B-24 heavy bombers called Liberators. We could pick up ships from as far away as 50 or 100 miles on the radar. I would give the pilot the bearing and distance to the target and continue giving directions until we were 10 miles away, and the target appeared on the bombardier's radar screen. From then on the bombardier essentially flew the plane until the bombs were dropped. This required close cooperation between radar operator and bombardier, so Kriete and I worked together on a trainer before we started training flights. There were some radar targets in Chesapeake Bay that we made our bomb runs on. Usually radar and bombardier instructors would go along. One difficulty we had was that the pilot had difficulty understanding my directions because I said "rite" instead of "right." Once I called out "ten degrees left," and he asked was that "ten degrees left?" I replied "that's rite." We missed the target.

After we completed our training, we had short furloughs home. Brownfield invited the crew to a party at his apartment in Hampton, Virginia and I got drunk for the first time in my life. We were assigned a plane and started the long flight to the South Pacific. We left around September 1, 1944.

We took the trip in short hops. We had stops at Dyersburg, Tenn., some field in Texas and Fairfield-Suisan airbase in California where I think we spent about two days. I remember going into Sacramento. Next, we flew to Honolulu where we spent a couple of days. Our radio operator, Sedilco, had been at Pearl Harbor when the Japanese attacked in 1941, and he showed the enlisted men around. Our next stop was the small island of Canton. It was memorable for the bedbugs in the mattresses assigned to us. Also I got an infection in the corner of one eye which swelled until the eye was almost closed. I could not get it treated until we got to Guadalcanal. Our next stop was Tarawa, the scene of one of the bloodiest battles of the war. I remember we went walking on the beach and picked up what we thought was a discarded shoe. The bones of a foot were inside. Next was Guadalcanal where I got my eye treated. We flew from there to Townsville, Australia.

Townsville in northeastern Australia looked very much like a town of our old west familiar from cowboy movies. I think we must have spent about two weeks there. Some of the other enlisted men and I rented horses and rode around the countryside. The plane we left in was not the same one we had flown across the Pacific.

Our next stop was Nadzab, New Guinea. I found to my delight that the APO number of Nadzab was that of my brother, Ted. Ted was a pilot in the Troop Carrier Command and had gone to the South Pacific some months before I did. We had no idea where his squadron was located, but Sedilco and I started hitchhiking and asking people and finally found him. He was surprised when we walked in. I think we were in Nadzab for about two days, then we flew on to our destination, Owi Island.

It may be helpful if I try to describe in words the geography of this part of the South Pacific. New Guinea is a large island (second largest in the world) shaped rather like a lizard and stretched out above Australia with its tail in the southeast and its head in the northwest. Above the head is the starfish-shaped island of Halmehera with the island of Morotai at its top. The Philippine Islands are north of Halmehera and Morotai, and to the east is the Celebes, a bigger starfish-shaped island, and farther east the big island of Borneo. North of the Philippines is the island of Formosa (now called Taiwan), and north of that is the China coast. This is the region I fought in during the war.

East of the neck of the New Guinea lizard is Geelvink Bay. In this bay are the islands of Biak, Japen and Noemfoor. We had taken Biak and Noemfoor from the Japanese in May and June of 1944. A mile or so off the south coast of Biak is the small coral island of Owi which was to be our home for about the next two months. It was here that our crew joined the 63rd Squadron (SeaHawks) of the 43rd Bomb Group. Owi was less than 100 miles south of the equator, but I do not remember it as being terribly hot. We set up our tents (one for the six enlisted men and one for the four officers) and built some crude furniture out of scrap lumber and bomb boxes. We were issued army cots and mosquito netting. We dug a well beside our enlisted men's tent and hit brackish water about 8 or 10 feet down. We could use the water for showers, washing our clothes and cooling beer on the rare occasions when we had some. The ocean was only about 100 yards away. We spent much of our spare time in the water. Generally, we wore very few clothes. Most of the time the food was terrible, but occasionally a plane would make the trip to Australia for fresh meat, eggs and vegetables and we would feast for a few days. Altogether, it was a fairly comfortable existence.

We all carried 45 caliber pistols in shoulder holsters when we flew. It occurred to us that we might have to use them some day, so we enlisted men went to what we thought was a deserted part of the beach to practice our marksmanship. We threw a can into the water and blazed away. Soon a very irate major came splashing through the surf to the beach. He and a nurse had been horsing around on an air mattress beyond the surf line where we had not seen them. He claimed we had almost shot them and he would see that we were punished. He ordered us to turn ourselves in to our squadron first sergeant. I do not remember whether he took our names, but if he did, I am sure we gave fictitious names. We decided the first sergeant probably had enough problems already, so we did not turn ourselves in. After all, how did we know if he was a real major; he was not wearing any insignia. Nothing ever came of this.

One of the first nights we were on Owi, I was awakened by a loud explosion. I thought a bomb had gone off just outside the tent. I ran out and jumped in the well. It turned out that it was an anti-aircraft gun sounding the alarm for an air raid. It was a false alarm. I think we got alarms when the raids were actually on nearby Biak.

On one occasion I climbed down the ladder into our well to get a beer. At the bottom I encountered a monitor lizard about two feet long. The lizard and I reached the top of the ladder in a dead heat and ran off in opposite directions.

The first combat mission we flew was to the port of Ambon on the island of Amboina which lies between New Guinea and the Celebes. We flew west from Owi over Geelvink Bay, then crossed a narrow neck of New Guinea into McCluer Gulf and on to Amboina. This was a short and easy mission (a "milkrun.") I think new crews were usually assigned easy first missions. We were to look for ships in the harbor and bomb any we found. We did not find any, so we bombed a secondary land target. Bombing land targets by radar is very inaccurate. It was an uneventful mission.

Since we flew at night, we usually left in the late afternoon and returned in the morning. We did not not want to be over enemy-held territory in the daylight. Before leaving we were briefed by the squadron operations officer, intelligence officer and weather officer. On our return we were debriefed about what actions we had taken, what we had observed and the weather conditions. Then the flight surgeon gave us a stiff shot of whiskey and we were told to go to bed. Sometimes I gave my whiskey to another crew member.

Shortly after I saw Ted in Nadzab he went to Sidney, Australia on furlough. Then his squadron moved to Biak. I managed to hitch a ride on a boat over to see him. He had about completed his tour of duty and left for the U.S. shortly after this visit.

Sometime in October we were given an intelligence lecture concerning the invasion of the Philippines and the move of our squadron there. On October 20, 1944 American troops landed on Philippine Island of Leyte.

I do not remember or have any record of where we flew to during October. My letters home were heavily censored. I am sure most of our flights must have been to the Philippines in support of the action there. I flew some missions with other crews. Crews that had missing members due to sickness or whatever would borrow from other crews. Also there was a "Ferret Detachment" in our squadron whose job it was to search for enemy radar stations. They had a plane in which the bomb racks had been removed and the bomb bay filled with electronic equipment. They flew with borrowed crews. I flew several missions with them. These were usually long flights. The longest I remember was about 18 hours.

In November 1944 we staged out of Morotai. We would fly to Morotai, fly one or two missions from there and then return to Owi. This put us closer to enemy targets. Morotai had been taken by our forces in September 1944. There were still Japanese troops on the island but they had been pushed back into the jungle and cut off from supplies. Most of the night we could hear artillery bombarding their positions. We all slept with our pistols close by to guard against infiltrators. Often we shared a tent with another crew. One man from each crew would spend the night in the plane to guard against infiltrators. This had tragic consequences for one crew with which we shared a tent. During an air raid their plane was destroyed and their crewman killed. Our new friends were deeply depressed by the loss of their friend and comrade-in-arms. When it was my time to spend the night in the plane, I would take our dog, Dingy, along for company. We never had a bomb raid on these nights.

One night we were in an outdoor movie when a Japanese plane came over strafing. He had sneaked in unobserved, and no air raid warning had been sounded. He came over at tree top level and we could see the tracers from his guns. They all went over our heads and none of us were hit. After this the alarm was sounded and the anti-aircraft batteries opened up on other attacking planes. I saw one or more planes caught in searchlight beams. When this happens all the anti-aircraft guns concentrate on the plane in the beam. I was to remember this later when our plane was caught by searchlights over Taipei. I think one of the planes may have been hit, but generally the anti-aircraft fire was very inaccurate.

The most exciting mission flown by our crew was while I was in the hospital in Finschafen. It was the first mission with Orion Rogers as pilot. Shortly after takeoff from Clark field, a red alert was sounded and every searchlight in the valley converged on them. The sky was full of tracers shortly thereafter. They were not allowed to land on the macadam runway. They put a few smudge pots on each side of a nearby field and directed them to it. They made it down O.K., and when they landed they counted 20 holes in the plane, some of them quite large. The automatic cutoff cables to two of the engines had been severed, but luckily more critical controls were not damaged. None of the crew were injured. Orion polled the crew, and they all agreed they would fly again the next night. I wonder how I would have voted!

One of our missions from Morotai was to the oil fields at Balikpapan, Borneo. A large force of heavy bombers had hit it during the day, and we were sent at night. As I have remarked, radar bombing is not very effective over land. The best we could do was to fly to the right spot on the coast and drop our bombs when we had flown the right number of miles past the coast line. I think we carried napalm bombs and were trying to set the oil fields on fire. I doubt if we did much damage, but I think other crews flying night bombing missions were more successful.

On another mission from Morotai, we flew to Brunei Bay on the northwest coast of Borneo looking for ships. I picked up one on the radar and we made a bomb run. The gunners said that they could see from the flash of the explosions that it was a destroyer, and that we had bracketed it with bombs on either side and perhaps one on deck. The bombardier and I both thought it looked like a good run. Later I did not find it on the radar screen. We were given credit for having sunk a destroyer. There is really no way of being sure at night. Air crews are always prone to overestimate their results.

One morning as we returned to Morotai from a mission we flew through a storm and were out of radio contact. Then, as we flew over the harbor at Morotai, the anti-aircraft batteries on land and on the ships opened up on us. It turned out that there had been an air raid just before we arrived, and the gunners thought we were another enemy bomber, although the Japanese never had a plane that remotely resembled a B-24. Fortunately, they discovered their error before they shot us down. In all the missions I flew I can only remember three times that we were shot at and this was one of them. One of these times we got a small hole in the tail of the plane, but I cannot remember which time it was.

Our squadron was supposed to move to the airbase at Tacloban on the island of Leyte in the Philippines as soon as space was available. This base had been taken soon after the invasion on October 20. It took some time for space to become available, since the base was needed for fighters and short range bombers that supported the ground fighting. As a result our squadron was fragmented during December. Part of the squadron was on Owi. Some of the support personnel went to Tacloban. My crew and some others with our planes went to Angaur in the Palau Islands. These islands lie about 500 or 600 miles east-south-east of Tacloban and are closer to the Philippines than Owi. Our troops had invaded them in September 1944. Some of the bloodiest fighting in the war was the battle for Peleliu, one of the Palaus. It is now generally regarded to have been an unnecessary battle as the Palaus were of little strategic value.

Angaur was a small island with many caves. There were still Japanese on the island hiding in the caves. I did not know that when I first arrived and took a solitary hike around the island without carrying my pistol. One night the men in a tent near us woke up and found a Japanese soldier in the tent in the act of stealing all he could carry. I am sure they were hungry, for we were too. Food was neither plentiful nor appetizng here. There were a lot of very large fruit bats here, but they apparently were not nocturnal for we saw them flying around at all times of day. There was a beach where the surf was good, and we spent some of our leisure hours body surfing. This was not a sandy beach and if you were not careful you could be thrown into jagged coral. After the war I read about the Palau Islands and found that the surrounding ocean had many poisonous water snakes.

The fighting for the Philippines was going on at this time, so most of our targets were in and around the Philippines. I remember one mission to Manila Bay. We found a ship in the harbor and made a bomb run. Unfortunately, the bombardier's radar did not work, and I had to guide us to the target and call for the release of the bombs using my radar. This is not a good way to bomb. I am sure we did not even come close. We had been apprehensive about this mission because the night before one of our planes had flown to Manila and had not returned. It turned out that our mission was uneventful. Later we learned that the plane on the night before had engine trouble and landed safely at Tacloban.

Our troops invaded the Philippine island of Mindoro on December 15, 1944. We were sent on a mission to look for a Japanese fleet that was sailing toward Mindoro to attack the invaders. We found the fleet and made a bomb run on one of its ships. They were expecting to be attacked, and as we made our run they took evasive action, and their anti-aircraft fired on us. I am sure we missed and think they missed us, but this may have been the time we got a minor hit in the tail.

Another mission flown from Angaur took us over the island of Cebu in the west central Philippines. There was a pattern on the radar screen that I had difficulty interpreting. As I was puzzling over the pattern, there was a lot of excited shouting over the intercom – something about trees. The strange pattern was due to a mountain that we had very nearly flown into. The waist gunners could see trees flashing past the window. I do not recall the crew being angry with me for almost letting us run into a mountain, but they should have been.

Some time during the fall I was promoted to Staff Sgt. and a little later to Tech. Sgt. This was the highest rank the radar operator was supposed to have. The engineer, radio operator and radar operator were Tech. Sgts. and the armorer and gunners were Staff Sgts.

We spent Christmas and New Years on Angaur. Somehow we got something intoxicating – it may have been rum and got drunk. Mother sent me a Christmas package, but it did not catch up with me until March.

In early January 1945 we moved to the Tacloban airbase. I think Leyte has one of the world's highest rainfalls. Our squadron area was a rather swampy place. We dug a well beside our tent to get water for showers and hit water at about a foot and a half. After some argument among the enlisted men on the crew, Sedilko got mad, built himself a house next door and moved out of the tent. I thought it was a rather cleverly built house constructed from old bomb boxes, palm fronds and mosquito netting.

I think I only flew one mission from Tacloban. I see from the letters I wrote home and mother saved that I had flown about 300 combat hours. My total for the time I was overseas was about 430, so I was well over half way through and entitled to a furlough in Sydney, Australia.

About this time our squadron commander, Major Sergeant, was killed in an accident as their plane was taking off from Owi. Our pilot, Brownfield, was made squadron commander. Because of this he could not accompany us on furlough. We left on January 26 for two glorious weeks in Sydney. Sedilko had a scheme for extending our stay in Sydney. Our plane stopped in Brisbane. We were to miss our flight the next day and take the train from Brisbane to Sydney. Since we were not on the flight we would not be checked in at Sydney and our names would not be put on the list for the return flight. We tried this, but it did not work. Years later I read an account of his experiences by Kent Zimmerman, a pilot in our squadron. He tried essentially the same scheme and it worked for him.

Sydney was a beautiful city. It was great to eat steaks and fresh eggs and vegetables and fruit and drink milk and to sleep in a real bed with sheets and not to worry about someone shooting you or dropping a bomb on you. But the best thing about Sydney was the girls. They were lovely and charming and eager to go out with American servicemen. Most of the Australian young men were off fighting the war. I dated several lovely girls in Sydney. I had never been much of a ladies' man, but I found myself quite popular with the girls in Sydney. Clausen and I had a room in a private home where the lady of the house would fix us a good breakfast at whatever time we got up. Bickford and Sedilko had an apartment nearby. I forget where Sloan and Simon stayed, but it was not far off.

Finally, our furlough was over and we flew back to Tacloban. I think I began to feel sick as soon as we returned. I remember a group of friends were drinking in Sedilko's house. I contributed a bottle of cherry brandy that I had brought back from Sydney. (Liquor was in short supply, and you took whatever you could get.) I did not drink anything because I was feeling so bad. One of the men there was Kingsbury, a navigator from another crew. Once he went outside to relieve himself in the bushes. Kingsbury was tall, and Sedilko's house had a low roof. As Kingsbury returned he banged his head on the roof and fell backward, ripping the door from its hinges and almost pulling the house down. We all thought it was funny.

Over the next few days I felt worse and worse. I would start for the mess hall for a meal, but as soon as I got close enough to smell the food I would become nauseated and turn back. I went to the dispensary, but tried to time my visits so as to miss the flight surgeon and avoid being sent to the hospital. A medical corpsman said he thought it was dengue fever and gave me some pills. One day I was put on garbage detail. Under the best of circumstances it is unpleasant shoveling stinking garbage into and out of a stinking garbage truck. Always since then whenever I have had unpleasant work to do, I have told myself that it is not as bad as working on a stinking garbage truck with hepatitis.

A few days later my eyes turned yellow, and I felt so bad that I saw the flight surgeon. He said that I had infectious hepatitis and sent me to the hospital. Eventually, about half the squadron got hepatitis. In the hospital they fed me intravenously, and in a few days I felt that I had recovered. When the doctor told me I would be leaving, I thought I would be returning to the squadron. I was disappointed when he told me I would be evacuated to a hospital in Finschhafen, New Guinea. The hospital in Tacloban was expecting casualties from the fighting in Luzon and Okinawa.

I was loaded onto a hospital ship. I think the trip to Finschhafen must have taken about a week. It was a fairly pleasant cruise. The food was good. I spent the days in my pajamas reading books and standing on deck watching the flying fish.

When I got to Finschhafen I was pleased to find that the APO number was that of George Whittington. George and I went to high school and the University of Tennessee together and were members of Sigma Chi fraternity. George entered the army a month or so after I did and ended up in the Transportation Corps. Some time before he got to Finschhafen, the ship he was on collided with another ship and sank. As I recall, George could not swim, but he managed to survive although many men on the ship lost their lives. I managed to get in touch with George and he paid me several visits. One of the things that patients with hepatitis must avoid is alcohol. I was not told because there was little chance that I could get any. However, George, like the good friend that he is, smuggled a can of beer to me on one of his first visits. I appreciated it, of course, but felt worse immediately after drinking it.

I was in the hospital about five weeks before I was discharged with orders to return to my squadron. It would not be very inaccurate to say that I hitchhiked back. Strangely enough, no one seemed to know where the squadron was. I was put on a plane to Biak where I stayed several days. While there I was put on KP in an officers mess. I must say that I resented being a servant for these rear echelon officers who had never heard a shot fired in anger. I found a crew that was flying to Tacloban, and the pilot said I could come along if I could furnish my own parachute but not otherwise (a very reasonable requirement). Unfortunately, I was unable to steal or otherwise acquire a parachute, and they left without me. Finally, I did get a flight to Tacloban. I hitched a ride on a truck from the airstrip to our squadron area and found it completely deserted. Someone told me the 63rd had gone to Mindoro, so I hung around the flight line until I could get a flight to Mindoro. When I got to Mindoro I found they were not there either, but someone had definite information that they were at Clark Field on Luzon. I got a flight to Clark and found them there.

Clark Field was a large airbase. It had been the primary base in the Philippines before the Japanese invaded in 1942. Only a few hours after the bombing of Pearl Harbor, the Japanese bombed Clark and wiped out most of the airforce in the Philippines while the planes were still on the ground. Clark was not as hot as Owi or as wet as Tacloban. We had much more contact with the native population than we had had before. I liked the Filipino people that I met. We could buy food from the Filipinos and send our laundry out. There were even tennis courts there, and I played when I had a chance. If I remember correctly, the courts were in the charge of Bitsy Grant, a well-known professional tennis player of the 1930s. Sometimes Negritos would come into our area and barter things like bows and arrows for food and clothing. Negritos are black pigmies with a Stone Age culture that live in the mountain jungles of western Luzon. They were probably the original inhabitants of these islands before the present population of Malaysian origin moved in. Clark Field was an interesting and fairly pleasant place.

As I have mentioned, our pilot, Major Brownfield, was now squadron commander. He thought that since we were in a civilized area, it was time we tightened up on discipline and abandoned our sloppy ways. I think this was a mistake. We had always worked efficiently with everyone doing his job. The relations between officers and enlisted men were generally friendly. Brownfield decreed that the enlisted men should fall out at six every morning for roll call and the assignment of the day's duties. We resented this. In order to get to the place where roll was called, we had to pass through the area where the officers had their tents. We always rattled our mess kits and were as noisy as possible, since the officers did not have to get up. They resented this. A friend of mine named Sympniewski (or something like that) agreed that it was not necessary for both of us to get up every morning, so we would take turns with the one attending answering for both. One morning it was my turn. The first sergeant went down the roll in alphabetical order. When he got to Harris I answered "here". He continued, and when he got to Sympniewski I answered "here" again. He paused.

"Sympniewski?" he said

"Here," said I.

"Where is Sympniewski?" he yelled.

"Here," I yelled back.

"Sympniewski! Step out of ranks," he ordered. I stepped forward. He came over and glared at me suspiciously.

"Do you mean to tell me that your name is Sympniewski?" he asked.

"Oh!" said I. "I thought you said Harris." Everyone thought this was very funny except the first sergeant who was a humorless sort. He put me on KP or some other detail.

Years later a pilot of the 63rd that I had flown with asked me if I thought Brownfield was a little chickenshit. He said that the officers and enlisted men on his crew were all good friends and generally ignored rank. One day when Brownfield was squadron commander, he came to the officers' tent and said they were fraternizing with the enlisted men too much. I told him that I thought Brownfield did become chickenshit after becoming squadron commander.

The missions we flew from Clark were to Taiwan and along the China coast from Hainan island in the southwest near Indochina to Shanghai in the northeast. Our military strategists wanted to isolate Japan from their sources of oil and other materials on which their war machine was heavily dependent. To this end planes and submarines patrolled the Japanese shipping lanes connecting them to Indonesia, Indochina and western China.

We had lines drawn on our maps indicating where submarines were operating, and we were not to bomb on the submarine side of the line. On one mission we found a target which as nearly as we could tell was right on the line. We talked it over and decided to bomb it. As we were on the bomb run, the target fired the colors of the day from a flare gun and we aborted the raid. We had almost bombed one of our own submarines.

We were given credit for sinking a cargo ship on one of our missions. I do not remember any details.

One night we were sent to bomb an Italian ship anchored in the Whangpo River that runs through Shanghai. The ship had been sunk once before by planes from our airforce based in China and been raised and prepared for operation by the Japanese. I think we probably missed it.

Sometime in April or May I was awarded the Air Medal. I first heard of this in a letter from Mother who had received a letter from Gen. Kenney, the commander of the 5th Air Force. I finally was told about it, and there was a brief ceremony in which those of us receiving decorations were congratulated by Brig. General Crabb. I think the policy was for the award of the Air Medal after 100 combat hours were flown and then an Oak Leaf Cluster for each additional 100 combat hours. By the time I had finished flying I had flown 430 combat hours and had the Air Medal with four Oak Leaf Clusters.

On one mission along the China coast we got lost and never found our target. We had to drop our bombs into the ocean. I should explain that as radar operator I controlled the radar set and had a scope on which radar reflections gave a map of our surroundings out to a distance of 50 or 100 miles. The bombardier had a radar bomb sight that took over for the last 10 miles of a bomb run. The navigator had a scope like mine. This usually made navigation very easy. You only had to look at the scope and compare it to the map, and you knew where you were. (This form of navigation is called radar pilotage.) I carried my own set of maps and usually knew as much about our position as the navigator, although this was not my primary responsibility. The navigator was expected to check our position by dead reckoning. On this mission I think our navigator, Ira Bloch, relied too much on radar pilotage. The section of the China coast we were flying along did not give strong radar reflections and the picture on the scope did not look much like the map. As a result we could not identify our position when we were near where our target should be. By the time we found our position, our time had run out and we had to drop our bombs in the ocean and turn back. Brownfield was very angry about this. We had risked the lives of the crew for no purpose. I think there was a hearing about this. Bloch blamed it on a malfunction of the radar. The squadron radar officer called me in, and I had to tell him that I thought the radar had functioned properly. A few days later we heard that Bloch had been grounded for combat fatigue. Thereafter, we flew with borrowed navigators.

One of our missions was to the capital city of Taipeh on the island of Taiwan. I think planes from other squadrons of the 43rd bomb group had bombed it during the day and planes from our squadron were to bomb it at night. Radar bombing of land targets is so inaccurate that the best we could hope for was to hit the city. We borrowed Kingsbury, the navigator on S.L. Flinner's crew. As we made our bomb run, we were caught with Japanese searchlight beams. After flying in complete blackness for hours, it is a strange feeling to have the plane light up so brightly that you could read a newspaper and to know that you are the sole object of attention of the antiaircraft batteries. Simon, the tail gunner, reported a night fighter following us. He never fired on us. Perhaps he was driven off by the antiaircraft fire directed at us. We had metallic strips called rope that we threw out to confuse the enemy radar, but it was not clear that it did any good. Through all of this, Kingsbury was on the intercom telling the gunners to carefully note the positions of searchlights and antiaircraft batteries so we could report it to intelligence on our return. His calmness in the midst of all the excitement struck us as funny, and we laughed about it later when we had safely returned and could laugh again. While in the searchlights we devoted our energies to sphincter control and had no time for humor. This may have been the time we got a hole in the tail of the plane.

I am rather uncertain about what crew I flew some of these missions with. In a letter home dated April 12, 1945 I said that Orion Rogers had replaced Brownfield as pilot of our crew, but I had not flown any missions after returning to Clark Field from the hospital. In a letter dated April 19 I said that I was looking for a new crew since our pilot (Rogers), engineer (Bickford) and radio operator Sedilco had finished the required hours and the navigator (Bloch) was grounded. In a letter dated April 29 I said that all of my crew had finished the required hours and that I had flown my first mission with S. L. Flinner's crew. After I had written the above paragraph, I got a letter from Orion Rogers. From his letter it is clear that I could have flown only two missions with him. One of these was on April 13 to the Shanghai area. The gunners reported a night fighter but we were not fired upon. Mission time 16:10 hours. The other was the mission to Taipeh in the paragraph above. Since Orion's report contains details that I did not remember I will quote it.

"April 15, 1945 to Taihoku (Japanese name for Taipeh), Formosa. Our bomb load was 500-pound fire (jelly) bombs. Our instructions were to drop our bombs four hours plus or minus five minutes after take off. As we approached the target there was no evidence of fires, but there were too many searchlights to count. As soon as the searchlights pinpointed us, the AA started. The sky seemed to be full of it. Shortly after Kriete said bombs away, the bombs of another plane hit the ground starting nice fires. As we turned eastward to clear the target area our bombs hit making a nice V-pattern. Later we commented that V for victory was appropriate since it was the last mission for most of us. One of the first three ships aborted. We overtook another. We were the only ship from the 63rd that dropped our bombs within the allotted window, four hours and three minutes. It was about 800 miles to the target so we had to operate in auto-rich. We had to fly about 200 miles an hour. That's moving right along in a B-24. We didn't tarry in the target area either. We headed due east. After a few very long minutes, we were out of AA range. The searchlights went out. Soon thereafter, the crew reported a number of night fighters. I cautioned them not to fire unless they fired at us first. The fighters seemed to take turns moving close in behind us. None fired, much to our relief. They broke off after about 30 minutes. We then turned southward and returned to Clark Field. Mission time 11:10 hours."

I flew one mission with the Ferret detachment that took us along the coast of Kyushu, the southernmost island of Japan. This is the closest I got to Japan. I think this was an 18-hour mission and the longest I ever flew.

On one occasion I was sent with some other enlisted men on a truck up to a naval supply dump at Lingayen gulf on the northwest coast of Luzon for the purpose of stealing a truck load of lumber for something that was being built in the squadron area. I suppose we could have gone through the proper channels to get the lumber, but the war would have been over before the paperwork was completed. We took along a bottle of whiskey as a gift for the guard who would look the other way as we loaded the truck and some additional whiskey for ourselves. On the way we were stopped by the military police near the town of Baguio, the summer capital of the Philippines. There were still Japanese troops operating in this area and no unarmed Americans were supposed to be there. We had not brought weapons with us. The military policeman said we were under arrest and took our names to report to our squadron commander. We gave fictitious names and a fictitious squadron, of course, so nothing came of it. I still think of it with amusement as "the time I was on my way to commit a burglary and was arrested for not carrying a gun." The war turns everything topsy-turvy. I think I made several trips to Lingayen for lumber.

As I remarked above, some time in mid-April my crew broke up. The pilot, co-pilot, engineer and radio operator had finished the required number of combat hours and had been grounded and were awaiting orders to return to the U.S. Some other members of the crew were within one or two missions of finishing up, and the navigator had been grounded. I was behind the others because of my stay in the hospital. I was assigned to another crew.

Its members were:

Flinner, S.L. . . . . . . Pilot
Dublin . . . . Co-Pilot
Kingsbury . . . . Navigator
Maker . . . . Bombardier
Schlereth . . . . Engineer
Peacock. . . . . Radio operator
Blair, Joe . . . . Radar operator
Amacher, William. . Gunner
Tulley . . . . Gunner
Ebert . . . . Gunner

For reasons I cannot remember, Joe Blair could not fly and I took his place as radar operator. My guess is that he had hepatitis like many of us did. I think that their plane was rather badly shot up and the tail gunner was badly wounded on a mission before I joined their crew. I am not sure whether Ebert was the tail gunner that was wounded or whether he was the replacement. I knew most of the crew and was glad to be assigned to them.

At one time in our group, air crews were grounded and returned to the U.S. after 300 combat hours. Then they changed it to 400. Then they changed again to a point system in which you got points for combat hours with additional points for flak, enemy interceptions, crash landings and so forth. Most of the missions I flew were relatively uneventful, so I had 430 hours when I was grounded in late May.

Sometime in June I got a letter from Mother telling me that my grandmother had died. I had grown up in my grandparent's home and had been very close to my grandmother.

After I was grounded I had to wait for the paperwork to be done. The work I was assigned was apparently not too arduous and I had time for tennis, swimming and a sight-seeing trip into Manila which had been badly damaged during the fighting but was now recovering. Clark Field was becoming a civilized place with tennis courts, a swimming pool and an enlisted men's club where you could buy a decent meal.

I think I left Clark about June 20 and then spent some time in a camp in Manila while waiting for a ship home. While there I ran into Brownfield who told me his wife was seriously ill and he was waiting on a flight home. Finally, I was put on a troop ship called the USS Howard Lykes and we started the long trip home. It took about a month. We changed course a few degrees every few minutes to make it difficult for Japanese submarines, although I think that by this time there was little danger. The ship was very crowded. For part of the crossing I was assigned to guard duty from midnight to 4 a.m. It was never made clear to me what I was guarding or whom I was protecting it from. The weather was very calm until we reached the California coast and there we saw some rough seas. We spent only a few days in a camp in San Francisco before being put on a train for Ft. McPherson, Georgia. As the senior noncom, I was nominally in charge of my car on the train and was supposed to post a guard at each end. There was really no point in this, so I did not do it. After a few days at Ft. McPherson, I was given a month's furlough and caught a train for Morristown. I must have gotten home in early August.

I remember that a few days after I got home I was talking with friends, and someone asked me how much longer the war would go on. I replied that the Japanese had fought tenaciously for a lot of worthless islands. I expected them to fight even more fiercely for every inch of their homeland. I thought the war would continue for another year. On August 6 an atomic bomb destroyed Hiroshima; on August 8 Nagasaki was destroyed by a second atomic bomb and the USSR entered the war; on August 15 the Japanese laid down their arms. So much for my ability as a prognosticator. One of the people in this group of friends was Charlie Bettis who was working at Oak Ridge and may have known that a bomb was being constructed.

All too soon my furlough was over and I received orders to report to an airfield at San Antonio, Texas to be discharged. I was hoping to be discharged in time to enter the University of Tennessee for the fall quarter which began in late September. I remember that I was supposed to catch an early morning train from Morristown. Mother said that there was no need to set an alarm clock since she could wake up at any time just by setting her mind to it. The next morning she came into my room in great alarm and said, "Edward, do you hear that train whistle? That is the train that you are supposed to be on. What shall we do?" I said that I thought the best plan was to go back to sleep. As a result of oversleeping, I was A.W.O.L. for a day, but no one seemed to care or even to notice.

The army had a point system for determining the order in which men were discharged. One received points for each month in service, additional points for overseas service, more points for combat and for decorations and battle stars. I had enough points to be in one of the first groups to be discharged, but the paperwork went very slowly. If I was not so eager to get into the university for the fall quarter, I would have enjoyed the month waiting. I did not have to work. The food was the best I had in the army. I played a lot of tennis, read a lot in the library and worked on the correspondence course on calculus that I had neglected.

Finally, they turned me loose and I took the train for Knoxville where I registered for the fall quarter two weeks late.

868th Bomb Squadron Crew

Standing Left to Right: Lt. C. Butch Werner, Lt. Chuck Ames, Lt. Joe Sullivan and Sgt. George Cubbage. *Sitting:* Capt. Bob Lehti, Sgt. Joseph MacColment, Sgt. Walter Rose, Sgt. Jack Ransom, and Sgt. Willie Wilcox.

63rd Bomb Squadron Crew

Standing: Clifford L. McHenry, Gunner; Sgt. Athill Irvine, Radio Operator; 2nd Lt. Thomas J. McCoetr, Navigator; Flight Officer Edwin D. Pheasent, Co-Pilot; Flight Officer Gordon B. Ball; Mickey, Radar Operator; 2nd Lt. Rodger W, Little, Pilot. *Kneeling:* Flight Officer James F. Hampshire, Bombardier; Cpl. David Fishoff, Tail Gunner; Sgt. Joseph L. Sosnowski, Flight Engineer; Cpl. Robert R. Richardson, Top Turret Gunner.

Arthur De Land

The Combat Diary and Log of Arthur De Land
Photo provided by Arthur DeLand

Enlisted in Buffalo, NY in Regular Army October 19, 1940. Was stationed in Signal Detachment at West Point, NY until transfer to Aviation Cadet Program in April 1942. Trained in Southeast Army Air Force Training Center: Pre-flight at Maxwell Field, Montgomery, Alabama; Primary in Stearman PT-17's at Bennetsville, South Carolina; Basic in Vultee BT-13A at Cochran Field, Macon, Georgia. Flew advance in AT-9 and AT-10 at Columbus, Mississippi. Graduated Class of 43A and commissioned 2nd Lt. January 13, 1943. Took four-engine transition in B24's at Smyrna, Tennessee. Flew 60 hours as co-pilot and 60 hours as captain with Instructor Pilot Captain Goldsworthy. Came out of Smyrna as 1st Pilot of B-24's. Then shipped to Pocatello, Idaho for four engine RTU. We were then sent to Herrington, Kansas for processing to Europe or Africa.

Standing, Left to Right: Edward Snead, C.P.; Arthur DeLand, Pilot; Weldon Richards, Engineer; How ard Blackwelder, Bombardier; John Meisenhelder, Navigator. *Kneeling: Left to Right:* Henry Johnson, Gunner; Willard Bryant, Radioman; William Manchester, Nose Gunner; Alan Rosenthal, Asst. Flight Engineer; Jack Jones, Radar Operator.

At Harrington, my crew and six others were selected to go to Langley Field, VA to train in Radar (LAB) Low Altitude Bombing for anti-shipping combat. This was in the Col. Stuart Wright Project in the 3rd Sea Search Attack Squadron of the 1st Sea Search Attack Group. I was promoted to 1st Lt. in September 1943 at Langley. I signed for a B-24J model aircraft in January 1944 and made five flights in it at Langley Field. My aircraft #4273396 was the first B-24J model with a nose turret to reach the 868th Bomb Squadron (H) "*Snoopers*." Before that, they were all "D" models without nose turrets.

COMBAT LOG OF ARTHUR DELAND

DATE 1944	TYPE	FROM	TO	TIME	REMARKS
1/26/44	B-24J	Langley Field, VA	Mitchell Field, New York	2:00	To process for overseas
28	B-24J	Mitchell Field, NY	Municipal, Memphis, Tennessee	7:15	
30	B-24J	Memphis, TN	Tucson AAB, Arizona	7:30	
31	B-24J	Tucson, AZ	Fairfield-Suisan, California	4:45	
2-5&6-44	B-24J	Fairfield-Suisan, CA	Hickam Field, Oahu, Hawaii	14:30	
8	B-24J	Hickam Field	Canton Islands, Phoenix Islands	10:45	
10	B-24J	Canton Islands	Nandi-Fiji Islands, Espirito Santos	7:15	
12	B-24J	Nand Fiji Islands	New Hebrides Islands, Guadalcanal	4:15	
13	B-24J	Espirito Santos	Solomon Islands, Munda Airfield	4:00	
15	B-24J	Guadalcanal	New Georgia Islands, St. Georges Channel	1:20	
18	B-24D	Munda Airfield	Bismarck Sea & Return	11:20	Strike #1 Sea Search
21	B-24J	Munda Airfield	Bismarck Sea & Return	12:05	Strike #2 Sea Search
23	B-24J	Munda Airfield	Local	1:15	Test Hop
24	B-24J	Munda Airfield	Bismarck Sea - Bombed Kavienk Field	11:30	Strike #3 Sea Search
26	B-24J	Munda Airfield	New Ireland Islands	11:40	Strike #4 } Secondary Targets after Sea Search
29	B-24J	Munda Airfield	New Ireland Islands	11:45	Strike #5 }
3/3/44	B-24D	Munda Airfield	New Britian Islands	9:45	Strike #6
6	B-24J	Munda Airfield	Area I	12:40	Strike #7
9	B-24J	Munda Airfield	Munda Airfield, Kavieng Airfield	0:25	Emergency - Lost #2&#4 engines on takeoff - U-turn and returned
9	B-24J	Munda Airfield	New Ireland Islands, Namatanai Airfield	10:30	Strike #8
11	B-24J	Munda Airfield	New Ireland Islands, Panapai Airfield	11:10	Strike #9
14	B-24J	Munda Airfield	New Ireland Islands, Heckled Rabaul	12:30	Strike #10
18	B-24J	Munda Airfield	New Britian Islands	9:30	Strike #11
20	B-24J	Munda Airfield	Local Namatanai Airfield	1:00	Test Hop
23	B-24J	Munda Airfield	New Ireland Islands, Piva Airstrip	11:45	Strike #12
28	B-24D	Munda Airfield	Bougainville Islands. Bombed Truk Islands	1:30	Staged thru Bougainville

DATE	TYPE	FROM	TO	TIME	REMARKS
28	B-24J	Piva Airstrip	Bougainville Isand, ret. Munda Piva	13:45	Strike #13
4/1/44	B-24J	Munda Airfield, Piva Airstrip	Bougainville Islands	1:45	Staged thru Bougainville
1	B-24J	Bougainville, Islands	Bombed Truk, Returned to Piva	13:00	Strike #14
2	B-24J	Bougainville, Islands	Munda Airfield	1:20	
4	B-24J	Munda Airfield	Local	1:10	Test Hop
12	B-24J	Munda Airfield	Green Island	2:10	Strike #15
13	B-24J	Green Islands	Bombed Truk Islands	10:00	
14	B-24J	Green Islands	Munda Airfield	2:10	
16	B-24J	Guadalcanal, Koli Airfield	Munda Airfield	1:45	
20	B-24D	Guadalcanal, Koli Airfield	Munda Airfield	1:20	
23	B-24D	Munda Airfield, New Georgia Solomon Islands	Momote Airfield, Los Negros Islands Admiralty Islands airstrip	6:15	Change of Station from Munda to Los Negros, Admiralty Islands
25	B-24D	Momote Airstrip Los Negros Islands	Woleai Islands	9:00	Strike #16 10000', lost #3 engine
29	B-24D	Momote Airstrip Los Negros Islands	Woleai Islands	2:55	Aborted mission & returned
5/1/44	B-24J	Momote Airstrip Los Negros Islands	Woleai Islands	9:20	Strike #17
6/25/44	B-24J	Mouerang Airfield Los Negros,	30 Mile ARC South of Truk - Search Admiralty Islands	8:45	Lt. Westerland with Haynes - search after downed at Truk
7/1/44	B-24D	"	Local	1:00	Test Hop
4	B-24D	"	Local	1:30	Test Hop
7	B-24D	"	Woleai Airstrip	8:40	Strike #18
10	B-24D	"	Woleai Airstrip	8:00	Strike #19
13	B-24J	"	Woleai Airstrip	8:20	Strike #20
16	B-24J	"	Woleai Airstrip	8:00	Strike #21
19	B-24J	"	Woleai Airstrip	8:15	Strike #22
20	B-24J	"	Local	1:45	Test Hop
22	B-24J	"	Woleai Airstrip Practice Bombing	8:00	Strike #23
23	B-24D	"	Local	3:00	
24	B-24D	"	Woleai Airstrip Practice Bombing	7:40	Strike #24
26	B-24D	"	Local	3:40	

DATE	TYPE	FROM	TO	TIME	REMARKS
27	B-24D	Mokerang Airfield Los Negros, Admiralty Islands	Local	3:20	
29	B-24J	"	Local	2:10	
31	B-24D	"	Local	2:20	
8/1/44	B-24J	"	Local	1:45	
5	B-24J	"	Woleai Islands Malakai	8:00	Strike #25
8	B-24J	"	Palau Islands Practice Bombing	13:25	Strike #26
10	B-24J	"	Local	3:40	
12	B-24J	"	Koror City, Palau Islands	13:10	Strike #27
15	B-24J	"	Local	1:30	
17	B-24J	"	2000' Kuoro City, Kuoro Islands, Palau Islands	14:00	Strike #28 *

MISSION STRIKE NO. 28* IS DESCRIBED IN THE ARCHIVES

At 2350K Lt. DeLand, piloting A/C #396, made a visual bombing run on Koror Island at an altitude of 2200 feet true. Fourteen 100-lb. incendiary bombs were toggled over the target and the remaining six, which hung-up, were salvoed in the water southeast of the target. All bombs were observed to hit on land. Several large fires were started on Koror Island. When A/C #396 was 20 miles from the target a series of terrific explosions took place and a very large fire spread throughout the target area. The fire was still burning when this aircraft was 80 miles distant from the target.

D.E.I. = Dutch East Indies

DATE	TYPE	FROM	TO	TIME	REMARKS
19	B-24D	"	Local	3:05	
20	B-24J	"	Koror, Palau	12:55	Strike #29
25	B-24J	"	Koror, Palau	13:00	Strike #30
9/3/44	B-24J	"	Kornosoran Airfield, Noemfoor Dutch East Indies	5:30	Change of station from Admiralty Islands To Noemfoor
6	B-24J	Kornosoran Airfield, Noemfoor D.E.I.	Practice Bombing Local	2:20	
6	B-24J	Kornosoran Airfield, Noemfoor D.E.I.	Ngesebus Islands, Palau Group	6:45	Strike #31
9	B-24J	Kornosoran Airfield, Noemfoor D.E.I.	Ngesebus Islands, Palau Group	7:05	Strike #32

DATE	TYPE	FROM	TO	TIME	REMARKS
9	B-24J	Komosoran Airfield, Noemfoor D.E.I.	Ngesebus Islands, Palau Group	7:50	Strike #33
16	B-24J	Noemfoor Airstrip, Dutch East Indies	Goronfalo Dock's, Celebes Islands	10:30	Strike #34
20	B-24J	Noemfoor Airstrip, Dutch East Indies	Manado Waterfront, Celebes Islands	9:30	Strike #35
28	C-47A	Noemfoor Airstrip, Dutch East Indies	Local	2:00	Check out in C47 Aircraft
29	C-47A	Noemfoor Airstrip, Dutch East Indies	Finschafen, New Guinea	5:10	Captain — 1st Lt. Phil
30	C-47A	Finschafen, New Guinea	Noemfoor, Dutch East Indies	6:25	Co-pilot — Hoffman and
10/2/44	C-47A	Noemfoor, Dutch East Indies	Finschafen, New Guinea	5:50	Captain — I flew crews
2	C-47A	Finschafen, New Guinea	Cairns, Australia	4:45	Co-pilot — down to Australia
3	C-47A	Cairns, Australia	Brisbane, Australia	5:00	Captain — for R&R. Then we
3	C-47A	Brisbane, Australia	Sydney, Australia	3:15	Co-pilot — would fly the
5	C-47A	Sydney, Australia	Brisbane, Australia	2:35	Captain — other crews
5	C-47A	Brisbane, Australia	Cairns, Australia	5:05	Co-pilot — back to base
6	C-47A	Cairns, Australia	Finschafen, New Guinea	4:20	Captain — to resume
6	C-47A	Finschafen, New Guinea	Noemfoor, Dutch East Indies	5:35	Co-pilot — combat status.
9	C-47A	Noemfoor, Dutch East Indies	Finschafen, New Guinea	5:40	Captain — We would
9	C-47A	Finschafen, New Guinea	Cairns, Australia	4:35	Co-pilot — alternate legs
10	C-47A	Cairns, Australia	Brisbane, Australia	5:00	Co-pilot — of flights as
10	C-47A	Brisbane, Australia	Sydney, Australia	3:00	Captain — Captain or
24	C-47A	Sydney, Australia	Brisbane, Australia	3:15	Co-pilot — co-pilot.
24	C-47A	Brisbane, Australia	Cairns, Australia	5:10	Captain
26	C-47A	Cairns, Australia	Finschafen, New Guinea	4:25	Co-pilot
26	C-47A	Finschafen, New Guinea	Noemfoor, Dutch East Indies	5:35	Captain
27	B-24J	Noemfoor, Dutch East Indies	Local	1:10	Local Test Hop
28	B-24D	Noemfoor, Dutch East Indies	Local	1:00	Local Test Hop
30	B-24D	Noemfoor, Dutch East Indies	Bombed East Coast of Boriveo and	16:00	Strike #36
11/2/44	B-24D	Noemfoor, Dutch East Indies	Morotai searched Visayan Sea	3:55	
2&3	B-24D	Morotai	Mindanao Sea for Leyte	10:00	Strike #37
3	B-24D	Morotai	Noemfoor, Dutch East Indies	2:40	

DATE	TYPE	FROM	TO	TIME	REMARKS
7	B-24D	Noemfoor, Dutch East Indies	Morotai	3:55	Strike #38
8&9	B-24D	Morotai	Sulu Sea, West coast of Negros,	11:00	
9	B-24D	Morotai	Noemfoor, Dutch East Indies	2:45	
11	B-24D	Noemfoor, Dutch East Indies	Local	1:00	
12	B-24D	Noemfoor, Dutch East Indies	Morotai	3:00	
12&13	B-24D	Morotai	Noemfoor, Dutch East Indies	13:20	Strike #39
14	B-24D	Noemfoor, Dutch East Indies	Morotai, West Coast Borned	3:00	
14&15	B-24D	Morotai	Hit Sandakan Airfield, ret. Noemfoor	14:30	Strike #40
19	C-47A	Noemfoor, Dutch East Indies	Hollandia, New Guinea	2:20	Captain
19	C-47A	Hollandia,NEW GUINEA	Finschafen, New Guinea	3:15	Captain
20	C-47A	Finschafen, New Guinea	Noemfoor, Dutch East Indies	5:30	
29	B-24J	Noemfoor, Dutch East Indies	Biak, Island	0:45	
29	B-24J	Biak, Island	Noemfoor, Dutch East Indies	0:45	
30	RB-24D	Noemfoor, Dutch East Indies	Cairns, Australia	7:20	Flew to Australia with Lt. Bryant to buy vegetables, milk & eggs for the Squadron mess
12/4/44	RB-24D	Cairns, Australia	Noemfoor, Dutch East Indies	7:20	
22	B-24J	Noemfoor, Dutch East Indies	Local	3:35	

```
Actual B-24 mission time for 40 missions . . . . . . . . .   =   460:20
B-24 times from Langley Field to Munda, Solomon Islands . . . .   =    63:35
Total B-24 test hops and practice missions. . . . . . . . . . . .   =    70:00
C-47 time. . . . . . .                                           =    97:40
              Total flying time overseas . . . . . . . . . . . .   =   691:35 hrs.
```

In addition to missions in the South Pacific, I flew five anti-sub patrols in B-24 out of Langley Field, Virginia, earning the American Campaign Ribbon.

NOTES:

At start of mission #8, I lost both #2 and #4 engines on a night take-off at about 600 feet altitude. We salvoed five 1000-pound bombs and I made a U-turn and returned to Munda Airfield. Hairy!!!

The spread in time between mission #17 and the flight on 6/25/44 was caused by: Started for R & R leave to Auckland, New Zealand and got to 13th Bomber Command at Guadalcanal. We were held there for two weeks while a change was made to send all crews to Sydney, Australia for R & R. I believe we were the first crew from the 868th to go to Australia.

When we returned to the Admiralty Islands from leave to our base on Los Negros, we found a very high percentage of the squadron personnel were down with diarrhea. In order to make-up a combat crew, Squadron Operations put together "bastard crews." A pilot from one crew, a co-pilot from another, a navigator from another, and so on. My Navigator, Lt. Gerard R. Westerland, volunteered to fly as navigator on the Lt. Haynes crew. They were shot down over Truk and I flew a mission to a 30-mile arc south of Truk to see if we could spot any survivors or debris. We couldn't find a thing.

Mission #28 to Truk was the first bombing of the island stronghold of Truk at that time. Lt. Donald Thomson's crew and I with my crew were the first to hit Truk. I was about five minutes behind Thomson and bombed on his fires because our radar went out. Bombed visually from about 12,000 feet.

My mission #36 was the longest I believe up to that date. I was supposed to refuel at Morotai but because of weather we couldn't land. So I had to make it back to the Noemfoor base. Had my Engineer, Tech Sgt. Weldon Richards, stick the fuel tanks after landing but he couldn't wet the stick. I believe we made the last 50 miles on fumes.

As you can see from my log, the 868th was involved with nearly every major Japanese target. My log is indicative of all other 868th combat missions. As you can see, we hit Rabaul, Truk, Woleai, Celebes Islands, Halmahera, Borneo (both east and west coasts), Palau Islands and the Philippine Islands. When I first arrived oveseas, the 13th Air Force was under the command of Admiral Nimitz; later we came under the command of General Douglas MacArthur. Nimitz of course favored the Navy and Mac's favorite was the 5th Air Force so the 13th AF received very little recognition. "History of the War in the Pacific," when published, should remedy this oversight.

After World War II, I was separated from the service in July, 1945. Flubbed around my hometown of Dunkirk, NY and finally joined the Dunkirk Police Force as a patrolman from September, 1948 to April 1952. At this time I was recalled to Active Duty and sent to Randolph Field, Texas, for transition in the B-29 aircraft. Came out of that as an Aircraft Commander and was sent to Okinawa to take over a combat crew. Flew 18 missions against North Korea and finally returned home and out of the service April, 1953.

Then flew a single-engine Beechcraft Bonanza out of Salt Lake City, Utah for a year and a half, and finally came to Albuquerque, New Mexico in November, 1956. Started flying for Carco Air Service which had the AEC (Atomic Energy Commission) contract to supply passenger and freight service to Los Alamos and Sandia Laboratory Personnel. I was Captain of the DC-4 and DC-3 aircraft.

Serviced most of the Air Force Bases on the continent plus trips to Alaska, Fort Churchill on Hudson's Bay, Canada, Panama for Sandia test work as well as four or five trips to Hawaii, Johnson Island and Kauai. So I got around. Served Carco Air Service as Chief Pilot the last two years until I had a heart attack in September, 1969. That shot me out of the saddle. I finished my work life as a carpenter and cabinetmaker with Lovelace Material center in Albuquerque. Worked until November, 1983 when I retired.

A SUMMARY: OTHER EVENTS

After World War II, my bombardier, Howard T. Blackwelder, stayed in and retired as a Lt. Colonel. My co-pilot, Edward Paul Snead got out, finished law school in Oklahoma and was appointed 5th District Judge. Served 15 or more years and retired in Roswell, New Mexico.

After losing my navigator, Lt. Westerland, over the island of Truk, I received Lt. John H. Meisenhelder as the replacement navigator. When my crew finished their 40 missions, Lt. Meisenhelder had not flown the required number of missions so he was sent to Australia on R & R leave with two other crews in the 868th Squadron C-47. Somewhere between Noemfoor and Finschafen, New Guinea, the aircraft disappeared. Rumor had it that they could have been shot down by a Japanese sub around Wewak, New Guinea. We used to go through there at 6000 to 8000 feet so it's a possibility. Wewak was still held by Japanese forces.

When I first arrived at the squadron, Major Francis Carlson was Commanding Officer. He was replaced by Major Leo Foster. When Foster rotated home, we received a B-25 pilot, Major James Barlow as CO. He was still there when I received my stateside orders. I went to Biak Island and two fighter pilots convinced the captain of the Merchant Marine tanker, the SS Lost Hills to take us with him to San Pedro, California. We left Biak and sailed to Finschafen, but the Aussies refused the tanker captain enough fuel to make the trip. So we went to Manus in the Admiralty Islands to get the fuel. We were on board 18 days and ate like kings all the way to San Pedro. Home for 10 days and then to Atlantic City, New Jersey for R & R (Rest and Relaxation). Separated from the Service in July 1945.

I was born in Sheridan, NY on October 2, 1918 so that makes me 83 years of age. I never expected to be here this long. Family moved to Dunkirk, NY when I was a year old. Attended Dunkirk Public School and graduated from Dunkirk High School in June 1937. So there you have the life history of one 1st. Lt. Arthur A. De Land, French Huguenot – Ancestors came to the colonies in 1637. Met and married my wife, Milly L. Jones De Land in Smyrna, TN on February 27, 1943 so this makes us man and wife for 59 years.

> Note: *This letter was received by Arthur DeLand on the date shown. Paul Snead was Art's co-pilot and they flew some 40 or 41 missions together more than 50 years ago.*

November 9, 1992

Dear Art,

A few snaps for your memory book. I have another roll of film in the camera; when I get it I will send along some more if worthwhile. I have the logs and have been flooded with memories of those times two lifetimes ago.

I remember the B-18's we flew out of Langley with some sort of radar sticking out the rear end. As I recall, if we encountered a submarine a light would flash on the dash and I would pull a couple of wires and release two depth charges from the wings. I think the idea was that the Germans would kill themselves laughing.

I remember the time we were directed into the rainstorm at Munda and the time you buzzed the tower next time we were up (not loaded with bombs.) Munda, I recall, as one of the prettiest landing strips we used, with that smooth crushed coral like a billiard table. We had just about arrived when Gay's crew went into the drink, and we moved into their tent. Toole was his co-pilot and survived but with a skull fracture. I had been in flying school with Toole, and he is in Arizona and still around.

It was nice up on the hill at Munda; never mind the snakes that crawled into the tent from the brushpile in back, the land crabs banging and clacking around at night feeding or making love or whatever, and a squadron naviga--tor who walked around crashing into trees. Doc Krug thought he had *locomotor ataxia,* never mind how you get it, but he also thought the squadron bombardier had *hydrocephalus* accounting for his big head. Someone asked the navigator how he passed physicals. He said he usually took a shot of booze before going in, and the doctors just assumed he was drunk and trying to get out of flying status; so, of course, they passed him.

Well, I suppose we were all a little crazy or we wouldn't have kept on doing what we were doing. Dorothy used to ask me how we ever won the war with units like the 868th, from my accounts of our shirt-tail war. After seeing the B-24's at Dayton, she wanted to know how we ever got home with that tin can.

I remember when Gerry went on Hayne's crew that went down and the search we flew the next day. Gerry had the idea that he could speed up his missions and go home early.

One of the Woleai missions I was back in the squadron with the daylight group and you flew the weather ship with the flight commander. You turned back and we went on to the target, and as I recall bombed through cloud cover without any real idea what we were bombing; then came home and got a mission ahead, so I finished with 41. Another time I went over for a briefing, then found that the weather ship had been cancelled, so I had Major Carlson get me out of the mission also, or I would have been two ahead, and I really didn't think I needed the experience.

I recall the door we dropped over Woleai and the breezy ride home; the time we got popped with flak there, and the time the frag bombs went off and peppered the airplane. I have a picture, probably you gave it to me, of the bomb run when we blew up the gun installation.

One of the things I remember about the long missions, including that 16-hour wonder, was that we would debrief, pop two ounces of booze, eat breakfast and sleep a few hours in the heat and wake-up; stumble around like the living dead for a day, then theoretically be fit for flying again.

Late in the game we had an overnight in the Halmaheras when the Japs came in and blew up the post office. I also seem to recall a pit stop there on one mission when someone wanted us to get a few hours sleep and hit the trail again, and you refused and we flew home to Noemfoor.

We almost collided with another B-24 over Morotai, Hoffman I think. I think we had the squadron commander that night, the Hollywood-type B-25 pilot.

I don't recall making a trip down to Australia with you in a B-24, so perhaps it was Freddie on that trip. I do remember the second trip to Australia in the DC-3, as I recall we had the executive officer along. Don't recall his name – Veeder called him "The Moke." You decided to try some single engine performance with the plane and he was a bit shook up. I also recall that we had something of an extended stay there because of engine trouble with the DC-3.

And I recall the time when it was over and we realized that we had bucked the tiger 40 (or 41) times and won!!!   ☺

I'm trying to retire from the practice of law this year, and hope to have a little more time and hope we can get together after the first of the year here or there. We may try the trip to Branson just for the heck of it, and I have a high school reunion next year; also back in the old home town in Oklahoma.

Incidentally, *How Did We Win the War?*

Paul

Hal Shirey, 1942 or early 1943, 868th Bomb Squadron Commander Col. Stuart Wright said, "Hal Shirey is the first authority on the low altitude bombardment radar soon to be of greatly expanded capabilities in the Pacific."

Radar Bench Set-up, Los Negros Admiralties Islands.
Photo provided by the Hal Shirey family.

Raymond E. Crawford

How a Combat Crew Is Put Together
and How It Performs In Combat
Raymond E. Crawford

2nd Lt. Raymond E. Crawford A-0742564 was graduated from the Roswell AF Flying School, Roswell, New Mexico, on April 12, 1943, Class of 43D. We (the whole class) were sent by train on 13 April to Blythe, California where it was very hot. Two days later we were put on a train to Clovis, New Mexico, only a hundred miles from Roswell. Some of the men had wives or girlfriends who came to the graduation. Because there was not enough time to make arrangements for the wives, they went along to Blythe and back to Clovis on the troop train.

Luck of the Draw

At Clovis we started transitional (beginning) training on B-24's. One day while there, a roster was posted in the operations office with all our names listed alphabetically. Every other man was designated a pilot, alternate names became co-pilots – no selection whatsoever. All through cadet school, William Adair Crawford was listed after me. On the pilot, co-pilot draw he became a co-pilot and I became a pilot and received a crew. I do not recall whether or not he went with us to the next station.

My next assignment was Pueblo, Colorado, traveling by train. My orders show I had a partial crew, but I think the crew did not meet until we arrived at Pueblo. Five airmen and bombardiers were assigned. Later, crew navigator, 2nd Lt. Serenus Mitchell, was assigned, but he was in the hospital at navigator school at Hondo, Texas. He caught up with us a week or two later. He flew with other crews also to get his necessary time in. He commented that the planes often came back on three engines and jokingly said he supposed that was just part of the training!

"Newt Fly This Thing"

I don't recall how long we flew without an assigned co-pilot, then 2nd Lt. Harold T. Newton was assigned to our crew. He was fresh out of fighter school and what a broken-hearted man he was – not so much to be assigned as co-pilot, which was a low blow, but to be put in bombers where you flew straight and level hour after hour. He would do nothing but occupy the co-pilot's seat. My flight engineer Sgt. Jack Arnold would reach past "Newt" to turn on the switches and do all the other things the co-pilot was supposed to do. Newt was very likeable and congenial, played guitar and sang to us on the ground and played checkers expertly. As the weeks went by and we had moved on to Salina, Kansas, we were up at 22,000 ft. one day trying to fly formation. I was having a terrible time. Newt had mentioned that in flying fighters they flew formation close enough to read the instruments in their buddy's plane, which probably was a slight exaggeration. Anyhow, I turned to Newt and said "Here, Newt, fly this thing" and I got up from my seat and went back on the flight deck. Sgt. Arnold took my seat. Well, very shortly Newt had our plane right next to the other plane and held his position until we were to break formation and go back to base. When Newt saw that he could do something that I couldn't do – he immediately became a real member of the crew. And a good co-pilot he was. One reason I was reluctant to make a fuss about Newt's early non-performance was that there was some shifting around of crew members going on and I was afraid we would get someone on the crew that we wouldn't like. It all turned out OK.

Checking Out Navigators

Now for some experiences with unassigned navigators. One day we were to fly from Pueblo to Sidney, Nebraska, go back west to the Denver area and on south to Pueblo. We flew long enough to get past Sidney, then I asked for a new heading. Navigator said to turn east, so I did. We flew above the Union Pacific railroad tracks for about an hour. Later I called for another heading toward the Rocky Mountains. By then I was using the radio compass, so I knew about where we were. Since my home at Alliance is about 90 miles from Sidney, I was somewhat familiar with the area. As we were flying east we flew over an air base, but I wasn't able to contact the base but we turned west from there to head for Denver. When we got back, the airmen in the back of the plane asked what we were doing flying over Kearney Air Base. The navigator admitted he was lost so I navigated back to Denver and Pueblo by radio compass. When we got back, the bombardier told me that the navigator was lost by the time we were in the air ten minutes! I still think he should have told me then. I suppose that a navigator could read the sun and the stars but not the ground. He never flew with us again.

Another day with another navigator we were to fly to Santa Fe, New Mexico from Pueblo to Trinidad and back to Pueblo. He was keeping us on course alright. However, I was using the radio compass and wasn't relying on him entirely As we passed Trinidad I asked for an ETA at Pueblo. No answer for quite a while. By the time he answered I could see the smokestacks from an iron smelter in Pueblo. He called and said we would land in 10 minutes. He was right, but I never found out whether he looked ahead and saw the smokestacks same as I did and guessed 10 minutes. I don't recall seeing either of those navigators again because our navigator joined up with our crew at that time.

Oops, Wrong Charts!

From Pueblo we were assigned to Smoky Hill Army Air Base at Salina, Kansas and flew there, making two trips and arriving the last time after dark. The next night we were to fly from Salina to Omaha, on to Kansas City and back to Salina. Not too long after leaving Salina we lost one engine, but that didn't worry us too much. We flew northeast long enough that I thought we should be turning southeast to head to Kansas City. Mitch gave me a heading but I could tell by his voice there was something wrong and he was hesitant. I wasn't worried because I was using the radio compass. Mitch was to be navigating by the stars and not supposed to look outside.

After flying for quite a while southeast and we were going past a big city I told Mitch to look out the window. He did and said "I suppose that is Omaha." Actually it was Kansas City. Later, still flying southeast, I called for a heading back to Salina and he said "If you know where it is, you just head back!" We headed west and arrived back OK but a couple hours late. I radioed that we were on three engines and as we were landing we could see crash trucks and fire engines at the far end of the runway. We were all wondering why they were there since we had come in several times on three engines and no big fuss was made. After landing, we found out that a plane had crashed on takeoff, hence the fire engines! The next day Mitch came to me and said "Do you know what happened last night?" I said no but I would like to know. He said that he took off from Pueblo and had not changed his charts for Salina. That's the only time he ever made a navigational error.

Try It With One Engine

We flew several times to the bombing range and dropped practice bombs from 22,000 feet with reasonable accuracy. One day after we left the bomb range and were headed back to Salina, my flight engineer Sgt. Jack D. Arnold told me that when he was in B-24 mechanics school at the Ford factory, they told him the B-24 would fly on one engine. He said he would like to know before we went overseas. Since we were still at 22,000 feet and within a hundred miles of Salina, I feathered all but #3 engine. The plane handled OK and lost about 100 feet per minute, so we could have made it back to Salina. After satisfying our curiosity on that item, we started the other three engines and continued back to base.

While at Salina one afternoon, word came that there was a B-29 down at one of the hangars. As we approached on foot from the back side of the hangar, we could see the nose sticking out past one side of the hangar and that tail sticking out the other side. Boy! We thought that was really a big airplane! As it turned out there were two B-29's there and we were seeing the nose of one and the tail of the other. They were a lot bigger than our B-24's, and they were roped off so we couldn't get closer than 25 feet to them. A captain was guarding them. Two colonels had flown them in. After completing our training at Salina, we were sent to Topeka, Kansa, where we were to get a new airplane and head overseas. I don't remember how we traveled to Topeka.

After a few days, they selected ten crews and put us on a train to Langley Field, Virginia, where we were introduced to radar low altitude bombing. We acquired another crew member – a radar operator – Sgt. Milton E. Ludlow. He was a likable person and fit right into the crew.

When it came time for our orientation flight, a Lt. North went with us. I was a bit nervous, having a stranger along on a strange airfield so I did a strange thing. We taxied close to the take-off position, checked the engines and called for clearance to takeoff, got the OK, wheeled out on the runway and pushed the throttles open. As soon as we started rolling, I realized the controls were still locked, so I chopped the throttles and applied the brakes. The tower called and asked what the problem was.

The first thing I could think of was one engine coughed and we needed to go back and check it again! Big lie. We unlocked the controls, taxied back, checked the coughing engine (it checked OK), checked the controls and took off OK. Lt. North was unfamiliar with the B-24 or he would have realized the strap he was leaning against was the control lock. He was to show us what areas were restricted and we were not to fly over. It was a wasted trip because ever after, as soon as we were airborne, we turned right and went out over the Atlantic Ocean. One of the first things I noticed was the white concrete silos for grain storage had Planter Peanuts painted on them rather than Kansas wheat!

Our Weather Officer?

There was a balloon hangar off the end of the runway and a little to the right. Many times our C.O. would come out of his office and if he could see half way to the balloon hangar he declared the weather fit for flying. We would take off into the "soup" and see nothing for several hours until we came back and usually the fog had lifted so we could see our way to our base. Since there was a blackout on the east coast, we could not see the lights on our runway above 500 feet. So we would line up on the lights on the bridge across the James River and as we got low enough we could see the landing strip lights and re-align.

One sunny afternoon we were scheduled to fly south from Langley Field out a ways from the coast and we flew alongside (for about an hour) hundreds of ships gathering for a convoy to cross the Atlantic Ocean.

Quite often we drew Sunday afternoons for our missions. After entering the fog and putting the automatic pilot on, there was not much to do or see. I happened on the the Boston Symphony and liked the music and made a point of listening to it each Sunday afternoon. I have been enjoying classical music ever since.

One night while we were out flying the blackout was lifted. We could not find our base among all the bright lights of the Norfolk Navy yard. So we went out to sea, had the radar operator lower the radar antenna and bring us to the mouth of the James River, then he quickly retracted the antenna on final approach to land.

Ready for Combat

At the end of our training at Langley Field we flew to Mitchell Field on Long Island, New York, to receive new radar-equipped planes to fly to Mather Field, California, near San Francisco. Our plane was 42-100035. The plane had very stiff controls. We flew to a repair depot at Oklahoma City, they tried to correct the problem, but didn't succeed. So we flew on to the the repair depot at Tucson, Arizona, where they did something that helped, but it took more adjusting at Mather field before it was made satisfactory. At Tucson I was able to see a friend of mine from home who was an aircraft mechanic. I suppose it took five days for us to get to California. Lt. Allen S. Clatworthy stopped at the nearest airbase for each member of his crew. It took him 13 days to cross the U.S. by air! (Maybe this should not be printed, but it is part of what happened.)

We left Mather Field on the night of February 25, 1944, heading for Hickam Field, Hawaii. As I recall we left at 10 p.m. so we would arrive at Hickam Field in daylight. As soon as it became daylight we started straining our eyes to see land, but could see none. Mitch said the island is dead ahead and we will be there at a certain time. He was right. It took 14 hours and 15 minutes elapsed time. Our plane burned 80 gallons of gas per hour, so we had plenty of reserve gas. I think some of the planes burned over 100 gal. per hour. I don't remember how much fuel we carried.

After leaving Hawaii on March 5, 1944 we flew to Palmyra Island. Second stop Fiji Island, then on to New Caledonia and to Townsville, Australia, on March 10. Lt. Kent Zimmerman made the same stops. He took off ahead of us on each flight. From Townsville we flew to Dobodura, New Guinea. The 43rd Bomb Group to which we were assigned was moving to Nadzab, New Guinea, so we were only at Dobodura a few days, March 14 to 18, 1944.

There were 12 crews trained at Langley Field and 12 crews left San Francisco, but Lt. Rudolph B. Schlesinger's crew never arrived in Hawaii. They just disappeared. Our radio operator never heard one signal from them. We were all saddened by that loss. We were the first replacement crews for the Scott Project, which were the first planes with the low altitude radar-equipped planes for nighttime bombing of Japanese shipping. A few days after arriving at Langley our assistant flight engineer, Sgt. Malcom Perry, joined the crew of Captain Charles Quinette, with the original Scott Project. Also Sgt. Thompson left our crew and Sgt. William P. Ferguson joined us. By the time we got overseas, Sgt. Perry had completed his combat duty and was ready to return to the U.S.

At Nadzab, the base was in the Markham River Valley, a wide flat area. Our tent living quarters were above the valley floor, less than a mile from the flight line. Our tents were among trees so it was not unbearably hot. I think we moved into a four-man tent that another crew heading back to the U.S. had vacated. I don't remember the food, but it must have been OK or I would have remembered it. I think we took K&C rations along on flights.

After a couple of orientation flights and some practice bombing flights, we were sent out on regular combat flights hunting for Japanese ships. We were assigned a certain area to search. If we didn't find shipping we had land targets to bomb – usually warehouse and storage areas on islands at the far end of our range. We usually took off just before dusk and landed after daylight the next morning. Only twice on the 25 missions we flew did we find ships to bomb. One night we flew across Borneo to Brunei Bay and found a merchant ship at anchor. On our first bomb run the bombs didn't release. On the second run, the bombs dropped but missed the target.

On June 3, 1944, we located part of the Japanese fleet. We picked out the biggest ship as our target, made a bomb run and the bombs didn't release. They were unaware of our presence. On the second bomb run our bombs did hit the target, as we could feel the concussion when they hit. As we turned to make our second bomb run, Lt. Newton looked out his side window and said that ship looked like it was a half-mile long. That was the basis for our reporting it as a cruiser. I don't remember how many other ships there were but there were several. One of the other crews was within radar range of the fleet. They said there was one less ship on their radar screen after we bombed, but they wouldn't confirm that in writing so we never got credit for a sinking. I'm waiting for our Group History to come out to see what the Japanese records show.

On our second bomb run, the Japanese put up lots of anti-aircraft fire and we were hit many times. The radio and radar were knocked out as well as the wiring to the fuel transfer pump. Sgt. Merle Rice was hit in the lower back and bled to death before we got back to base. Even though he was badly wounded, he held the flashlight for Sgt. Arnold while he put wires to the fuel pump back together so we could get gas to the wing tanks. After the bomb run, No. 3 engine lost power, so I feathered the prop. However, by flashlight, we couldn't see any oil leaks or missing parts so we re-started the engine and it worked OK. I still don't know why it lost power. For a while it looked like we would have to ditch at sea. But after Sgt. Arnold got the fuel transferred and we got #3 engine running, we figured we could get back to base. I think we had staged out of Wakde Island and returned there.

The hydraulic lines were shot out, but we had one application of brakes in the accumulators – which turned out to be enough. After landing, we stayed by the plane until Sgt. Rice's body was removed, then we were de-briefed, ate and rested until there had been enough repairs done on the plane to fly it back to Nadzab in late afternoon. I'm sure Sgt. Arnold stayed with the plane and helped repair it. It had over 100 20mm shell holes in it and these were not repaired there. Mainly the hydraulic lines were repaired so we would have brakes for the next landing. We flew to Nadzab with bomb bay doors open and wheels down because of lack of hydraulic power. The plane was in the repair depot for the next month during which time all four engines were replaced because they had 500 hours on them. News of this flight was heard of by a friend of mine in Oklahoma four days later. My name was given.

At our Langley Field reunion in 1991, Fred Cheuvront told me that had we ditched after our fleet experience that a Catalina flying boat was following us and would have picked us up if we survived the water landing. He was in group operations and knew of our predicament. That was nice to know even after all these years. We were recommended for some medals, Silver Star or DFC. Instead we received a letter of commendation from General George C. Kenney.

According to my records, we did not fly again until early July, so I think we were sent on rest leave to Sydney, Australia, for a week where we could enjoy the mild temperature of an Australian winter, the big city and of course the company of Australian girls and Australian beer. I stayed at a Red Cross lodging place at Kings Cross. We could ride street cars to get to the main downtown area. The week went all too quickly!

Black Sunday

April 16, 1944 became the most disastrous day in 5th Air Force opera-tions in which the target was Hollandia in preparation for an invasion on April 25. The weather was threatening rain and the flights were delayed three hours. The raid on Hollandia proceeded as scheduled, but a terribly heavy and vicious weather front moved in, cutting off usual return flights and causing landings at alternate bases, ditchings, bail cuts, and disappearances. Losses of aircraft were 35 to 57 planes and 54 crewmen, depending on whose account you read. No planes were lost to enemy fire.

After I read the account of Black Sunday by Michael J. Claringbould, I wondered if I contributed to the disaster. We were on a search flight, taking off in the evening of April 15 and returning early morning of April 16. I have wondered if we saw the front in its early stages and didn't consider it danger-ous; whether it was farther east and we did not see it, or whether if we saw it, we didn't properly report it. I don't recall that it was even raining when we landed. After de-briefing and eating we went to bed. Later when we awoke

after noon it was raining hard. Then we kept hearing the reports of low
ceilings, overcrowding at alternate fields and crashes.

One night one of the ground crew went with us. As we were coming
to Nadzab the next morning, Sgt. Arnold suggested I show our passenger
that the B-24 would fly on one engine. So I feathered three engines and flew
along for a short time before we started the three engines again. We were
meeting the daylight flights going out. When they saw us, I'll bet they thought
we must have had a really rough mission!

The "Sackwagon"

While we were at Nadzab our plane acquired the name "Sackwagon."
I don't remember who came up with the name or who had the name and
picture painted on the side. I think Lt. Newton took care of the whole project.
I think the name came about from the amount of sack time several of the
crew got on the long flight with nothing to do as long as the automatic pilot,
co-pilot, navigator, engineer, radio operator and radar operator were alert on
the job. Lt. Newton claims that as soon as we were in the air and on autopilot, I went to sleep; which is probably more truth than fiction.

One evening the squadron commander Major Sargeant decided to go
on the mission with us. After being delivered to the airplane by truck, I checked
the tires for cuts, as I always did, but never found any, while Sgt. Arnold went
up on the wings to see that the gas tanks were full and caps put on properly.
I sat down in the shade of the wing. Soon the CO asked shouldn't we be
loading up. I said as soon as Sgt. Arnold says the plane is ready, we will go
and I continued to sit there. I don't suppose that made me any goody points
with the CO. When we went on our bomb run, the CO intended to watch the
bombs explode. No one told the bombardier, so as soon as "Bombs Away"
was announced, he closed the bomb bay doors, cutting off the CO's view.
Later during the night the CO was sleeping on the flight deck and someone
came through and walked on his flying glasses. So for him the whole mission
was one disaster after another. Later on Major Sargeant was killed piloting a
B-24 that crashed on take-off at Owi and burned.

One afternoon we made a flight north of New Guinea to the Admiralty Islands, landed, refueled and were loaded with bombs. Our destination
was Biak Island. We took off in the night so as to arrive at Biak a little after
daybreak. It may have been the day of invasion by our troops, because as we
approached Biak the naval ships were shelling inland a little ways from the
coast. We could see the flames from the big guns on the ships, then a bit later
the shell bursts on the island. We made our bomb run in the same area as the
ships were shelling and as soon as possible headed back to Nadzab. Later
some one came through the bomb bay and reported three bombs hung up.
The lowest bomb did not release and the two above were resting on top of it.

Top Left to Right: Raymond S. Hewis (Nose Gunner), Ohio; Darmus D. LeGate (Radio), Oklahoma; T/Sgt. Jack D. Arnold ("The Best Engineer, regardless"), San Antonio, Texas; Milton E. Ludlow (Radar), Indiana; William P. Ferguson (Tail Gunner), Pennsylvania. *Bottom Row, Left to Right:* Airplane Driver Lt. Raymond E. Crawford, Nebraska; Lt. Harold T. Newton (Co-Pilot); Lt. Serenus Mitchell (Navigator) Indiana; Lt. Edward St. Onge (Bombardier), New York.   *Photo provided by Raymond E.*

So, Lt. St. Onge, my bombardier, opened the bomb bay doors and went back on the cat walk and manually tripped the rack on the lowest bomb and all three fell into the ocean. I think we dropped six 500 lb. bombs at Biak.

In July of 1944 our group moved from Nadzab to Owi Island just off the south side of Biak. The Air Force was warned that Owi was "taboo." The all-knowing Air Force thought it was a native superstition, but soon, the first troops there started coming down with typhus fever carried by a tick that lived in the grass. I think the island was sprayed with DDT. By the time our crew arrived, the threat of typhus had diminished. However, Sgt. William Ferguson, a gunner on my crew, got typhus. We went to see him in the hospital; he had a terribly high fever and felt he was about to die. A few days later he was evacuated to a hospital at Nadzab and we never heard any more about him; presumably he recovered. I think we flew with one crew member short after that.

The landing strips at Owi were coral and stretched nearly from waters edge to waters edge. They were good and solid. It was from Owi that we started bombing Davao, Mindanao as an alternate target when no shipping was found. We made several runs on the harbor installations at Davao. We never encountered any night fighter, nor Ack Ack or searchlights. One other time we did get caught in searchlights and could see A/A shell bursts a little below us. We probably weren't in the lights more than a couple minutes, but that was long enough.

I think it was at Owi that I became Squadron Engineering Officer. There needed to be a flying officer in the position. I was mostly a figurehead as there was a ground officer by name of Lt. Noonan who was really the engineering officer. Because of the position, I was assigned a jeep with my name on it. Lt. Knobby – 63rd Sqn. Eng. Officer.

One day as I was on the flight line word came that Bob Hope was to dedicate an airplane "Ken's Men" in honor of General Kenney. In the ceremony, Bob Hope made mention of his show the night before and someone yelled out "we didn't see it – we weren't back yet," so Bob Hope, Jerry Cologna and Patti Page put on an impromptu show of about half an hour. I happened to be at the right place at the right time.

When our crew was first assembled, co-pilot Lt. Harold T. Newton and radio operator Sgt. Darmus D. Legate found that they both liked to play checkers, and so the friendly rivalry ensued. Over the months that they played, once in a while Legate would play to a draw, which encouraged him to play again, but he never won a game. I'm sure "Newt" must have played other men in the squadron. He had played the runnerup to the champion checker player in South Carolina at age 16. One evening at Owi arrangements were made for "Newt" to play six opponents at a time, blindfolded, making one move at a time at each board, having a man on his side move his man as he called the moves by number. "Newt" won four games and got a draw on two. I saw it happen.

On the night of October 18, 1944 we flew a ferret mission up along the east side of the Philippines, hunting for enemy radio and radar stations. Nothing spectacular happened except that the radio operator reported very heavy traffic in radio transmissions. He said that something big must be going on. We landed back at Owi on the 19th. A few days later we learned that a landing had been made on Leyte Island, Philippines, on October 20 and the subsequent proclamation by General Douglas MacArthur "I have returned."

Move to Leyte

We were soon staging out of airstrip at Tacloban, Leyte. On our first flight out of Tacloban, we had come in from Owi, were loaded with gas and bombs and took off just before dark. The runway was made of punched-plank, steel matting laid on sand not far from the beach. As we were taking off, Newt said you'd better have the thing in the air because we just ran out of runway. We were just lifting off. By the next morning when we came back, they had laid another thousand feet of steel matting.

Another time at Tacloban, we didn't get off before the fighter planes came in to land. They got priority because they were usually short on gas. It got dark as they continued coming in. I was sitting in our plane listening to the radio. I heard the tower say, "Plane on final approach, if you are friendly blink your lights." Pilot did not blink and the A/A guns shot him down. It was a Japanese plane loaded with land mines. Luckily, the land mines did not explode. A bulldozer came quickly and pushed the wreckage off the strip. The rest of the fighters came in and then we went on our mission.

Not long after this one of our 63rd crews had been west of Leyte, searching and locating several Japanese ships. They made their bomb run and dropped their bombs but the A/A fire was intense and two engines were shot out. They threw out whatever was loose in the plane to lighten it as much as possible. They were several hours from base. When they came in on final approach, a Japanese plane came over and dropped some bombs on the strip just ahead of them, so they had to pull up and go around. Luckily the bombs didn't explode and damage the runway, so our plane was able to land the next time around. That plane never flew again, it was cannibalized for parts. The engines that had been feathered were repaired and used again, but the engines that brought the plane home were never used.

That crew never took off again with a load of bombs, but would take the ferret plane any time assigned. The ferret plane often stayed out 18 hours, but this crew stayed out 21 hours once. We thought they had disappeared.

While at Owi, Lt. Newton became Squadron Suppy Officer. Somehow he came across equipment and supplies to make carbonated water. Also located Coca-Cola syrup and served us Cokes as supplies were available. My records show that we did not fly between September 15 and October 10, 1944. I think we may have gone to Sydney, Australia on rest leave for the second time. Sydney shuts down on Saturdays so people could go to the horse races. I went too. On the first race I missed the finish because I was looking to my left for the horses and they came from the right! They ran them clockwise down there.

After coming back from leave, we flew two missions in October and four missions in November. During this time Lt. Newton qualified as first pilot, and he checked out the other co-pilots in the squadron.

On December 4, we flew a mission to north of Manila and bombed some rail yards. On December 6 we flew a mission to Negros Island and landed back on December 7, completing our required combat flight time, having accumulated 422.55 hours and 25 combat missions.

I think my crew all went back to the states by whatever transportation became available – mostly by ship. I agreed to stay on as engineering officer of the 63rd squadron as we moved up to Tacloban. I had been hearing that pilots who were returning to the U.S. were being retrained to fly B-29's and would soon be back bombing Japan. So I was in no hurry to get home. I had neither wife nor girl friend at home!

Other crews began flying "the Sackwagon." It was parked by the air-strip at Tacloban one day when a Japanese plane dropped a string of bombs on the runway. One bomb exploded close enough to the "Sackwagon" to set it afire and it was demolished. Also my "Lt. Knobby" jeep was destroyed, but worst of all Lt. Noonan was killed along with some other men. Some other planes were destroyed also.

Boy Scouts of America

One day after the 63rd Squadron had moved to Tacloban, I got a jeep to drive into Tacloban, which was a small town perhaps seven or eight miles from the airstrip. On the way I came to a circle where several roads came together. In the middle of the circle was a statue four feet high of a Boy Scout on a pedestal with a plaque on it, which read "Boy Scouts of America." That made me feel not quite so far away from home. The town was a disappointment, only a few stores and houses along side a dirt road. I didn't even stop.

When the Navy was shelling the Island of Leyte ahead of the landing, a Boy Scout with a flashlight signalled the Navy that they were over-shooting the area where the Japanese were dug in. They redirected the fire to the proper area. After landing, this boy became known to our troops and they asked where he had learned to signal code. He had learned it in the Boy Scouts.

I stayed with the squadron as it moved from Tacloban to Clark Field north of Manila. I flew a mission to Yulin harbor on the south side of Hainan Island off the south China coast. I flew co-pilot with Major Brownfield, the 63rd C.O. at the time. That was my last combat mission, March 25 and 26, 1945. On April 24, 1945, I left the 63rd Squadron to go to Fifth Air Force Headquarters where I joined Lt. Gen. Ennis C. Whitehead's personal flight crew as co-pilot. Major Glen E. Ream was pilot (from the 64th Squadron) and Capt. Fred W. Epplen was the navigator. Epplen had been in the 63rd Squadron as had assistant flight engineer Sgt. Leonard "Red" Lawson. Sgt. Gordon Bavor from headquarters Squadron was radio operator and Sgt. Fred Kleinfelder as flight engineer completed the crew. The general had a B-17 that we flew taking him where he needed to go and took other people and papers as ordered. Much of the time we had nothing to do, except be ready in case we were needed. I continued that duty until we arrived back in the states on October 15, 1945, in a war-weary B-24 J from Okinawa.

Pearl Harbor Day

December 7, 1941. I was attending the University of Nebraska at Lincoln. I came back "home" from a movie when I heard on the radio that Pearl Harbor had been bombed by the Japanese. I had never heard of Pearl Harbor and only knew Hawaii was out in the Pacific Ocean somewhere.

I had been called by the draft in August 1941. I had another year to complete in Nebraska University and asked and received a six-month deferment, which wouldn't get me through school. I heard of a civilian pilot training program and found that by taking that I could finish the last semester in school. The catch was that at the end of course I would have to enlist in one of the Air Forces, Army, Navy or Marine. Since I was due to be drafted, that requirement was not a deterrent. I wanted to know whether or not I could pilot a plane.

Subsequently I was ordered to report to Ft. Leavenworth, Kansas, across the Missouri River from Kansas City, Missouri, on July 2, 1942. From there we were put on a train and sent to Santa Ana, California to start Aviation Cadet Training. From there we went to Oxnard, California for Primary training; to Bakersfield, California, for basic training and to Roswell, New Mexico, for advanced training in twin-engine aircraft. This takes me full circle to the beginning of this narrative. When I went into the Army Air Corps, as it was known at the time, I thought I would either come back alive and in one piece or not come back at all. I never worried about which one. I had confidence in our airplane and my crew. The rest was in God's hands.

After Thoughts

I was promoted to Captain in October, 1944.

Our navigator, Lt. Serenus Mitchell was a good poker player. He had all his Air Corps pay sent home. It took longer to get out of the states than he anticipated and he had borrowed some money from other crew members. By the time we went on our first rest leave he had paid back what he owed and had enough to finance the rest leave. He always said he was going to open a beer joint when he got out of the service – which he did. One night while we were on Owi Island he came into our tent about 10 at night and said that there was a poker game a few tents away and he was going to sit in for a while. He came back one hour later and said I got the sign for my beer joint tonight. He had won $2000. He sent it home the next day.

In order to clean out the flight deck before we landed at the end of our missions, someone on our crew found that by taking the oxygen hose off the regulator (we never flew high enough to need oxygen), stick the end out the side window and use it as a vacuum cleaner.

Bill Craig

Crew Overcomes Bad Luck and Tragedy
Bill Craig

My crew was one of those who ended the war in Ie Shima. As pilot, I graduated from pilot school at Lubbock, Texas in Class 44-D. Went to command pilot school in Liberal, Kansas, picked up a crew and did overseas training at Boise, Idaho in B-24s.

The original crew was: Bill Craig, pilot, Don Zech, co-pilot, Don Christopherson, bombardier, Pat Davis, navigator, Bill Hall, engineer, A. Shearer, armorer gunner, Sam Wertz, radio operator, Wally Iskra, tail gunner, Gerry Riordan, nose gunner and Jack Quinn, gunner. We finished at Boise and took a train to Langley Field along with 49 other crews. When we got there we all lined up and ten of us stayed at Langley for LAB training and the rest went to Europe.

At Langley, Jimmy Smythe was added to our crew as the radar operator. As I recall, ten of us went by train to Mather Field, CA where we picked up a brand new B-24 to be delivered to the 43rd Group at Biak, New Guinea. One of the humorous things you asked about was the troop train, which took just about a week from Langley to Mather. We had numerous stops along the way and various guys wanted to visit home for the last time. Needless to say the opportunity was there and many of them took advantage of it. How we ever got all of them to San Francisco upon our arrival is still a mystery.

We picked up the B-24 at Mather, flew it to Hamilton Field and waited for orders to fly to Biak. We spent New Year's eve 1944 in San Francisco. So far, so good. Then things started to happen. Our first leg to Hawaii was uneventful. We were to take off for Christmas Island on our way to Biak when we crashed on take off at John Rodgers Naval Air Station, Hawaii. It was very early in the morning and we had just reached 100 mph when the number 3 engine exploded, broke the lock on the right landing gear and the right wing tip dug into the ground and around we went. We were on fire as soon as the front bomb bay gas tank scraped the runway. Pat Davis, the navigator was killed as the top turret came loose and crushed him. Fortunately the rest of us escaped with a few minor cuts and bruises. We buried Pat at Schofield Barracks and then went on to Biak via ATC. Incidentally, Pat was moved to the Punch Bowl Cemetery in Hawaii after the war and is buried just a few feet away from Ernie Pyle.

I wish that was the end of the bad news but it isn't. On one of the island stops Don Christopherson found an unexploded cartridge and it blew up in his hand as he was inspecting it. He was flown home and suffered damage to his hand and to one of his eyes. After we arrived at Biak Sam Wertz had to be sent back to the States as he was allergic to the tropical weather in New Guinea. So there we were with three of our original members already gone, but we did pick up a new black B-24 and flew it to Leyte to deliver it to the 63rd.

When we got there we found out that the group had moved to Clark Field so we went on to there and made the final delivery. Roy Rose was assigned to us as our replacement navigator. Incidentally we flew to Leyte without a navigator. We just flew north until we reached what we presumed to be the Philippines and followed the coast line until we found the Tacloban airstrip on Leyte.

We flew a couple of missions before I went into Manila with a few of the guys where I apparently picked up some sort of bug and came down with amoebic dysentery. I was sick as could be – lost 45 pounds in the next ten days – and was sent to a General Hospital in Leyte. While I was gone my crew members flew as subs with the other crews. I think they flew a couple with Major Butts, the 63rd CO. When I returned to the squadron I was shocked to learn that Jimmy Smythe and Jack Quinn were lost in action while flying missions as subs. I flew a few more missions before the end of the war.

One of the most interesting things I did was to fly about 30 POW's from Okinawa to Clark Field as they were returning home. Our 24's had been outfitted with plywood seats in the rear bomb bay as we were getting ready to fly troops to Japan if the war continued. We flew over to Okie from Ie Shima and waited for them to be sent out to us. Most of them were British, having been prisoners since before we were even into the war. Some were Americans including a Catholic priest. I never felt quite so humble as I did with these men who were so grateful to us for helping to get them back home. One of the British, with tears in his eyes, came over to me and said that many of the British perished during their captivity but that most of the Americans made it through. Then he said, "You Americans are the greatest people on earth." The priest told me later that none of the prisoners had ever bared their soul to him as that man did to me. I still get tears in my eyes thinking about it.

December 7, 1941

As far as remembering my reactions to Pearl Harbor I'm a little hazy. I think it happened on a Sunday and I heard about it along with my close buddy, my cousin Jack. Being just a kid I don't remember knowing much about the overall worldwide situation with Japan. Our first thoughts were that they were a bunch of little guys and that they were crazy for picking on us and that we would plow them under in a couple of weeks. This sounds quite naive now, but it seemed to be how a couple of young kids thought back then. I signed up to be an aviation cadet as soon as I became 18 and went into the service in 1943 – graduating in pilot class 44-D.

My crew members preceded me home since they had more combat hours than me. I did fly a B-24 home in Operation Sunset. Landed back at Mather Field on November 11, 1945. Took a train to Indiantown Gap, Pa. – was discharged and arrived back home to a loving family on Thanksgiving Day. I married my high school sweetheart on January 5, 1946 and we celebrated our 62nd wedding anniversary last month. We had four sons, one of which graduated from the Air Force Academy in 1968.

In reminiscing about time with the 63rd I always remember the times when we got together around a tub of beer [after a once in a while beer ration] telling jokes and singing songs. I don't think we could sing those same songs in mixed company, but they were sure fun back then. I also remember the guys returning from Japan after the war when they brought back some sake. We really had a party that night. As I recall we thought sake was whiskey and mixed it with fruit cocktail from the mess hall. We had to hold Butts down because, as the song went, he was going to burn the s–house down. Of course, going through the typhoons was something I will never forget. Another thing, since I was grounded because of sickness, I had to go from Clark to Ie Shima in the naval convoy. Riding out the typhoon was hell, even the sailors were sick.

I get a kick out of reading some of the current writings that say that flying a B-24 was difficult. Some of my son's friends who flew in Desert Storm marvel when you tell them that we took off an overloaded airplane, leveled off at 1000 feet flying just a few miles over stall speed, flew for 12 to 20 hours and returned home. While we think of the way they flew planes like their fighter jets as being super human, they say that it took "guts" to do what we did and thought nothing of it.

John
P.
Harmon

The following is a write-up that my navigator John P. Harmon wrote of a mission we made. John Harmon died in the spring of 1994. I would like to include this story in this book as the description of the mission was very typical. It was certainly no big success story. You will notice the date of the mission was 19 Dec. 1943. On 24 Dec. 43, Christmas Eve, we were sent out again. I always felt they sent us out on Christmas Eve to get even for the trouble we caused.   JAMES SMITH, Radar

Weather Not Fit For Man or Beast
John P. Harmon, Navigator

Dec. 19, 1943
APO 503
5th AF, 43rd Grp; 63rd Sq.
Operations "Shack"

16:30 Hours: The briefing is short for this "Armed Reconnaissance" mission to the Bismarck Sea area north of New Britain; look for shipping close to shore along the west coast of New Ireland. Most likely barges, that lie hidden along the shore during the day and move south to Rabaul at night. Weather? Look outside – sheets of rain. Wind? Swirling and unpredictable. Visibility? One eighth of a mile. Prior to Radar, a reconnaissance mission such as this would have been "Scrubbed."

Crew:	**P**	Clarence "Tex" Molder	**CP**	Donald C. Requa
	N	John P. Harmon	**B**	Paul J. Indyke
	E	Manley B. Gross	**AE**	William R. Harner
	R	Charles G. Meinke	**AR**	Baxter A. McCamish
	G	Robert C. Jackson	**AG**	John P. Bernicky

Radar: James Smith

17:00 Hours: The tarp covered "Six by Six" bounces and slips along a water-soaked road to the revetment area. There the "props" of the assigned B-24D bomber are "pulled through." A precaution taken before each flight. It assures that oil has not collected in the lower combustion chambers of the R1800 Pratt and Whitney engines.

The bomb bay, loaded earlier, contains two "sticks" of bombs. Each "stick" consists of a 500, 1000 and 500 pound bomb set to release individually in that order.

17:20 Hours: All crew members are in take off position. A reluctant "Putput" slowly staggers to life. The pilot toggles the starter switches on the instrument panel. Engaging each engine in turn when the shrill whine of the inertia starter reaches its peak. The first engine fires with a blast of sound that overpowers the drumming of the rain on the aluminum skin. It sets up its own pattern of vibration replacing the slight swaying caused by the wind. Engine number three backfires, belching smoke and fire. In its own way, protesting this ominous weather. The storm poses obstacles for the mission but is ideal for an enemy waiting to move men and material over open water with little or no chance of observation.

Secured on the Navigator's desk is a Mercater projection. Marked are the coordinates indicating the positions of Dobodura, and the sunken hull of a German ship lying off the coast of Buna. Navigators use the hull as a reference point when approaching the airstrip at Dobo. Also marked are coordinates of checkpoints on the north coast of New Britain and the west coast of New Ireland. The northernmost point is just off the coast at Kavieng.

17:35 Hours: It is unbelievably dark. Inside the plane one hooded light bulb focuses a spear of light on the navigation desk. In the cockpit, the eerie glow of the "black light" on the instruments belies the time of day.

Slowly the throttles advance. The B-24, heavily loaded with 4000 pounds of bombs and 2100 gallons of high octane gasoline is reluctant to move. Blue darts of flame flash from the exhausts when the "props" develop enough power to start the huge bulk rolling. Retarding the throttles the instant the plane starts forward prevents speed build up that is inconsistent with visibility.

The darkness outside suddenly retreats as first, one landing light and then the other alternate to illuminate the sea of water that is the taxi way. The B-24 creeps slowly forward, its progress impeded only slightly by the nudging application of one brake or the other. Two rows of lights marking each side of the runway appear.

17:50 Hours: With landing lights off, guided only by the faint glow of the runway markers, the darkness again prevails. At the light, marking the end of the runway, firm application of the left brake swings the B-24D in a tight arc. The row of lights marking each side of the runway stretched out ahead, disappearing into the rain and mist. The runway length is only adequate at best, and the splashing water will slow the takeoff roll. The warm moist air will not help wing lift.

Because of the many negative aspects of the takeoff, every inch of runway must be available. To regain the portion of runway lost in the turn, backing the B-24 to the end of the runway is mandatory. By locking the right brake and running up the right outboard engine the left wheel rolls back. Alternating first the right and then the left brake and engine, the plane moves back until the tail assembly extends over the very end of the runway.

18:00 Hours: Assured of a full takeoff roll, only the readiness of the B-24 to fly remains. The controls, ailerons, elevator, rudder and flaps must move smoothly through their full travel as observed by crewmembers.

Also verified is the prop pitch and all of the other details on the check list. Runup of the engine is crucial. Each engine is, in its turn, run up part way to check the mags and then full throttle while setting the turbocharger for maximum allowable manifold pressure – PLUS a little more. Only partially retarding the throttle after each engine runup prevents the spark plugs from oil fouling while the other engines are being put through their paces. The last engine to runup remains at full power. With brakes locked, advancing the other throttles bring all four engines up to full power. The thunderous roar and trembling of the aircraft adds to the anxiety of the crew.

Through a small bit of Plexiglas in the fuselage by the navigation desk, the underside of the left wing, two engines and one landing gear strut are visible. The rain, blasted into a fine mist whips under the wing. The "Saint Elmo's Fire," a flashing blue ring of static electricity, frames the spinning props and discharges in flashing bolts of lightning, into the ground. The engines strain against their mounting bolts. The turbochargers, crimson from the blast of scorching exhaust, cram power boosting oxygen into the manifolds. All four "Hamilton Standard" propellers tear at the air. Despite the tremendous weight involved, releasing the brakes initiates a powerful forward surge, thrusting mission into a night of suspense.

18:10 Hours: As the B-24 dashes for the end of the runway momentum builds. The "Davis" wing takes over more and more of the load and the landing strut, observed through the Plexiglas, begins to lengthen. It flexes up and down, absorbing the shock of the uneven runway surface. Then, water, blasted from a small lake on the runway by the landing gear, cascades over the side of the fuselage retarding the forward speed.

The landing strut settles, then lengthens again as the B-24 accelerates. The trees at the end of the runway flash to mind each time the strut settles. A glance at the remote compass indicates the deviation card is correct. Now, the strut, relieved of its load no longer flexes. The tire skips once - twice then the wings take over and that hulk is actually airborne.

18:12 Hours: Gear up - power reduced - trim tabs set.

18:17 Hours: Flaps up - starting a single needle width left turn to a compass heading of 359. With no horizon for reference, the rate of turn and climb are extremely difficult to maintain in the wildly turbulent air. Atmospheric conditions will make this a long mission if we cannot break out on top. Hopefully, the breakout altitude will be livable. The radar screen comes to life, its sweeping arm turns the sunken hull, to the left, into a bright yellow blip. The familiar coastline, beyond, lends orientation to the otherwise dark, forbidding surroundings.

Tremendous flashing of lightning rip the sky, remaining momentarily embedded in the eye of the beholder. The radar screen identifies the storms greatest density enabling the B-24 to bypass the most violent turbulence.

18:55 Hours: Altitude 8000 feet. There is no letup in the fury of the storm. If anything, turbulence escalates with increased altitude. Descending to 4000 feet brings relief from the cold but only slight decrease in turbulence.

There are no signs of storm moderation. The plane continues to slip through the passes between radar-located hot spots and boring through vicious lightning-filled thunderheads when no other alternative presents itself.

19:42 Hours: The southern coast of New Britain becomes a glowing yellowish colored mass on the radar scope. It shatters the monotony of the nonreflective sea, and hints an extremely important aspect of the landfall. The plane will not cross the coastline precisely as intended. The westerly drift was not unexpected. The winds, no doubt, are whipping the sea below into a froth.

19:59 Hours: A time and the radar established position west of Talasea translate into a wind of 20 knots from 40 degrees. The new compass heading is 59 degrees towards a point north and a little west of Rabaul. The north coast of New Britain glows on the radar scope. All blips on the radar screen that do not correspond with known or charted islands are suspect. Mission orders dictate an attack on suspect blips.

No targets appear, nor did we expect any along the New Britain coast. Targets would most likely appear between Rabaul and Kavieng to the north.

21:07 Hours: Radar confirms the previously established turning point northwest of Rabaul. The new compass heading is 296 degrees. The west coast of New Ireland is on the radar screen to the right. This is where we expect to find ocean going traffic of supplies and replacement troops sent by Japan to bolster the defense of Rabaul. Typically, they try to slip through under cover of darkness.

To stop this traffic is why the mission battles the turbulence and lightning. By cutting the supply lines, the manpower odds the enemy possesses could be minimized or eliminated. If he has no gasoline his planes are impotent. If there is no food the troops cannot sustain themselves in the field.

21:10 Hours: Disaster – it could be described no other way – complete and total disaster. The radar images disappear. Our eyes are gone. We can no longer see to interdict the enemy – we can no longer see to get back to base. We must feel our way through this ominous night.

A radioed position report, made accurate by the 21:07 landfall and recently calculated wind, informed Dobo of the location and circumstances of the mission. A request for orders brought the response "return to base." What else? Such a simple thing to say – so difficult to do.

Anticipating orders when disaster struck, the B-24 negotiated a 162-degree compass heading. Clearing all known obstacles between the plane and

Dobodura, 8000 feet might also find some stars and get the mission out of this nerve wracking turbulence.

At 8000 feet – no indication of change in the elements that have so completely engulfed the mission. Finding the weaker passes through the storm without radar proves impossible. Now, the only perceptible change, in the night sky, is a darker blackness as the plane bores into the core of the towering cumulus clouds.

22:00 Hours: ETA (est. time of arrival) On the sunken hull 23:39. Descending slowly towards warmer air and Dobo strip. Increased speed, possible because of the descent, hastens the mission's return. Unfortunately, increasing speed intensifies the effect of the turbulence. In response to a request for Dobo weather during the last position report, the radio now spells out in code: "Rain – visibility one half mile." What this mission needed, desperately, was luck.

Pressures within the storm are no doubt affecting the plane altimeter readings. Hoping for advanced warning of the sea's proximity the mission approaches 2000 feet with the trailing antenna extended.

23:30 Hours: Leveling out at 1500 feet. In response to a request for runway lights, the control tower acknowledges "runway lights on."

23:42 Hours: Is the plane over the runway? There are no lights – nothing but blackness and rain. All eyes strain to glimpse some clue of the plane's position – nothing but rain. The present heading is on a collision course with the Owen Stanley mountains, minutes inland from Dobodura. Continuing on course means disaster!

23:43 Hours: In a steep left bank the B-24 commences a 180 degree turn. A radio message spells out–"PROCEED TO KIRAWINA". Commencing a climb to 3000 feet, the mission turns toward its new destination.

Two hours and 36 minutes, of elapsed turbulent time, since the last positive position renders the present position questionable. All subsequent positions were established by dead reckoning, a choice of last resort. Now the mission, headed for an unfamiliar destination in the Trobrian Islands, must contemplate a landing strip not intended for B-24 bombers. It lies an hour and 30 minutes somewhere ahead.

00:20 Hours, 20 December 1943: A radio message "RETURN TO BASE" – nothing more – no explanation, raises many questions. Is the weather worse at Kirawina than at Dobo? Was Kirawina under attack? Commencing a 180 degree change of course to return to Dobo the mission again faces the daunting presence of the Owen Stanley mountains – WHY?

The turbulence seems somewhat less as the plane descends to 1500 feet. Flashes of lightning in the clouds confirm the storm's continued presence. ETA on Dobo is 00:58.

00:55 Hours: A call to the tower for runway lights produces no answer – another call – no answer. The radio is "out."

The plane is not only blind but now it can not hear! There is no way to know if the base receives the radio transmissions.

00:58 Hours: Calculations place the plane directly over the runway-nothing but black night and rain! There are no lights to guide the B-24.

01:03 Hours: Executing left turn and a compass heading for Kirawena is the only alternative. While climbing to 3000 feet a message from the B-24, of destination and ETA (02:35), is not confirmed by base. The plane, blind and deaf, hurtles through black space toward an island and airstrip ill prepared to receive it.

02:00 Hours: Position and weather reports continue on the speculation that they will be received. The fuel, at this point is no problem.

Compass headings, drift, variation, all of those calculations so critical to navigation are checked and rechecked. No errors are found. If the wind has remained constant and the compass headings are not affected by the violent turbulence, the position report should be accurate. If the tiny island of Kirawina is to be found in this weather there is no allowable error. The search for it must be made at very low altitude. Fortunately there are no mountains to prevent the prepared search plan.

02:20 Hours: A fleeting thin spot in the clouds – then another – "WONDER OF WONDERS" the B-24 clears the last wispy fragments of the clouds and bursts into bright moonlit world with a sea of glass stretching endlessly before it. Directly ahead lies Kirawina. After eight hours and 10 minutes of buffeting turbulence, six hours of it without radar and the last hour and 25 minutes without radio, nothing – but NOTHING could describe the relief.

An absolute necessity now, is the skillful placing of the landing gear on the first few feet of that short, short runway. A gradual let down to a position for a straight-in approach commences. A runway light request, radioed to Kirowina tower brings no acknowledgment, and no lights. The radio was not transmitting – small problem at this point, for the moon is bright enough to find the strip.

As the plane banks to the left for a long straight-in approach, the sky ahead fills with bursts of black smoke. A veritable carpet of "ACK -ACK" lies across our approach. Kirawina AA is FIRING. Tracers come streaming out to greet the mission. They come in that strange looping arc that, at first seems to be way off the target but then, bend back to what appears to be a inevitable hit.

The plane, gear and flaps down – landing lights on, banks steeply in violent evasive action. Making a diving 360 degree turn, the B-24 again enters the approach to land. The tracers die away and the runway lights glow in the distance. The B-24, in a power-on approach skims over the last 100 yards to the runway and, when the throttles are closed, settles solidly on the first 100 feet of the strip. Hard braking action compresses the nose wheel strut and the landing roll is made in a tail high position.

02:30 Hours: The FOLLOW ME jeep is on the scene before the plane completes its 180 degree turn at the extreme end of the airstrip. It leads the plane to operations. Flexing muscles, stiffened by inactivity, relieves the tension. The ebb and flow of questions concluded, the officer in charge is asked to radio Dobo of our landing. Other personnel issue blankets and lead us to tents.

While billeting is in progress, the air raid siren screeches. "Washing Machine Charley" no doubt, on his night fly nuisance raid. If so, the runway was the safest place to be.

As blankets are tossed onto folding cots the "Red" alert sounds. "ACK-ACK" fills the sky directly overhead. Maybe – just maybe, that shallow trench in the coral is the place to be. Approaching the trench the decision to enter is hastened by a sound, not unlike that of a startled flight of a covey of Hungarian Partridge. An explanation of the source of the sound is not necessary. It is self-explanatory. The first bomb blast is very close – the second CLOSER – if there is another, most certainly it would fall amongst the flattened bodies in the trench – it didn't.

The first reaction, after the events of the night, was one of exultation. Individuals, whose expertise was called upon, performed their duties in commendable fashion. Those whose specialties were not called upon can feel no blight. They took the same risks and, to a large degree suffered the same anxiety. Most certainly they would have suffered the same consequences had this flight not been executed in a successful manner.

Frustration, total, abject frustration overcomes the first rush of exultation at the realization that the mission was a total failure. Nothing, absolutely nothing was accomplished. The enemies' plans were not deterred by anything that had been done.

In final analysis it appears that wars, as well as other endeavors are decided by partial failure and partial success. The degree one way or the other, depends upon which attribute prevails and by how much.

Howard
S.
Booth

Too Young to Vote But Old Enough to Command a B-24 Crew in Combat
Howard S. Booth

On December 7, 1941 – The Day of Infamy – I was 17 years old, a high school student sitting at home shortly after 12 noon in upstate NY listening to the radio when I heard of the attack. I was shocked and then mad. The next day I ran home at noon time to catch the broadcast of the President's speech to Congress and cheered wildly when Congress approved his declaration of war. I was sworn into the Army Air Corps on December 14, 1942 and was actually called into Service in February 1943. I graduated from twin engine flying school on 15 April 1944, a 2nd Lt., at 19 years of age and went directly to B-24 Transition School in Smyrna, Tenn., graduating in July '44. Then to Westover AAF where I picked up my crew, thence to Charleston AAF base where I actually flew with my full crew while still 19 years of age. My birthday was August 17, which accounts for the fact that the war ended a couple of days before my 21st birthday in 1945.

I have lots of stories about my young age such as flying into the Glen View NAS as I was finishing up training on the B-24 in July '44 and not being old enough to buy an alcoholic beverage in Chicago. And being kidded by my crew before the November 1944 Presidential election by being asked who I was going to vote for as I was not yet old enough to vote.

Crew:

Pilot	Lt. Howard S. Booth
Co-Pilot	Lt. Joseph G. Parrish
Navigator	Lt. Wilfred H. Parker
Bombardier	Lt. Thomas S. Ireland
Radar	Lt. Richard C. Landsman
Engineer	Sgt. James L. Derden
Radio Operator	Sgt. Donald McDonald
Ass't: Engineer	Sgt. Joe H. Repovg
Ass't. Radio Operator	Sgt. Dwane Reed
Armorer-Gunner	Sgt. Robert E. Evans
Ass't Armorer-Gunner	Sgt. Michael Hunter

After finishing phase training at Charleston AFB, where we trained for high-altitude bombing of Europe, we were transferred to Langley AFB in December 1944.

At the completion of training in April 1945 we were ordered to travel by troop train to Salinas, California. As we were leaving our Navigator, Lt.

Sutherland, was taken by acute appendicitis and underwent emergency surgery. We traveled west without him and he never did rejoin our crew.

In Salinas we picked up a brand new B-24J, serial no. 451027, manufactured by Ford at Willow Run; painted black with radar installed and oxygen equipment removed. After making a calibration flight and a second flight to record fuel consumption, we flew to Mather Field, California to await orders to fly overseas.

An ATC Navigator was assigned to fly overseas with us. In late April we left at 6:30 p.m, landing at John Rodgers in Hawaii 13:58 hours later. The next day we flew to Canton Island, thence to Tarawa, Los Negros Island, and then Biak where we delivered the aircraft. We were taken to Lae, New Guinea from where we were assigned a new Navigator, Lt. Parker, and taken by C-46 to Clark Field, Northern Luzon, Philippine Islands, where we joined the 63rd Bomb Squadron, 43rd Bomb Group.

On May 19, 1945, I flew my first mission (squadron regulations required each First Pilot fly his first mission with another crew) with Major Link and his crew. We flew to Nanking, China, carrying 3500 gallons of gasoline and four torpex bombs. Major Link made a search of the river by diving fast from 7,000 to 1,000 feet then climbing back to 6,000 feet from which the run on the target was effected. Lt. Page, flying his last mission, was the Bombardier and Lt. Rocks, the Navigator. The bomb run was of the ETA type and at the last minute the navigator called for a correction to the right, the bombs paralleled the target, falling into the Yangtze River. The target was a railroad terminal and docks, as no ships were sighted in the search of the river.

As the bombs were released we received light and inaccurate flak, however searchlights were accurate and showed a Japanese single-engine night fighter on our tail. "Rope," strips of lead foil, was dropped, to cloud up radar reception on the ground. We broke from the target and nothing further was seen of the night fighter. We arrived back at Clark Field around noon of the 20th, having logged 17 hours, 40 minutes.

On the evening of May 26 I flew my first mission with my crew. Copilot Parrish was sick with dysentery, therefore, Lt. Jake Grover, of Olean, New York, flew in his place. We carried 3500 gallons of gasoline and four 500 lb. general purpose bombs. The mission was to search the Yangtze River for shipping. We encountered a bad weather front near the Pescadore Islands and had a very difficult time getting through it. Upon reaching the Yangtze River we located a destroyer escort, made two runs on it, the first of which was a free pass but the bombardier missed by 200 to 300 feet.On the second run we encountered small arms firing, inaccurate, but missed the target again due to evasive action by the ship. We had been making the run at 1000 feet altitude approaching him broadside. At two miles distance he started moving at full speed (31-35 knots) and the bombardier couldn't kill course. The bombs fell 50 to 60 feet astern of the ship. Jake and I wanted to make a third pass strafing with our 50 caliber guns but then decided we would be ineffective and headed home.

Around 0700 hours, east of Weng Chow, we found a small island along the coast with the appearance of an old volcanic crater with a harbor in it (We called it Shangri-La). Three small freighters were anchored there. Strafing was almost impossible with a B-24 due to the steep terrain; however, we did make three passes. The first was effective and put one freighter out of commission, possibly sinking him as he exploded, but the second and third passes were ineffective due to gun malfunctions. Flight time was 18 hours, 20 minutes.

On May 30 we left Clark Field, heading for the Yangtze again, carrying 3500 gallons of fuel and four 500 pound Torpex bombs. At the target we found a Fox-Tare-Charlie alongside a burning FTC that had been bombed earlier by Lt. Canevari. We made two unsuccessful runs on it; nothing unusual was encountered on the flight and we landed after 17 hours flight time.

June 2nd. I drew a ferret mission, whereby I flew a special B-24 that had the bomb bay converted into a radar compartment with several radar officers who were trying to locate, track and monitor radio signals on the ground. We were to fly box patterns around Shanghai, then to Canton for weather information and radar counter measures, but we lost our radar search set north of Formosa and headed home by dead reckoning. The weather was very bad and we nearly flew into the mountains of northern Luzon. The Ashland control sector at Lingayen advised that the weather at Clark was Savannah 5 (field closed) so I landed at Leng, an emergency, and fighter airstrip at 0130 hrs on June 3rd. At daylight, we taxied out to the end of the very short runway and then noted all of the base personnel rushing out to see us take off on the short strip. By running up full power with the brakes locked and no flap we released the brake and at the end of the runway dropped the flaps, ballooned into the air and we were flying. Flight time 11 hours, 20 minutes.

June 4. We again had a ferret mission with the same mission plan as on June 2nd, Our radar again failed us north of Formosa so we started home. Due to a lot of high cloud cover we had to dead-reckon our way home and came very close to the Formosa Mountains. On the west shore of Formosa two fighters passed us, one on each side, but apparently didn't see us. Due to blackout regulations the control sectors steered us down the Lingayen Valley to Clark Field, where Doodlebug put us right over the field where we landed with 9:40 hours flight time.

June 7. We had a sea search in the Yangtze River with 3500 gallons gasoline and four 500-lb. general purpose bombs. Takeoff was scheduled for 1930 hours but I wanted to beat an oncoming storm so I was ready at 1920 hours. The storm hit while we were lining up on the take-off runway and the airfield was closed. At 2000 hours upon learning that the mission could not be canceled, I made an instrument take-off in very heavy rain, in a southerly direction, which was slightly uphill. We ran off the end of the runway and I ballooned the plane into the air, only to come back down into the Kunai grass where we hit very hard, but bounced into the air and were airborne.

We left the valley totally on instruments and remained so until we arrived at the target area. Just south of Formosa we ran through a terrific weather front, and then another one north of Formosa. Our search of the Yangtze River began at dawn while there was still a lot of haze on the river. We bombed a ship, then determined that it was already sunk in shallow water. It was then daylight so I climbed to 5500 feet, flew over Shanghai and bombed an airfield. We encountered very heavy flak and got one hole in the bomb bay. We saw fighter planes taking off so I dove, exceeding the red line speed, to the ocean where we flew a few feet above the water for some distance until we felt that we were out of the fighters' range. Flight time 17 hours, 30 minutes.

June 7. Flew another ferret mission to Shanghai. I have no notes other than it was successful. Flight time 17 hours, 5 minutes.

June 22. Flew a ferret mission to Hong Kong, then south to Indo-China. A successful mission. For my part I merely had to fly on instruments, flying timed turns and exact patterns as requested by the radar operators. Flight time 17 hours, 45 minutes.

At this point we moved from Clark Field to the Island of Ie Shima, NW of Okinawa. My crew traveled by LST, skirting a typhoon as we traveled.

August 8. We took off for Tsushima Straits for a shipping reconnais-sance, carrying a full load of gas, including one bomb bay tank, and 12 Composition 'B' (Torpex bombs). Our radar was inoperative so we flew back and forth between Japan and IeShima attempting to fix it, finally giving up for a bad attempt, we dropped a flare in the darkness to make certain the area was clear, then jettisoned our bombs that were not yet fuzed, yet they all exploded. Four hours, five minutes flying time.

August 9 – the following night. I took off for the Sea of Japan on a reconnaissance mission to last until the middle of the morning. (A pretty shaky mission considering that we would be a lone aircraft without any fighter defense in broad daylight). On takeoff in the dark I noticed a very definite power failure, but was too far down the runway to stop. To apply the brakes would surely shear the landing gear and being loaded with bombs and a full load of gasoline, including two bomb bay fuel tanks, we would, in all probability, blow up. I shouted to my co-pilot to re-check the flaps. He misunderstood and raised them to 10 degrees, our airspeed jumped from around 98 mph to nearly 110 mph and we went off the end of the airstrip, 242 feet above the water, and started mushing downward. The engine instruments were still reading ok. Cowl flaps were checked, they were closed as they should be. The engineer opened the bomb bay doors and I salvoed the four Torpex bombs, but held on to the two bomb bay fuel tanks. We then realized that we had extreme detonation in our #3 engine. The RPM and manifold gauges were oscillating and the cylinder head temperature hit the stop. Oil temp was 102 and oil pressure dropped to 60. I was now down to 50 feet altitude, staggering along at 125 mph, and couldn't see a thing outside as it was so black out. I couldn't turn as the airspeed was too low so I flew, just skimming over the water. We carried a radio altimeter, accurate from 0 to 300 feet.

The plane had good three engine operation and, as #3 engine cooled a little, co-pilot Joe Parrish fed a little power back, then eased off, then fed back a little, and we gradually picked up airspeed to 140 mph and gradually began climbing. I continued straight on course attempting to get all out of it that I could and finally went into a gradual turn and started back to Ie Shima, attaining 3000 feet of altitude before leveling off. We hadn't used up much fuel and were still severely overloaded. We landed with around 3350 gallons of gasoline aboard.

After taxiing back and shutting down the engines, the engines were checked and #3 checked out OK with a ground run up, raising considerable suspicion as to why I returned. But when the engine was opened up in the morning the oil screen was completely covered with metal filings and it was concluded that the engine would have blown its cylinder heads had it run much longer.

August 10, the following night, I completed a mission. About three minutes after takeoff from Baywood Base, air traffic control called me and said the war was ending. We asked if we were to continue the mission and were advised in the affirmative. Eight Torpex bombs were dropped on the docks in Fusan, Korea, and blew up railroad marshaling yards. In addition to bombs, we carried one bomb bay gas tank. We snooped around an island, not on our charts, located at 37 degrees 30 minutes north and sighted 15 merchant ships by radar in an island harbor. We also picked up two more ships by radar at 4 a.m. We returned to the area at dawn and found them to be destroyers, which we shadowed until we were convinced they were headed for the island and the 15 merchant ships, the existence of which we visually confirmed after dawn.

The mission was to search for remnants of the Japanese fleet; shortly after daybreak we were supposed to be able to make radio contact with B-25 units who would be in the area and, if we had any findings, we were to direct them into the target area. We were unsuccessful in making contact with the B-25s so we climbed higher and higher, while continuing with code transmissions by the radio operator and then voice contact by me, but no contact. We then headed home convinced that the war must be over, but after landing we found it was not. Flight time 14 hours, 25 minutes.

August 13. We took off for a weather reconnaissance of Tokyo. Our batteries boiled over in flight so we returned to base immediately after salvoing four Torpex bombs. After quick repairs and bomb re-loading we again took off and after 1-1/2 hours of flight I began to notice an odor, my eyes burned, I began to get sleepy and my navigator complained of a sore throat. Both inverters operated at the same time so we unplugged one. The connection started arcing and the voltage regulators were red hot. I returned to base, very happy to get on the ground before an explosion occurred. Flight time 6 hours, 35 minutes

On August 14 we flew to Tokyo, without bombs, as it was to be a reconnaissance flight. We carried a *Times* reporter aboard. Our mission was to go up the east coast of Japan, then into Tokyo and the inland sea, radioing weather as we flew. Almost immediately after take-off we lost our liaison radio set, but despite losing the long-range radio, we went up the coast to check on a typhoon. In doing so I went through the worst storm of my life. We were thrown around the sky wildly, and the plane seams leaked water from the torrential rains, shorting out our radios. After breaking out of the

Looking through a mud-spattered window at Howard Booth and his plane.
Photo provided by Howard Booth

storm we hit clear weather near Tokyo when our radar picked up aircraft off to our starboard. As the radar operator tracked them, he was convinced that they were going to fly into us as he couldn't tell if they were at a higher or lower altitude. We then picked up several aircraft visually, passing directly in front of us, traveling from our right to left in a steep descent, one just missed our nose. The interesting thing was that they had interior lights on, for what purpose we couldn't imagine. They appeared to be Japanese, two-engine Betty bombers.

The radio operator could not get the radios to work, which precluded our being able to radio weather information back; therefore we flew back home to report what we had seen. We landed at 0615 hours and learned that the war had ended at 0600 hours. Flight time: 10 hours, 55 minutes.

Last Mission

On August 22 we went on another recon to Tokyo. In flight our radar went out, the Loran became inoperative and the navigators sextant was broken! We came home by dead reckoning, pitch black outside, and upon landing I began taxiing on a coral strip, using my landing lights alternately, when I saw a Diesel roller up ahead. Apparently my lights approaching in the dark scared the operator, T/5 Sam Foster, 73rd Aviation Engineers, as he hopped off the machine and ran. Meanwhile the machine started rolling backwards toward the plane. We tried to shut off the engines, but the fuel mixture control on the #1 engine stuck and didn't shut off immediately. The roller came to rest on a loose piece of coral, acting as a chock, stopping about two inches from the propeller blade. Flight time 10 hours, 35 minutes.

Epilogue

Not being certain if the Japanese were going to surrender peacefully, we began training to fly slow formation at 500 feet for the purpose of dropping paratroopers into Japan. Thank heavens we didn't actually have to do it!

Thereafter, knowing that eventually we would fly our plane home, we spent our time making certain that it was in perfect operating condition as well as cannibalizing damaged aircraft belonging to the 7th AF on Okinawa to make certain that we had the necessary spare parts, if needed, as we flew home.

Ultimately, we flew home via Okinawa, Guam, Kwajalein. Honolulu, arriving at Mather AFB at 0930 November 3, 1945, where I received a receipt for "One war-weary B-24."

As I look back on it I realize that our activities did not change the course of the war one iota. However, it was not for lack of trying . . . and our entire crew arrived home safely.

The
Williams
Mission

Standing: left to right: Sgt. Joseph Virok, Asst. Engineer-Gunner; Sgt. Morris (Morry) Rifkin, Gunner; Sgt. Bill Dew, Flight Engineer; Sgt. Lorenzo Munoz, Gunner (Sgt. Munoz was replaced by Sgt. Dale Thompson, Radar Operator at Langley Field); Sgt. Luther Cummings, Gunner, and Sgt. Vernon Phillips, Radio Operator. *Front Row:* Lt. Bennie Siler, Co-pilot; Lt. Bill Williams, Pilot; Lt. Robert Williams, Navigator, and Lt. John Pruzinsky, Bombardier. (Lt. Bennie Siler and Sgt. Dale Thompson were killed in action.)

Note: Bill Williams received this account from Marc Rifkin about two years ago. In the same time period, former Radio Operator Vernon Phillips (now deceased) visited Bill Williams and left his diary of the mission with him. This was the 16th mission for this crew.

Both these accounts and the official combat report from the Air Force Archives, Maxwell AFB, are included in this memoir. Marc Rifkin, who found "The Williams Mission" on the Internet, wrote: As a young child, my mother often told me the story of my father's last mission. It was, in fact, the Williams mission. He was the top turret gunner, S/Sgt. Morris (Morry) Rifkin. He never spoke of his war experiences to anyone but my mother. He was the gunner wounded in the leg who sat in the co-pilot's seat and broke his shoulder in the crash. He was in the hospital when he found out I had been born on March 15, 1945. The mission occurred on March 28, 1945.

He was awarded the Distinguished Flying Cross, a Purple Heart with one oak leaf cluster and an oak leaf cluster for his Air Medal. My father was the "old man" of the crew (he was 25 years old).

The Williams Mission

The following story was prepared by the Squadron Public Relations and submitted to the Blue Network in Manila:

The B-24 was especially designed for night missions, but this time she was out in daylight, alone, poking in and out along the French Indo-China Coast hunting for stray Jap ships trying to sneak through our aerial blockade.

The plane belonged to the 63rd Bomb Squadron of the Fifth Air Force's 43rd Bomb Group and her crew had sunk many a ship at night. This was their first daylight mission.

At half-past ten in the morning they spotted an enemy convoy of four large merchant ships protected by three destroyers, two destroyer escorts and one light cruiser. This was a target for a large formation of bombers protected by fighter cover and flying high enough to keep out of reach of the warship's guns.

But Lt. Williams and his crew were out to sink ships – and their bombs had been set for low-level attack.

They lined up for a run and came in at 300 feet with every gun in the convoy shooting at them. They dropped three bombs on the biggest merchant vessel, but they were duds. As the plane pulled away, the tail gunner, Sgt. Morris Rifkin, was wounded in the leg and the tail section of the ship was riddled with bullets.

Five minutes later they were coming in for a second run at the same altitude and this time they let go with their five remaining bombs. Two of them were hits; there was a violent explosion and as the crew looked back they saw the ship list sharply to port and belch black smoke. But Jap guns destroyed all the plane's trim tabs and elevator controls.

And as it peeled away from the target two silver-colored Oscars came diving out of the sun in a frontal attack. They slammed a 20 mm. shell into the cockpit and killed the co-pilot, Bennie Siler. Then they wheeled and made another pass from the rear of the bomber. This time they killed Sgt. Dale Thompson, the radar operator, who had

Sgt. Dale Thompson relaxes by his tent at Clark Field. (Sgt. Thompson was killed in action.)

gone back to take the wounded tail-gunner's place. The navigator and the bombardier, who were manning the waist guns, were also slightly wounded on this pass.

Now the Jap fighters came diving down again in a frontal attack and shot out the bomber's No. 3 engine. On their fourth attack from the front they made hits on the No. 1 and 2 engines and destroyed the top turret guns. But one of the Oscars was hit and was trailing smoke when last seen. The remaining one made several more passes but the bomber escaped into a cloud cover and headed for home.

The hydraulic system was destroyed, the radio was shot out, a severed fuel line was gushing gasoline into the bomb bay, the No. 3 engine was gone, another was damaged, the compass and other instruments were shattered, the controls were cut, two men were dead and two more injured.

The wounded were given first aid, all loose equipment was jettisoned to lighten the plane, the gas leak was repaired, the co-pilot's body was removed to the bomb bay and the crew members alternated in his seat to help the pilot.

The plane had no altitude and their first problem was to get her up. Straining with all their might, they managed gradually to nudge her higher. But the weight was too much for them; they took the interphone wires and tied the controls back and in that way slowly gained height.

Gasoline was low and they had only two good engines and they might or might not make their base, but they decided to fly her out. For six hours she limped along, and the crew didn't know if they could land her when they did get there.

They made the field and they had to crank the landing gear down manually. The nose wheel stuck, and they had to kick and cut and pry it loose. They couldn't contact the tower because the radio was gone. They dropped signal flares but they didn't go off. With the wheels down the plane lost altitude rapidly. They had no choice; they circled once and came in to land.

The plane came down heavily, and at the moment of contact the navigator, acting as co-pilot, hit the crash bar. She was on the ground and for a moment it seemed that they had made it.

Then the right wheel collapsed, the big plane slewed violently around, skidded and crunched into a crumpled heap. She was a complete washout.

But miraculously she didn't burn and, more miraculously, all but the men who had been killed in the air came out of her under their own power. All of them were badly shaken up, and five of them were bruised and battered enough to require hospitalization, but none were seriously injured and they'll all be back to sink more Jap ships.

THE WILLIAMS MISSION
Diary of Radio Operator – Vernon Phillips
Photographs provided by Bill Williams

On March 27, 1945 we briefed at 5:30 p.m. and received our emergency maps, etc. Our target was a recently sighted convoy of warships and merchant vessels that had left Singapore headed northward and hugging the coast of French Indo China. Captain Welch and crew with John L. Wood as radio operator had already taken off at 10:00 a.m. for sea search carrying no bombs. No sightings reports had came from them. Our take off was 0330 March 28. We headed straight for Indo China intending to search from one hundred miles south of harbor. Everything was routine except that it was well after sunrise and not a cloud in sight when we reached the area. There were hundreds of Chinese on native sailing vessels everywhere, mostly fishing trawls, but nothing that looked like Japanese vessels.

We crossed a peninsula that had a small town on it and what was apparently a naval academy or naval training school. We were about 4,000 feet and could easily see a large group of uniformed men running from the building to bomb shelters. They began firing light ack ack and machine guns and we found two small holes in the elevators, but we dropped no bombs and continued searching for the convoy. There were many small coves and bays going back into the island and small mountains. Over and near one mountain about 1,000 feet high that perhaps came out of the ocean, we could see two merchant vessels at quite a distance. We circled around and decided to make a skip-bomb run directly over the mountain then drop to 200 feet at 200 miles per hour for bomb release. Gunners were instructed to strafe and we went in. Upon clearing the hill we could see the composition of the convoy – one light cruiser, two DD, two DE, five large transports. They began firing heavy and accurate ack ack as soon as we came into view.

Down we went and bombs away – we climbed to the right and got out of the thickest fire I'd seen. The bombs (two 500 pounders) had missed being short and off course. They damaged one destroyer, however, which was very close to the transport we ran on. Sgt. Rifkin was injured with flak in his right leg. There were several holes in the fuselage and tail sections, otherwise no material damage. We moved out to take a look at Sgt. Rifkin then made another run – same way – 200 feet, 200 MPH. We ran along way over the 10,000 ton transport. I was crouched by the auxiliary power unit and looking through the bomb bay doors. The transport looked close enough to touch. I saw our delayed fused bombs strike one 50 feet short, two directly on deck and three a bit long. All exploded almost at the same time. The 10,000 ton freighter broke in three parts and sank immediately. I could see huge sections of the deck along with the men on them blown 50 feet in the air and one stack disappeared before it moved from my view. The light cruiser and DDs were throwing everything at us. The navigator was slashed across the face and was bleeding freely. Holes appeared all over the flight deck and explosions were seen and heard on either side of me. The smoke was thick and I could hardly see. No. 3 engine was on fire and smoking heavily.

We got the bomb bay doors closed and managed to climb to 2,000 feet and headed inland to turn around toward the sea. Two fighters (oscars) immediately closed in the first pass and a 20mm shell struck radar operator Dale Thompson right above the eyes and blew his head half off. He fell to the floor and Rifken took over the tail guns in spite of his leg wound. The navigator came back and manned a waist gun. Gunner Joe Virok was in the Martin upper turret when a 20 mm struck the left gun knocking him onto the floor. He wasn't injured, however, and he jumped back in and fired the other gun manually. The shell had knocked half the Plexiglas cover off the turret and the left gun out. Benny Siler, the co-pilot, was on interphone so he told me to go back to the waist after I had tried to bandage the navigator's face. I started back and another 20 mm struck Bennie in the forehead killing him instantly. The bomb bays were so full of smoke I couldn't see all the way through as I passed by the bomb bay tanks. I could see a large stream of gasoline pouring from a severed line. In the waist I operated a waist gun but scored no hits on the fighters. Luther Cummings knocked down one from the nose turret. Rifkin stayed by the tail guns. One waist window was knocked off to make it easier to handle the guns. I re-manned the other one. After 15 minutes of almost steady attack, we hit the clouds and lost the fighters.

Dale and Bennie were dead. Everyone aboard was injured except me. No. 3 engine was out and No. 2 had a cylinder out. Almost all the controls were shot away. Elevators were almost out. It took all the strength of two men to hold the nose in level flight. No flaps, no rudders, one aileron and three engines. The navigator gave a course of 75 degrees which we turned on to and began trying to gain altitude. The plane was holding its own and Joe Virok patched up the leak in the gas tank with tape partially, and we dressed wounds and after an hour we gained to 2500 feet. My radio was completely dead. Antennas were flying loose in the wind and the trailing wire was cut to four feet long. Side tone could be heard from UHF and command sets but I doubted if they were putting out a signal. I began calling "Mayday, Mayday, this is cocktain 8, this is cocktain 8. We are badly damaged and have dead and wounded aboard. Our course is 75 degrees, 7-5 degrees, our position is 12 degrees and 30 minutes north, 112-45 minutes east (later 13 degrees north, 113 degrees, 15 minutes east).

We were about 800 miles from home, but the B-24 continued to fly. We prepared to ditch at any moment. I removed all the items from my musette bag and put some of them in my pockets, buckled on my pistol and canteen, then my May West and waited. We took turns co-piloting. Bennie had been lifted over the co-pilots seat and laid in the bomb bay on the catwalk. Dale was covered with a turret cover and everyone remained at gun positions for two hours out to watch for fighters again.

After three hours of flight, we contacted a P-38 close by who was also lost. He said he would notify air-sea rescue and went on his way. Our UHF was apparently working faintly. IFF was turned to emergency. At about 4:15 p.m. we reached Subic Bay and could see that the navigator had done a good job. We were still flying O.K. so we didn't attempt a landing there, but continued to Clark Field. There we couldn't contact the tower who apparently didn't see us as there were three B-25's preparing to take off so the runway was obstructed. We attempted to circle around but had almost no control over the plane except on a straight course. Luther Cummings and I went back to the waist to prepare parachutes to use as brakes. When we hit the ground the landing gear went down alright and was apparently alright. With no flaps, we lost altitude rapidly and failed to reach the runway. We struck at 160 MPH as the pilot gave it full throttle to try to reach the runway. I remember seeing the right gear give way and the wing struck the ground. Then I saw or felt nothing more. I awoke in the ambulance and didn't even wonder what had happened. It was from the morphine they had given me.

The plane had strewn metal for 200 yards, a wheel here, a rudder there. The tail turret was torn off completely. Joe and Bob had both struck the power switches immediately upon hitting the ground and it didn't burn. I was pulled out from the tail, knocked out and every one else had managed to get out by themselves. Bob, John, Rifkin, Pruzinsky, and I remained in the 24 General Hospital for six days. Rifkin was evacuated to Leyte; he had a fractured shoulder bone. I only had cuts and sprains on my knee and hip with small cuts all over my body.

Dale's body was thrown 50 feet from the plane and Bennie was severed half in two when the catwalk bent from impact. They were buried in Manila on March 29, 1945.

We were back on flying status April 7th and the correspondents from several US papers had taken our story and radioed it to the states. We were recommended for the Silver Star and received the Purple Heart and the Distinguished Flying Cross.

THE WILLIAMS MISSION
As described in the Air Force Archives – Maxwell AFB

Lt. Bill Williams receives the Silver Star.

Now reports of a convoy off the Indo-China coast came in and at 2022/1 # Lt. Bryant took off in #898, without bombs, to locate it. He found a destroyer escort, a large merchant vessel and either one destroyer or a light cruiser all strung out along the coast just north of Vanfong Bay. He reported his sightings to the 309th Bomb Wing ground station.

At four o'clock in the morning Lt. Williams took off in #676 with eight 500-lb. bombs. He found the convoy a little before eleven, in broad daylight. It was two miles east of Tre Island and it consisted of two or three destroyers, two destroyer escorts, one light cruiser, one Sugar Able Love, one Fox Tare Able, two other large merchant ships, and one Sugar Dog.

This was a formidable target for a lone bomber on a bright, clear day. But Lt. Williams was out there to sink ships. He set up a bomb run at 300 feet on the choicest target – the big oil tanker. Every ship in the convoy fired everything they had as the bomber came in – and they had plenty, ranging from small machine guns up to large-bore naval guns. Some of it was accurate: the tail gunner was wounded in the leg and there were several hits in the plane's tail section.

Nothing Can Stop The 63rd Squadron

Three bombs were dropped on this run and they strung nicely across the ship – but they didn't explode. The crew didn't hesitate; they came around and in on another run at the same altitude. The ack ack was thicker than before this time; all the trim tabs and the elevator controls were shot out. And the radar operator, who had gone back to replace the wounded tail gunner, was himself slightly wounded on this run.

Five bombs were dropped this time and they strung the entire length of the ship, two of them direct hits on the port side. There was a heavy explosion; the tanker burst into flames and began to list sharply. She was claimed as sunk; that oil would never service Jap warcraft.

But as the bomber peeled off – the crew marveling that their ship was still in the air after two runs through hell – two silver-colored Oscars came out of the sun in a screwing dive at 12 o'clock. On the first pass a 20 mm. shell slammed through the cockpit and killed the co-pilot instantly. The Oscars came in on another pass from the rear. This time their cannon killed the radar operator. The third pass was again from the front; this time the enemy planes crashed a 20 mm. shell through the dead center of the spinner on No. 3 engine and knocked it out. They made several other passes; the crew isn't sure how many. But the top turret gunner had the satisfaction of seeing his tracers enter one of the Oscars and of watching it trail smoke as it dived for cover in the clouds.

And eventually the bomber found cloud cover – and headed for home. It had been a pretty rough go. One engine was gone, another was damaged. The electrical and hydraulic systems were out. The radio was out. Instruments were out. Controls were shot out. The fuel lines had been hit and there was a bad leak in the bomb bay. Holes riddled the plane. And there was plenty of blood. Two men lay dead. Others were wounded, but none seriously.

Everything that was loose was thrown out to lighten the plane's load. The co-pilot's body was taken into the bomb bay and other members of the crew took turns helping the pilot. The plane was dangerously nose/heavy; so heavy that two men using all their strength could not hold her up. Finally they used the brake pedal strap and a wire from the interphone system to tie the control wheel back. They flew the crippled plane that way for six hours.

They made the field, but with no flaps, the plane came in too fast. The bomber had to be crash landed, and she ended up a total washout. But the men who were still alive all walked away from her. Five of them were hospitalized, but their injuries were superficial, and all but one were back on duty within a few days. The exception was one of the gunners whose shoulder blade was chipped.

What It Takes To Win The War

This mission would go down in the Squadron records along with many others testifying to the courage and the flying skill of the men who fly the big night bombers. When some weeks later, the official communique from Gen. MacArthur's headquarters could say that the Jap shipping lanes along the China Coast were practically deserted, it was sacrifices and achievements like this that made the claim possible.

Bill Williams Remembers December 7, 1941

As to my recollection of December 7, 1941, I was attending a military school, New Mexico Military Academy in Roswell, New Mexico in my first year of college. I was 16 years old and with some other cadets were playing a pick-up game of basketball, when someone came into the gym to announce that the Japanese had bombed Pearl Harbor. Some of the cadets had parents in Hawaii and many had fathers in the military there. They immediately ran to the office and tried, with little success, to contact their families in Hawaii. It was several days before school officials were able to get news from Washington that all cadet families were fine.

I signed up for an Air Corps pilot training program as soon as I turned 18, February 9, 1943. I was called up several weeks after and subsequently received my wings and 2nd Lt. commission while still 18 years old. After B-24 training and crew training at Davis-Monthan Field and Langley Field, we went overseas in December 1944. We began flying missions when I was 19 years old, and I often now wonder how my crew had the guts to trust their lives with someone with so little experience. Thank god they were patient, forgiving of my mistakes, and very brave. Without them we would never have survived.

Our crew was one of the most decorated in the Pacific theater. All of my crew members received Purple Hearts, Distinguished Flying Crosses, and Air Medals with numerous clusters. I was the lucky one who did not get a Purple Heart. We carried an extra gunner on this mission, Cpl. Cashmer Sydnewski. It was his first combat mission.

After we had flown our 400 hours and qualified for rotation, the crew went back to the States. I had agreed to stay on as Operations Officer, for promotion to Captain, and did not return for discharge until November, 1945.

F. Neal Fugate

Crew Flew in the Last 63rd Bomb Squadron Anti-Shipping Bombing Mission Before the Japanese Surrender

F. Neal Fugate

Background

I enlisted in The Enlisted Reserve Corp for the Army Air Corps Aviation Cadet Program (ERC) on December 15, 1942, my 18th birthday, while a freshman at the University of Nebraska. In February 1943, this group of ERC college students (from coast to coast) was called to active duty. After 30 days of Basic Training, the members were assigned to various U.S. colleges in the College Training Detachment Program (CTD).

After three months at the University of Washington in St. Louis, it was off to San Antonio for Aviation Cadet processing and into the Preflight Cadet Program on August 1, 1943. I received Primary Flight Training at Oklahoma City, Basic at Garden City, Kansas, and Advanced at Brooks Field, San Antonio. This was the first B-25 program for advanced Aviation Cadets. I was commissioned on June 27, 1944, Class 44-F. I was 19 years old.

I received B-24 Transition Training at Fort Worth, then on to a Replacement Training Unit at Tonopah, Nevada; Radar Bombing Training at Langley Field, Virginia, and overseas to the Southwest Pacific to join the 63rd Bomb Squadron, 43rd Bomb Group.

Retired in June 1972 (29 $\frac{1}{2}$ years) as a Lieutenant Colonel with the Air Force Reserve, Nebraska Air National Guard (F-80 jet fighters); then some time in the California Air National Guard. I served two years of active duty in the Korean War call-up (1951-1952) as a Flight Commander in the 173rd Fighter Squadron, and then as a Fighter Pilot (F-84G's) with the 20th Fighter Bomber Wing, which had a special all-weather mission carrying an A-Bomb.

The 20th trained at Langley Field and flew 105 F-84G's across the North Atlantic in May 1952 to England. The 20th Headquarters and my squadron, the 55th, were based at Wethersfield RAF Station, 40 miles northeast of London. I was appointed Wing Flying Safety Officer while there, returning stateside and civilian life in December 1952.

In my senior year at Law College, University of Nebraska, in September 1949, I flew an F-80 in the Allison Jet Trophy Race, Cleveland Air Races, taking second place. My civilian law career has been primarily with corporate America. I retired in 1982.

One of the main points I want to convey in this memoir is the selection of the 63rd Bomb Squadron as part of the initial occupation force in Japan in August 1945. It was explained to us before we flew from Ie Shima to Atsugi Air Base that the 63rd Squadron was being honored by having been selected from all the other Heavy Bombardment Squadrons in the Pacific because of its combat performance. I thought this might be relevant in this history of the 63rd. How many members of the 63rd are aware of this honor? A P-51 squadron and a B-25 squadron were also selected for this duty at Atsugi Air Base.

Introduction

Since the 63rd squadron flew long, all-night, single-ship flights, the missions were essentially boring. The missions flown from Clark Field, Philippines over Japanese targets were 17 – 20-hour missions (5:00 p.m. to 10:00–12:00 a.m. next day) with front bomb bay fuel tanks and only four 500 pound bombs. Missions out of Ie Shima were essentially 12-hour missions (7:30 p.m. – 7:30 a.m. next day) without bomb bay fuel tanks and eight bombs.

Because of our rather specialized missions (anti-shipping) and the fact that we didn't interface with other flights within our own squadron or with the daylight bombers, I suspect the mission "excitement factor" for the 63rd would register on the low side.

Having said that, the listing of our crew is included:

> 2nd Lieutenant Forrest N. Fugate - Pilot
> Flight Officer Robert A. Scott - Co-pilot
> 2nd Lieutenant Wilfred H. Parker - Navigator
> Flight Officer Richard R. Fletcher - Bombardier
> Corporal John J. Rukert - Flight Engineer
> Corporal, James S. McGuire - Radio Operator
> Corporal, William M. Bynne - Armorer Gunner
> Private First Class Charles E. Smith - 1st Gunner
> Private First Class Henry Beherns - 2nd Gunner
> Private First Class, Herbert A. Pink - 3rd Gunner

When we were sent to Langley Field, Virginia for radar bombing training in February 1945, our 1st Gunner, Charles E. Smith, was replaced by a "Mickey" man, Radar/Navigator Lieutenant, Ned Caldwell.

First Mission

On our first combat mission (I had flown one 18-hour mission on May 30 - 31, 1945, as an observer, with another crew as an introduction to combat missions) we were assigned an experienced co-pilot, Felix (last name, I believe). If no enemy shipping was located in the designated target area, the secondary target was Shanghai, at 10,000 feet.

On this, our first mission, we were unsuccessful in locating any shipping targets, so we went for Nanking up the Yangtze River at 10,000 feet for a

2:00 a.m. "nuisance" raid. On our initial bomb run, there was a disagreement between my navigator and my "Mickey" man (radar operator who was also a graduate navigator) as to which direction our bomb run was to be made; meanwhile, we're on the bomb run throwing out chaff and the searchlights were revolving, unable to locate us – probably because of the chaff. Because of the disagreement, I pulled off the bomb run and we re-entered from another (presumably the correct) direction; this time without chaff, since it had all been expended on the previous run. The searchlights locked on us and it was brighter than high noon at 10,000 feet, a very uncomfortable feeling while straight and level on the bomb run.

After bombs away, I took evasive action, whether it was needed or not. But if they had anti-aircraft guns with the same lock-on capability as those searchlights, we might have had some trouble that night. To the best of my knowledge, we were not fired upon – fortunately. Perhaps they had no idea that bombs were going to be dropped and after they were dropped, it was too late.

The conclusion of this story is that back at Clark Field, my navigator and "Mickey" man had it out with each other, including physically (with no harm to either), but not in my presence. After this altercation, the navigator advised me that he would not fly missions with the "Mickey" man and that it was either him or the other guy.

As a 20-year old airplane commander, I could use, and needed, some assistance with this decision and discussed it with Major Butts, 63rd Squadron Commander, and also with the Operations Officer, Captain Patton. In any event, it was concluded that since the navigator had made this type of decision, it was fair that he leave the crew.

As a result of this vacancy, the Squadron Navigator, Captain Paul Rumbarger, who was not presently assigned to a crew, but needed additional combat hours for a completed tour, was assigned as our crew navigator. This was great for us, as he was a skilled navigator – and compatible with all the other crew members.

Hit Over Korea

One of the designated target areas was the Korean coast line. On one of these missions, we were hit by gunfire on our second 1,000 foot-run over a ship that was anchored near the Korean shoreline.

The first run, at night, was a "free one," ordinarily, in that the ship below, if it heard you, wasn't aware that we had radar and a radar bombsight aboard. Also, of course, the ship wouldn't want to give away its position by firing at an overhead aircraft, who may not know that there is a ship below. As a result, I can't remember ever being fired upon on the first run. Actually, most of our hits were first run successes.

This time, however, we swung around for a second run, since we didn't score on the first. On this run we were hit on the underside of the plane, with the only serious damage being the loss of our hydraulic system. We had a "parachute-assist" landing back at Ie Shima.

Ferret Mission

One mission that we flew, without bombs, was the Ferret Mission, in which the bomb bay of a B-24 had been converted into a bay of radio and radar frequency detection equipment, with two operators, checking out radio and radar frequencies of the enemy. This mission was flown at night also, as would be expected, and was passed among the various flight crews of the 63rd, but I don't recall how often this type of mission was flown or how many of the other crews got this duty. We only flew this mission once.

The "Combat Line"

In our flight briefings we were assured that any sea vessels (shipping) beyond a certain designated line was the combat zone and therefore fair game. Later, much later, like within the last year or two, I have read statements and one statement, attributed to U.S. Navy personnel that U.S. submarines were operating in the Inland Sea of Japan during World War II.

One of the 63rd's target areas was the Inland Sea, and I flew at least two missions in this area.

It gives me an eerie feeling to know this, since we could not specifically identify the ship or type of ship with our radar and we would bomb without further identification. I know of no problem in regard to this, but it is now somewhat disconcerting.

The missions into the Inland Sea were interesting. At 1:00 a.m. we'd enter into the Inland Sea at 1,000 feet altitude through the approximately two-mile wide mouth of the sea with various lights visible around the shore line. Of course, once you're in the Inland Sea area looking for targets, you're completely surrounded by the enemy and in the event of a problem a very potential POW.

Combat Whiskey

I guess it's known that a double-shot of combat whiskey was served up to the crew members upon their return from a mission. This wasn't a fringe benefit to the non-drinkers, so their drinks were available to the others, which wasn't particularly appealing to me as a socially-only drinker.

But the point being, for night-time mission crew members, a serving of a double whiskey at 8:00 a.m., either with or before breakfast, may qualify for "the cure being worse than the disease."

Flight Boots, Boots, Boots and More Boots

This begins in Tonopah, Nevada Army Air Field in the period of October 1944 to January 1945 where we trained in RTU. For our high altitude practice missions (20,000 feet) we would check out from supply, leather, wool-lined flight boots that were considered a very valuable piece of personal equipment, along with the sunglasses, the watch and the leather jacket.

These boots that were issued just prior to flight time and only to those who would be flying the 20,000 feet missions; they were not available in all sizes, since they were in very short supply. You might be issued your correct size, or you might receive a pair of medium size when you needed large or large when you needed extra large, etc. This would necessitate removing your shoes so your feet could fit into these smaller sizes.

And there was a rule, strictly enforced, that these boots were not to be worn, walking or otherwise getting to your assigned aircraft on the ramp. They were only to be worn while in the aircraft, being put on and removed while in the aircraft. These procedures seemed reasonable since the boots were in short supply, even though it was quite inconvenient for the crews.

Now jump forward to May 1945, after our radar bombing training at Langley Field, Virginia, and we're being processed for our overseas assignments out of Hamilton Field, California. A full complement of personal equipment is issued, including a pair of brand new flight boots in the correct size and a parachute bag which is then pretty much filled with this newly issued gear. We flew a B-24 from San Francisco to Hawaii and beyond, island hopping to Lae, New Guinea (where squadron assignments were made) and then on to Clark Field and the 63rd squadron, hauling this parachute bag of flight equipment.

In July 1945, when it was time to move up (from Clark Field to Ie Shima) everything we owned had to go with us aboard the B-24 we were flying to Ie Shima, including our 8-man tent which was our home. We'd been lugging this parachute bag with all this equipment since leaving San Francisco and yet we were flying missions at 1,000 feet (mostly) in the southwestern Pacific and the flying boots seemed superfluous – very superfluous. So we checked with squadron supply to see if we could turn in these boots and have them taken off our records. This was OK with supply and the word spread and I assume every pair of these boots in the 63rd was turned in. Say 20 crews, 10 crew members, means 200 pair of boots, which had never been worn.

But supply also had logistic concerns, moving up also, but by sea, compliments of the U.S. Navy with limited cargo space assigned. Within a day or two (we moved with very short notice) there was a pile of flight boots probably ten feet high in front of the supply tent and they were set fire, eliminating once and for all the problem of transporting these flight boots. (A "logistics pyre.") At that time, of course, I recalled our experience back at Tonopah when we could have really used those boots.

Our Last Mission

As documented in the Narrative Report that follows:

63RD BOMBARDMENT SQUADRON (H)

43RD BOMBARDMENT GROUP (H)

Office of the Intelligence Officer

APO 245

14 August 1945

SUBJECT: Narrative Report of Mission FFO 226-A 3-4

TO: COMMANDING GENERAL, 5th Air Force

APO 710

ATTENTION: A.C. of S. A-2

1. The million mark for tons of Japanese shipping sunk and damaged by the 63rd Squadron was in sight. After almost three years of smashing at the Nip, the Seahawks were knocking on the door. But time worked against us, for the strike of the night of 13/14 August was the last of the war. Three Seahawk crews did their best for the record, and ended the night with 13,000 tons definitely sunk, bringing , the grand total to 967,020 tons, sunk, damaged, or probably sunk.

2. Two planes were scheduled to search the Blind Bombing Zone west of Kyushu-Honshu, and one to search off Southern Korea and in the Tsu Shima Straits. Bomb load for the first two was 12 x 500 lb. Torpex, plus 2700 gallons of gasoline, and for the single plane 9 x 500 lb Torpex and 3100 gallons of gasoline.

3. First off from Ie Shima on the Kyushu-Honshu search was 2nd Lt. Forrest H. Fugate in plane 025. Airborne at 1938/I, he set a direct course through the East China Sea to the south tip of Kyushu, arriving there at approximately 2230/1. Within ten minutes he had made his first run on a shipping target.

4. At 3340N-12920E, the crew found a stationary Sugar Dog. Two 500 pounders were dropped on a 90 degree heading from 1200 feet. They fell 100 feet to the right with no damage.

5. Leaving this small boat, the crew went after larger game. Nearly two hours later, they found what they were looking for – A convoy consisting of one Sugar Able Item, one Lugger, and three U/I medium sized vessels, moving on a 130 degree course, 5-8 knots, at 3430N-13015E. The first bomb run was set up at 0020/1, with the largest of the convoy singled out as a target. Driving in at 1000 feet on a 70-degree heading, the bombardier dropped three 500's, but course was off and they fell 150 feet left. On the next run, from the same altitude and on a reciprocal heading, course was plotted still further off, and the three bombs dropped 500 feet to the left. With two such deviations under his belt, the bombardier lined up correctly for the next and final run on the freighter.

Two 500 pounders scored direct hits on the stern. It looked like an ammunition factory had exploded. Tracers flew in every direction, and the blast was of such velocity that the waist windows of 025 were shattered to bits.

Ammunition continued to fly for five minutes, and finally the torn hulk of the 5000 ton Sugar Able Item sunk, as much a victim of its own cargo as the accurate bombs of the B-24.

6. The remaining two bombs were dropped on the lugger while 025 circled to observe the kill of the larger ship. At 0052/I, from 1000 feet, and on a 320-degree heading, 2 x 50 lb. bombs fell 75 feet left of the boat with nil apparent damage. No further ship sightings marked the uneventful trip home, and 025 landed at base at 0843/I.

7. Plane 812, with 2nd Lt. Thomas Burwell at the controls, took off from base at 2030/I, but turned back due to a gas leak, after two hours of flying. 12 x 500 Torpex were jettisoned in the water at 2248/I, from 3000 feet at position 3130W -12905E. The plane landed safely at 0050/I.

8. 2nd Lt. P. Cressor and his crew just got in under the wire. On this, the last mission of the war, they flew combat for the first time. The job they turned in was a superlative one, for two ships sunk, totaling 8000 tons, would have been unusual even for the hardiest veteran in the outfit.

9. Cressor was off from base in 969 at 2018/I. His mission was to search the Blind Bombing Zone off southern Korea, and he proceeded directly there. After two hours of search, however, no shipping had been found, and he crossed the Tsu Shima Straits to the other search area. In short order plane 969 picked up the first shipping target, identified by flare as a Fox Baker, moving on a 320-degree course, 10 knots, at 3430N-12940E. On the first bomb run, at 0210, from 1000 feet, on a heading of 90 degrees, the three 500s fell 500 feet over. On the next run, 3 x 500 Torpex strung diagonally across the Fox Baker, scoring three very near misses. The ship exploded in a sheet of flame, and within 15 minutes had sunk.

10. turning to a second, and comparable indication, Cressor found another Fox Baker at 3430N-12845, plying the same course. At 0230/I, a run from 1200 feet and on a 210 course was set up. Three 500's were dropped, with one bomb scoring a direct hit amidships. Fire followed the large explosion, and the ship was observed to be listing 20 degrees shortly after the bomb run. The 4000 ton Fox Baker sank in 12 minutes.

11. On the initial pass over this last ship, meager, light, but accurate A/A holed 969 in the tail. At 0235/I, while Cressor circled to observe results of the last bombing, two U/I planes were spotted in the vicinity. One closed to 300-400 feet blinking wing lights, but did not open fire. The B-24 crew did not attempt to fire. The crew returned to base with no further incident, landing at 0700/I.

12. Weather enroute to and from the target was generally good, with only a 3-5/10 Strato-Cumulus undercast from 1-4000 feet. Over the shipping targets, a 4-6/10 Stratus undercast from 900-1500 feet and a haze.

Appendix 1
Biographies:
Edward W. Scott Jr.

Stuart P. Wright

Baylis E. Harriss

Official Air Force Biography

Brigadier General Edward W. Scott Jr. Retired, Died Oct. 16,1968. General Scott was commander of the European Exchange Service. In this position he was responsible for the command and management of all exchange activities for both Army and Air Force personnel located in Europe and the Middle East.

Born at Hollandale, Miss., Aug. 18, 1916, General Scott attended high school in Mississippi and received his bachelor of science degree from Mississippi State College in May 1939. As a graduate of the ROTC program he received a commission in the Army Reserve in 1939 and participated in the aviation cadet program. In March 1940, the general received a commission as second lieutenant in the U. S. Army Air Corps.

General Scott's early assignments were with the 9th Bomb Group in New York, Panama, Trinidad and Surinam, and later with the 6th Bomb Group in Guatemala. He was then assigned to the Southwest Pacific as a squadron commander and later as Commander of the 43rd Bomb Group. He then assumed command of the 90th Bomb Group.

From November 1945 to October 1947 General Scott was assigned to Headquarters Fifteenth Air Force, Colorado Springs, Colo., as statistical control officer and then to Headquarters, Strategic Air Command, Andrews Field, Md.

Following graduation from the Armed Forces Staff College in February 1948, General Scott was assigned to the Office of the Comptroller, Headquarters U. S. Air Force, where he served until August 1951. From August 1951 to August 1953 he held positions at group and wing level, assuming command of the 95th Bomb Wing, Biggs Air Force Base, Texas, in September 1953. In 1956 he commanded SAC XRAY in Japan and became special assistant to the commander, 810th Air Division, in May 1957. In August 1957 the general assumed command of the 22nd Bomb Wing at March Air Force Base, Calif.

General Scott was assigned to the University of Alabama in June 1960 as professor of air science of Air Force ROTC Detachment 10. In July 1962 he became vice commandant of the Air Command and Staff College. From July 1963 to June 1966 he was commandant of the Air Command and Staff College. He assumed his present position on July 1, 1966.

General Scott's awards and decorations include the Silver Star, Legion of Merit, Distinguished Flying Cross with two oak leaf clusters, Air Medal with four oak leaf clusters, Air Force Commendation Medal with oak leaf cluster and the Army Commendation Medal with one oak leaf cluster.

Official Air Force Biography

Major General Stuart P. Wright. Retired June 30,1957, died April 18, 1982. Stuart Phillips Wright was born in Dallas, Texas, in 1903. He graduated from Terrill High School there in 1921, and attended Dartmouth College and Texas University.

Appointed a flying cadet in June 1927, General Wright completed primary and advanced flying schools a year later and was commissioned a second lieutenant in the Air Reserve. Receiving his regular commission as a second lieutenant of Air Corps Jan. 6, 1930, he was assigned to the First Pursuit Group at Selfridge Field, Mich., and in March 1933 was transferred to the 18th Pursuit Group at Wheeler Field, Hawaii.

Ordered to Mitchel Field, N.Y., in July 1936, General Wright was assigned to the 97th Observation Squadron, becoming operations officer of a Ninth Bomb Group squadron in April 1939, and assuming command of the First Bomb Squadron, Ninth Bomb Group in July 1940. That November he took the First Bomb Squadron to Rio io Hato Air Base in the Republic Panama, and in March 1941 assumed command of the Ninth Bomb Group in Trinidad. A year later the general became operations officer of the Sixth Bomb Command at Albrook Field in the Panama Canal Zone. Moving to Army Air Force headquarters, Washington, D.C., in August 1942, he became operations liaison officer in the Directorate of Communications, and in October 1943 was appointed chief of a Special Project Section studies there.

The following April General Wright assumed command of the 497th Bomb Group at Clovis Field, N.M., taking it to Saipan in the Marianas Islands three months later. In February 1945 he joined the 73rd Bomb Wing, also in the Marianas, and that April was appointed communications officer of the 20th Air Force in the South Pacific. Three months later he was transferred to the Air Communications Office at Army Air Force headquarters as chief of the Equipment Programming Section, becoming deputy air communications officer there in April 1946. Entering the National War College that September, he graduated the following June.

Joining the Strategic Air Command, General Wright was an electronics officer at SAC headquarters, Andrews Air Force Base, Md., becoming chief of the Electronics Section, SAC, there in August 1948; and retaining that position when SAC headquarters moved to Offutt Air Force Base, Neb., three months later. In September 1950 he was appointed deputy commanding general of the Air Proving Ground Command at Eglin Air Force Base, Fla. Transferred to the Far East Air Forces in March 1953, he was designated deputy commander of the Fifth Air Force (Rear) in Korea.

His decorations include the Legion of Merit, Distinguished Flying Cross, Bronze Star Medal, and Air Medal. He is rated a command pilot, combat observer and aircraft observer.

BAYLIS E. HARRISS. Born Galveston, Texas. 1915. Died in crash of Stearman cropduster, Madras, Oregon, Nov. 1959 at the age of 44.

Commanding officer, 868th Bomb Squadron, (H) March 10, 1945 until the end of the war on Okinawa. The following is quoted verbatim from Squadron Historical report for the month of April 1945.

Major Baylis E. Harriss, Commanding Officer is but thirty years old and was born in Galveston, Texas; however he has maintained his residence in Clovis, N.M. and Tucson, Ariz. He attended Columbia Military Academy, St Edwards University at Austin, Texas, and the University of California, School of Agriculture.

He then became interested in flying, later becoming a commercial pilot, with over a thousand flying hours to his credit in 1941 when he joined the RAF for active combat service. While in the RAF, he received a wealth of experience under all combat and flying conditions, and in various types of aircraft. Major Harriss has a total of 2430 hours with the RAF, 1300 of which are combat hours. 450 hours were flown in 52 combat missions, 300 hours were flown in fighters, 550 hours in medium bombers while 900 hours were compiled in the Ferry Command Staging out of London.

Major Harriss flew missions to France, Italy, Germany and Czechoslovakia, and was in a formation that smashed the famed Skoda works. His experiences and adventures would make a first-rate thriller. As Squadron Leader of the 408th Bombardment Squadron, he flew Lancasters, Halifaxes and Hurricanes. He also had considerable time in Spitfires, Bostons, Beau Fighters and innumerable American types. His daring and brilliant achievements in the air and against enemy targets soon distinguished him and he received many commendations and awards. Major Harriss now has the Order of the British Empire, the British Distinguished Flying Cross, the British Star, the American Volunteer Commemorative Medallion, the Allied Service Medallion, and the British General Service Award.

In July 1943 Major Harriss joined the 8th Air Force in England and in November 1943 was returned to the United States. In October 1944 he was ordered overseas on active combat duty. During his career in the Service he has gained invaluable knowledge in flying tactics, administration, planning of missions and the handling of men. It is this latter asset that has so marked him as an able leader, one that inspires utmost confidence in his fellow men. His ability to understand the other man's problems and especially the importance of ground personnel in a flying outfit has greatly endeared him to the men under his command. He had a faculty for cutting red tape, and getting to the core of things.

After leaving the service, Baylis and his wife Mildred ran a ranch in the Avra Valley out from Tucson, Arizona, where they raised cattle and horses. Baylis also had a flying service and cropdusting was a part of this. It was while doing this in an old Stearman that he was killed outside of Madras, Oregon in November 1959.

Appendix 2
Original crews of the Scott Project and the Wright Project

The Captain L. Coleman crew in B-24D 42-40475, The Swan, was missing on 3 December 1943 while on a night reconnaissance mission from Dobodura, New Guinea, in the vicinity of New Hanover Island. The last message from the plane was "Why aren't lights on?" It appears that the plane was off course to Dobodura because it crashed into the thick jungle inland from Cape Ward Hunt some distance north of Dobodura. The crew in the photograph were aboard and a Pvt. Joseph Thompson.

The plane was located by John Douglas, Chief Field Officer for Michael John Claringbould of Aerothentic Publications. As yet, the remains have not been recovered by Central Identification Laboratory in Hawaii. Sgt Frank's dog tags were recovered at the crash scene providing positive identification of the plane.

As reported by Andy Anderson in the July 2002 43rd Bomb Group Association Newsletter.

(See photo of Coleman Crew on following page)

R-E-S-T-R-I-C-T-E-D

HEADQUARTERS
FIRST SEA SEARCH ATTACK GROUP (H)
LANGLEY FIELD, VIRGINIA

SPECIAL ORDERS)
                :   E X T R A C T
NUMBER   195)

1. The following named Officers and Enlisted Men, 2nd Sea Search Attack Squadron (H), 1st Sea Search Attack Group (H), assigned. to Project Number 96189 are further assigned to Movement Order Number 3, this Headquarters, dated 25 Sept 1943, effective the date of movement:

2nd Lt JOHN E. BREWSTER, 0-854474 (0141) FK-600-BB 10 42-40972 Technical Office

Crew No. FK-600-AB 1 42-40904

Capt. ROBERT L. COLEMAN, 2nd Lt KENNETH L. CASSIDY, 1st Lt. GEORGE E. WALLINDER, 2nd Lt. IRVING (NMI) SCHECHNER, T/Sgt. Paul (NMI) Miecias, S/Sgt. Albert J. Caruso, T/Sgt. William L. Fraser, S/Sgt. Robert E. Frank, T/Sgt. Robert C. Morgan, M/Sgt Robert J. Turner.

Crew No. FK-600-AB 2   42-4101

1st Lt GEORGE M. BIDDISON, 2nd Lt RICHARD T. BURKE, 2nd Lt STUART E. CAMPBELL, 2nd Lt HAYWARD K.SCHANDORFF, T/Sgt Robert C. Temple, S/Sgt Michael L. Eisenkerch, T/Sgt Joseph C Callewaert, S/Sgt Heavrin J. Reagan, T/Sgt James E. Bray, T/Sgt Kenneth A. Kelley.

Crew No. FK-600-AB 3   42-40896

Kneeling, left to right: 2nd Lt.Arthur H. Millard – Pilot, 2nd Lt. Harold C. Way – Co-pilot, 2nd Lt. Mervyn O. Cadwah – Navlgator,and 2nd Lt. Char les E. Swindler – Bombardier. *Standing:* T/ Sgt. Ralph H. McMillan – Rad1o Operator, T/Sgt. Rudolph J. Rypyse – Flight Engineer, S/Sgt. J Richard Everson – Asst. Flight Engineer, T /Sgt. Leslie G. McCulla – Radar Operator, and S/Sgt. William Desrnond – Armorer-Gunner.

Crew No. FK-600-AB 4   42-41058

Capt. WILLIAM F. HAMILL, 2nd Lt CHARLES P. POMERHN, 2ND Lt T. B. (io) ALLEN JONES JR, 2nd Lt BEN (NMI) SCHNEIDER, T/Sgt Walter (NMI) Tadys, S/Sgt. Edward J. O'Brien Jr, T/Sgt Donald J. O'Brien, S/Sgt. Myron (NMI) Lewis, T/Sgt Lloyd M. Locker, S/Sgt William V. McCarthy Jr.

Crew No. FK-600-AB 5   42-41049

Ist Lt CHARLES F. QUINETTE, F/O JOE B. BARTON, 2nd Lt JOHN D. SIZEMORE, 2nd Lt ROBERT C. RYAN, T/Sgt Raymond J. Danyow, S/Sgt Joseph W. Pepitone, T/Sgt Laverne A. Landefeld, Sgt George D. Haulenbeek, T/Sgt Milton (NMI) Rubin, S/Sgt George F. Olvera.

Crew No. FK-600-AB 6   42-40955

1st Lt GROVER C. HALLMAN, 2nd Lt JOHN W. CODY, 2nd Lt CLIFTON C. BOWEN, 2nd Lt FREDERIC G. CHEUVRONT, T/Sgt Raymond, (NMI) Gates, S/Sgt Stephen (NMI) Kosch, T/Sgt Attelio A. Rosati, S/Sgt William A. Reese, Sgt Creighton H. Bonner, T/Sgt Frank L Remaniak.

Crew No. FK-600-AB 7   42-41050

1st Lt WILLARD L. BURGHOFF, 2nd Lt JACK E. CARNALL, 2nd Lt BILLIE W. THOMPSON JR, 2ND Lt EDWARD B. CRAWFORD, T/Sgt Russell G. Laraway, S/Sgt Thomas F. Prout, T/Sgt Arthur J. Haack, S/Sgt Russell E. Brown, T/Sgt William E. Kelly, S/Sgt Alfred (NMI) LeBlanc.

Crew No. FK-600-AB 8 42-41053

1st Lt STEPHEN (NMI) RING, F/O JOHN B. AHRENS, 1st Lt JOE B. KINSEL, 2nd Lt J0SEPH A. STEVENS, T/Sgt Robert C. Parker, Sgt Walter J. O'Leary, T/Sgt Michael (NMI)Lengyel, S/Sgt Raymond W. Comerford, T/Sgt James G. O'Kane, Sgt Ralph H. Machold.

In late February 1944, Lt. Alvin McGehee, Lt. Henry Kreider, Sgt. Howan Dust, and Sgt. Liggett Gilliam were killed in an emergency landing at the Cape Gloucester fighter strip with a runaway prop on one engine. Most seriously injured was Lt. Joe Schwarber with broken ribs and a lacerated ear.

Crew No. FK-600-AB 9 42-41041

1st Lt ALVIN E. McGEHEE, 2nd Lt HENRY H. KREIDER JR, 2nd Lt KENNETH N. CARSON, 2nd Lt JOSEPH A. SCHWARBER, T/Sgt Howard O. Dust, S/Sgt Liggett N. Gilliam, T/Sgt Dowaine J. Woiderman, Sgt Burton C. Burman, T/Sgt Harry T. Hardin Jr, Sgt John F. MacPherson.

On November 4th, 1943, the Hafner crew went out and reported three direct hits on a cruiser. An hour later they sent a routine position report from near Rabaul, but no further transmissions and they never returned. Hafner and crew were our first casualties. Reported by Arthur Millard, Crew #3.

Crew No. FK-600-AB 10   42-40972

1st Lt WILLIAM M. HAFNER, 2nd Lt ARTHUR C. ARMACOST III, 2nd Lt DAVID R. EPPRIGHT, 2nd Lt CHARLES F. FEUCHT, T/Sgt James G. Lascelles, S/Sgt Arthur P. Fredrickson, T/Sgt Alfred W. Hill, S/Sgt William C. Cameron, T/Sgt Raymond S. Cisneros, Sgt Richard M. Salley.

Crew missing in action – Gasmada, New Britain. May have been shot down by our own Navy PT Boat.

Crew No. FX-600-AB 11   42-41043

1st Lt JAMES J. HARRIS JR, 2nd Lt GEORGE J. BOLLES, JR., 1st Lt JAMES B. HAMILTON JR, 2nd Lt DOUGLAS H. WRIGHT, T/Sgt Gardiner A. Corrigan, S/Sgt Lewis V. Nason, T/Sgt Joseph E Moskalak, S/Sgt J. K. (io) Johnson, T/Sgt Richard B. Friend, Cpl William H. Skidmore.

Crew No. FK-600-AB 12 42-40475

Capt CRAIG S. McINTOSH, 2nd Lt HARRY O. STAPLES, 2nd Lt JOSEPHI I. CONCHA, 2nd Lt HAROLD A. HOODS, T/Sgt Herbert J. Geuder, S/Sgt Gustave J. Sakowski, T/Sgt Horace (NMI) Roland, S/Sgt Richard H. Wertz, T/Sgt Joseph A. Wynne, Cpl David (NMI) Tesser.

R-E-S-T-R-I-C-T-E-D

HEADQUARTERS
FIRST SEA SEARCH ATTACK GROUP (H)
LANGLEY FIELD, VIRGINIA

3 August 1943

SPECIAL ORDERS)   _ _ _ _ _ _ _
              E X T R A C T
NUMBER 155   )

6. The following named O's and EM, 3rd Sea Search Attack Squadron (H), 1st Sea Search Attack Group (H), are assigned to Movement Order Number 1, this Headquarters, dated 3 August 1943. Colonel STUART P. WRIGHT, 0-17920, FP-617-AD 1, 42-40832, is Provisional Flight Leader and is designated Provisional Flight Commander. Capt ERNEST R. BARRIERE, 0-431828 (0145), FP-617-BD 5, 42-40822, Technical Officer.

NO PHOTO AVAILABLE

Crew No. FP-617-AD 1   42-40832
Major LEO J. FOSTER, JR., 2nd Lt. JOHN A THOMPSON, JR., 2nd Lt. CECIL D. COTHRAN, JR., 1st Lt..VINCENT R. ZDANZUKAS, T/Sgt. Samuel C. Pona, S/Sgt. Howard L. Eastabrooks, T/Sgt. Bernard B. Nachbe, T/Sgt. Albert R. Smith, S/Sgt. John (NMI) Dohan, Jr., T/Sgt. Leon L. Armstrong.

Crew No. FP-617-AD 2   42-40836
Major FRANCIS B CARLSON, 2nd Lt WILMER B. HAYNES, 1st Lt CLARENCE L. HARMON, Jr., 1st Lt. JUNIOR M. BARNEY, T/Sgt. Glenn M. Chandler, S/Sgt. James D. Justus, T/Sgt. Lawrence E.De St. Croix, T/Sgt. Ray F. Davis, S/Sgt. Michael (NMI) Blendy, M/Sgt. Thomas W. Milton.

Crew No. FP-617-AD 3   42-40854

Capt. JOHN F. ZINN, JR., 2nd Lt. CHARLES V. CONRAD, JR., 1st Lt. JAMES E. POPE, 2nd Lt. SAMUEL L. PELLEGRINI, T/Sgt. Raymond W. Trimble, S/Sgt. Jacob A. Stief, T/Sgt. Clarence W. Patterson, S/Sgt. Sylvester P. Harmon, S/Sgt. Dale (NMI) Burch, Cpl. Jerome (NMI) Sosin.

NO PHOTO AVAILABLE

Crew No. FP-617-AD 4   42-40833

Capt. FRANKLIN T. E. REYNOLDS, 2nd Lt. VINCENT D. BROOKS, 2nd Lt. GEORGE (NMI) DESKO, 2nd Lt FRED A. WHEATLEY, T/Sgt Albert G. LeBlanc, S/Sgt Elmer R. Ruff, T/Sgt Herman C. Goldtrop, T/Sgt Kenneth T. Evans, S/Sgt John E. Young, Sgt Robert L. Lambert.

Crew No. FP-617-AD 5   42-40822

Capt. ROBERT W. LEHTI, 2nd Lt. JOSEPH L. SULLIVAN, 1st Lt. CROWELL B. WERNER, 2nd Lt. CHARLES F. AMES, JR., T/Sgt. Walter A. Rose, S/Sgt. Jack V. Ranson, T/Sgt. Joseph A. McCalmont, S/Sgt. George A. Cubbage, S/Sgt. John S. Wilcox, S/Sgt. John A. G. Stanford.

NO PHOTO AVAILABLE

Note: On the night of August 31, the Robert Easterling crew made a bomb run and was never heard from again.

Crew No. FP-617-AD 6   42-40839

1st Lt. ROBERT E. EASTERLING, 2nd Lt. EUGENE H. WHITE, 2nd Lt. JOHN R. BULL, 2nd Lt. WILLIAM A. S. FURLOW, JR, T/Sgt. Grover R. McDonald, S/Sgt. Charles J. Sottong, T/Sgt. Eugene J. Gossen, T/Sgt. Gentile W. Cespino, S/Sgt. Anthony A. Pellegrini, Sgt. Anstess H. Weir.

Crew No. FP-617-AB 7   42-40838

1st Lt. CARLES L. ROCKWOOD, 2nd Lt. CHARLES R. BOWDEN, 1st Lt. FRANK M. SYLVESTER, JR., 1st Lt. NED B. ESTES, T/Sgt. Charles R. Bespole, S/Sgt. John A Plocek, T/Sgt. Harold A. Dennis, Jr., T/Sgt. William J. Prosser, T/Sgt. Robert W. Cunfer, Sgt. Robert F. Sandreczki.

Crew No. FP-617- AD 8   42-40651

1st Lt. KENNETH E. BROWN, 2nd Lt.HARVEY E. CURRAN, Capt. WILLIAM P. SCHUBER, 2nd Lt. HENRY B. WISE, T/Sgt. John H. Terpstra, S/Sgt. Frederick E. Preye, T/Sgt. Christoff G. Kilzer, T/Sgt. David (NMI) White, S/Sgt. Sidney (NMI) Schwartz, S/Sgt. Rudolph F. Nelson.

Crew No. FP-617-AD 9   42-40653

1st Lt. FREDERICK A. MARTUS, 2nd Lt. FOSTER M. HILL, 2nd Lt. JOHN C. BURT, 2nd Lt. ROBERT L. McLEOD, T/Sgt. Joseph (NMI) Ouimette, S/Sgt. Donald C. Peterson, T/Sgt. Thomas W. Owen, T/Sgt. Leroy (NMI) Rubin, S/Sgt. Augustus J. Sayko, S/Sgt. Harold W. Shirey.

Note: On the night of September 28-29, 1943, Lt. Fred Martus and crew, returning from this mission, crashed on landing at Carney Field and all were killed. (Sgts. Leroy Rubin, Augustus J. Sayko, and Harold W. Shirey did not fly this mission.)

NO PHOTO AVAILABLE

Crew No. FP-617-AD 10   42-40639

1st Lt. GEORGE A. TILLIINGHAST, JR., 2nd Lt. LOUIS J. BECK, 2nd Lt. EARL (NMI) COX, 2nd Lt. 2nd Lt. ROBERT E. TRESSEL, T/Sgt. Curtis A. Pond, T/Sgt. Edmund (NMI) Paradis, Jr., T/Sgt. Andrew J. Moore, T/Sgt. Louis A. Guerra, T/Sgt. Charles G. Redhead, T/Sgt. Floyd E Hune, Sgt. John J. Purvis, Cpl. Vincent P. Hoover.

Ernie Pyle Memorial on Ie Shima Island
Photo provided by Fred Peters